BURNED BY THE ROCK

Inside the World of Men's Championship Curling

Jean Sonmor

Macmillan Canada
Toronto, Ontario, Canada

Canadian Cataloguing in Publication Data

Sonmor, Jean
  Burned by the Rock: inside the world of men's championship curling

Rev. ed.
ISBN 0-7715-9183-7

1. Curling – Canada – Biography.   I. Title.

GV845.S67   1991   796.964′092′2   C92-094297-0

TOC

1 2 3 4 5   GP   96 95 94 93 92

Cover design by Alison Hannas

Cover photo by Labatt's/Michael Burns Photography

Macmillan Canada
A Division of Canada Publishing Corporation
Toronto, Ontario, Canada

Printed in Canada

To the curlers, for their generous help and for their passion, which surprised, delighted and warmed me through a long, difficult project,

and

to my mother, Kathleen Sonmor, for a lifetime of love and support.

TABLE OF CONTENTS

ACKNOWLEDGMENTS

IN MANY WAYS this book is a collaboration between the curlers and the writer. The subjects described here were unfailingly generous with their time and their confidences. For the love of the game, they were all willing to answer questions for as long as it took to get the record right. For that alone, they are unique in the world of sport.

Any errors or inadequacies of understanding are mine alone.

This book began with a wider lens, intending to encompass women's curling too, but time and space ran out. Hence many busy people who are never mentioned here gave hours of their time, opening up a fascinating world that now sits neatly stacked in three dozen green steno notebooks. I am deeply grateful for the help and I hope I will be able to use their contributions in another project.

Dave Parkes of the Canadian Curling Association, Doug Maxwell of the Ontario Curling Federation and Jeff Timson of Labatt's were unstinting in their willingness to check facts or offer explanations. Julie Kirsh and the library staff at the *Toronto Sun* were astonishingly able to ferret out weird and wild facts. When all else failed, they never let me down.

Neil Harrison was always a bright spot with a fine memory and a ready quip. If he didn't know the answer he knew whom to ask. Thanks also to Bob Weekes, editor of the *Ontario Curling Report*, for his kind assistance and for entrusting me with his only complete set of back copies of his newspaper.

Perry Lefko, curling writer of the *Toronto Sun*, offered the early encouragement that helped get the project off the ground. I am also grateful to my employers at the *Toronto Sun* for putting up with me through this difficult process. Features Editor Luke Betts endured the most.

And to Joanne Ashdown and Denise Schon of Macmillan, a salute to their professionalism and kindness—especially at the bleakest of moments. Sincere thanks also to my editor, Barbara Schon, who was resolutely positive and hardworking even under the most killing schedules. Thanks also to Ian MacLaine of Canadian Press for loving curling both as a sport and a culture, and for reading the manuscript for errors.

And thanks especially to Ann McGrath and her son Peter, to Janice and Tim Hawkings and to Maureen and Gunther Fadum who put me up, kept me sane—and even moderately punctual—as I travelled across the country. And to Kay Duncan and Kathleen Sonmor, thank you for the million kindnesses that have made the past 14 months bearable.

The deepest debt is owed to Regan, Jacob and Brendan Devine, a magic trio who make everything worthwhile.

J.S.
June 1991

INTRODUCTION

CANADA FROM END to end, from Hay River in the Northwest Territories to the tip of the south shore of Nova Scotia, teems with curling clubs—1,300 of them. Some are one-sheeters, a few still use natural ice, but in all of them the culture is uniquely Canadian. In each of the buildings, somebody cares for the ice, somebody thinks about the club's entry in playdowns for the Labatt Brier or the Scott Tournament of Hearts, and likely somebody dreams about winning big.

Altogether, 750,000 Canadians pull on their sliders each year, limber up and head out to throw the rock and play the one game in which Canada is the undisputed kingpin. These Canadians are farmers, fishermen, stockbrokers. They run computers, hairdressing salons or supermarkets. The mix is as diverse as the country.

And from a distance so are the clubs. And yet even in Hay River or Rankin Inlet you'll find people who've been to the Royal Canadian Curling Club in downtown Toronto and felt at home.

Much of that is because the rhythms of a curling club don't alter with geography. Once the door closes behind you, you can't tell if you're in Nipawin, Saskatchewan, or Cranbrook, British Columbia.

It's 4:30 on a dark Sunday morning in January and Mike Warren is scraping the snow off his blue Acadian. Like 1,000 other curling icemakers across the country, Warren has to be on the job early on Sunday. It's a big day at the club and the ice will bear the scars of Saturday night's activities.

He's always amazed at the ruin that can be wrought on a sheet of curling ice by a novice's gritty street shoes. Today will be especially hard, he knows, because yesterday's Bank of Montreal Funspiel attracted dozens of first-timers.

For 13 winters Warren, the fresh-faced, soft-spoken icemaker at the Royal Canadian Curling Club in downtown Toronto, has been struggling out of bed before dawn to do a job few appreciate and fewer understand. For although the game of curling is best suited to night owls who love togetherness and partying, the icemaker has to be a morning person with a strong streak of the loner in his soul.

The little blue car noses its way through Toronto's untracked snow from Rhodes Avenue in the Beaches to the downtown corner of Broadview and Queen on the southern fringe of Chinatown 2. As he turns into the driveway of the squat old building, his eyes scan the handsome buff paint job and take in the elegant gold lettering. Both are his own handiwork. Last summer he spent countless hours painting and scraping until the old girl looked as if she'd had an expensive facelift. It was an appropriate gesture: the club is celebrating its 100th birthday in 1991.

On paper, the club is owned by 100 members who bought their stakes without realizing the real estate would one day be worth millions. Some day these people, if they collapse the club, stand to make big money. But until then it's Warren who has the feeling of ownership. After all, he's the one who's there every day coddling the pipes and the electrical system. He's the one who carefully builds up the ice at the sides so no one notices the five-inch wow in the centre. And when something's wrong at the club, he's the first to hear about it.

This morning he'll be on the ice by 5 A.M. and this afternoon at 5 P.M. he'll be spelling off the barkeep and pouring drinks. He was only 22 when he saw the job advertised on the board at Manpower and thought he'd take a shot at it. He'd never been in a curling rink before, but the job sounded interesting and it had to be better than the noisy, smelly print shop where he'd worked before.

That was 1978 and since then he's seen eight managers come and go. He's even endured the retirement of his teacher and mentor, icemaker Horst Reichart. And his attachment to the sport and the curling lifestyle has grown steadily.

It's been 10 years since Royals bought Ice King, the machine that pares hours off the tedious job of scraping the ice. In the old days, Warren and Reichart scraped by hand with an 18-inch wide blade. Now, working alone, Mike still has to do the tricky areas around the hack by hand before he guides the machine out onto the sheets to finish the job. Next he'll pebble the surface with the sprayer. Then he'll finish by dragging thirteen 44-pound curling stones up and down every sheet to polish it to perfection. The ice must be keen, fast and ferocious even for the very first curlers of the day.

This morning the job will take him four hours. So now, while most of the city sleeps, he's hustling to get the sludge off and the ice finished before the first curlers show up. Other icemakers he knows have cut the scraping to a couple of times a week but he insists it must be done daily to keep the ice really good.

He likes the feeling of accomplishment when the club curlers tell him the ice is the best in the city. He discounts the superlative but he knows that if the ice is heavy and sluggish the rocks won't curl as predictably and the game won't be nearly as much fun—for him or anybody else. Warren knows that, above all, fun is what the 250 or so curlers who will find their way to Royals on this snowy Sunday will be looking for.

Thinking about this, he cranks up the music—pure sixties rock— and gets down to work. The coffee will have to wait until the ice is finished. Outside on Broadview Avenue dawn is breaking and the city is waking up, but inside the windowless club Mike takes no notice. He works steadily, alone with the Stones, the Grateful Dead and his own profound sense of order.

When he comes off the frozen surface, finally ready to make the coffee, his fair moustache will be fringed with icicles and his teeth will be chattering. Even his parka and heavy wool shirt won't be enough to keep the cold from his bones on a morning like this. The Royals, like most of the older curling clubs, has no heating system. When it's cold outside, it's often colder inside. Sure he'd like a heater, but the club doesn't have the funds for big-deal improvements, and everybody knows that one year soon there will be a crisis with the 40-year-old electrical system. The ice compressor they bought two years ago cost $27,500. They're crossing their fingers they won't have another bill like that for a while.

Some of the staunch Royals regulars fear for the future. As drinking and driving rules tighten up and their club's bar income decreases, they wonder if the Royals can survive where other similar clubs have folded. But Warren dismisses the idea. The game is too addictive, the club is too strong, for a financial crisis to plough them under, he says.

He's a good testament to the addiction. He had never even seen the sport played when he took the job. But he was immediately intrigued, and three years later won the Southern Ontario Icemakers' Bonspiel. Just to prove it wasn't a fluke he repeated the win in 1990.

But that's the limit of Warren's curling ambition. You know within a couple of years, he says, if you've got the eye-hand co-ordination, the nerves, the strategic powers of mind to excel.

"Besides, you have to love the sport so much, you're willing to spend thousands of hours practising." So Mike's curling ambitions are limited to making a good showing at the Icemakers' Spiel. He understands what drives fellow icemaker, Kevin Martin, the 24-year-old who won the 1991 Brier, but it's not his schtick. Martin chose to be an icemaker so he could be close to the sport and get plenty of time to practise. Warren simply likes the life.

Now 35, he insists he'll be an icemaker until he retires. Nobody ever gives up icemaking to do something else, he says. Oh sure, an icemaker might move from a public club to a plush country club to make more money, but he doesn't go off suddenly and take a salesman's job.

Warren, like most other curlers, recognizes a special fraternity among curlers that contradicts the image of impersonal Toronto or tough Montreal. Curlers from any part of the country can drop into Royals and feel welcome. It's a curling village in downtown Toronto where partying and practical jokes are not yet the lost arts they are in most of the rest of the workaholic city.

Among the best of the Royals' story-tellers are the members of the Sinners' League, average age 70. They'll start ringing the bell around 8:30 this morning, anxious for a cup of Mike's coffee and a few minutes of chat before the game.

Conventional wisdom tells us that that's about all they should be doing at 70—drinking coffee and talking. But although most make hearty fun of their own curling prowess, they are obviously proud to be still playing a game some of them started when they were teenagers or younger.

Sunday at the Royals is a relaxed day for a casual game and a friendly drink. Instead of curlers with an edge and something to prove, there are special-interest groups like the Riverdale Men's League where most of the members are gay. Although this league, with its 48 players, might be unique in Canada, nobody at Royals takes much notice. It's just some curlers out to have some fun and along the way affirm their community. Winning is the least important part of their game.

The mixed league that plays Sunday evening is another social league. The same curlers might be quite competitive during the week but on Sunday night the object is to have fun.

Jazz musician Don Thompson, a 50-year-old with a long grey ponytail, started playing at 14 in Edmonton. He loves the game for its strategy and he loves the good times that go with it. At 20 he stopped dreaming about making it to the Brier and started focusing on his career as a musician. For years after he moved to Toronto to study the saxophone, he could only curl in hastily arranged pick-up games because he was always on the road. Now that he stays put more, he makes a point to curl Sunday nights because it's the one night he knows he won't be working. "I wish I could curl more," he says. "It's a great game. It's relaxing and I love the strategy."

Architect Dave Craddock agrees. Although he regularly curls during the week, he'll show up on Sunday to spare, and afterwards you might catch him enjoying a plate of Rose Marie's fine Chicken Kiev with Thompson and sharing a drink or two before heading home.

Sometimes when the mood is expansive on a Sunday night, you'll find Thompson at the keyboard of the grand piano in the lounge, playing a tune or two while the curlers gather around appreciatively. The feeling in the club is casual and jolly, and very unlike hard-edged Toronto and the ambience of some of the more "socially competitive" clubs.

People who are interested in that scene usually move on to other clubs where they spend $20,000 or $40,000 and buy a lifestyle that includes racquet sports and figure skating for the kids, explains Craddock. Royals, where the membership costs a mere $300, tends to attract a young unmarried crowd looking for fun. And over the years they have not been disappointed.

Across the country Royals has always had the reputation of knowing how to party. Upstairs there's a huge dancehall, and Beer Night at the Royal Classic bonspiel in early November is legendary. But reputation now exceeds reality.

In 1988 the police raided the club on the weekend of the Classic. For years—decades even—nobody had thought much about keeping strict bar hours. Royals wasn't a booze can, but it was known around town that if something was going on you could usually get a drink after hours. On a fateful November night Metro's finest decided to test the theory. They found 200 people quaffing champagne at 4 A.M.

After that, the board of directors clamped down—worried that the club might lose its liquor licence. It was bad enough that the manager had to spend a week at LCBO training school learning how to run a club.

"Now it's just a curling club," says one disappointed member.

"The lights are out and the doors are locked tight by midnight on a Sunday night."

But in this, as in most things, Royals is typical of the trend in curling clubs across the country. The raid on the champagne party was just one landmark in a steady decline in drinking and hilarity.

These are tamer times. Because of the stricter drinking and driving laws and a general shift in the social acceptability of drinking, everybody, everywhere, is more cautious. There are still wild exploits at bonspiels and Briers but they aren't talked about with as much indulgence as before, and they don't inspire the same spate of imitators.

At the Beaver Curling Club in Moncton, New Brunswick, where B-52 night is a traditional highlight of any Moncton event, the bartenders noticed a big decline in the action from the 1985 Brier even to the Moncton 100 bonspiel in 1990. It used to be standard practice for some of the more resolute partyers to order $100 or $200 worth of B-52s at a time. One year the profit in shooters alone was said to be $25,000.

A B-52 is aptly named after a bomber. It's a lethal combination of Kahlua, Triple Sec and Irish Cream. In Moncton, curlers, even competitive ones, have been known to down great quantities of the concoction. With every drink the customer gets a set of plastic airforce wings. In the past, competition to have the longest string of wings has been intense. Some revellers have been seen walking around with pins up one arm and down the other.

Lately, though, such displays are not as universally admired and drink sales are way down. "In the 1985 Brier you couldn't get in the door," remembers one employee who worked the upstairs room at the Beaver. "They got going pretty good during the Moncton 100, too, but it wasn't nearly as crowded."

And at the Nutana Curling Club in Saskatoon it took a blizzard to break open the party in 1988. After the Bessborough Classic no planes could get out because of a big winter storm. What an excuse for a party! It was the biggest and best anyone can remember.

In every province curlers of a certain age can remember parties that lasted from Thursday to Monday morning. On bonspiel weekends the partyers would plan to stay up. They'd hire babysitters to look after the kids, and if they slept at all it would be in one of the club's comfy armchairs.

Sure there are still all-night parties. *The Heart of the Nation* daily newsletter at the Scott tournament, the Canadian women's championship, still makes honourable mention of the last to leave the lounge at night. And the organizers of the Labatt Brier will rank the top 10 bars in town. But it sounds a little old-fashioned and the sizzle is fading.

A couple of years ago, the Manitoba rink at the Scott were determined to party. Their dedication to fun got them approving nods from the old-timers until it came down to the crunch and they racked up a disappointing record. Then everybody had something to say about going too hard.

Banquet night at Thunder Bay's Heart to Heart Bonspiel is honour-bound to last all night. The reveller who outlasts all others and remains upright long enough to lock up the basement party room after everyone has gone to bed earns the title "Dungeon Master." The honour is somewhat akin to winning the spiel.

But there's a touch of wistfulness about the competition. People used not to have to be bribed with honours to stay up all night and party. Those were the days when wild drunken exploits were cherished as badges of honour.

How this shift in values will affect curling is still unclear. Obviously, curling clubs are losing their cachet as meccas for the wild and misbegotten. But whether that will help or hurt the country's love affair with the sport is still an open question.

The newly amalgamated Canadian Curling Association would like to preside over a rebirth of the image of curling. They don't make official pronouncements on the subject of alcohol but it's clear they're pleased to have curling gradually joining the ranks of regular sports. They sit on their civil service perch in Ottawa, in a building that also houses the figure skating and synchronized swimming associations, and carefully deflect any references to the sport's bacchanalian past.

They prefer to talk about their five-year marketing plan—a plan to update the image of curling and bring in youngsters and women. Several years ago a study showed, or at least broadly hinted at, the obvious—that curlers were primarily men over 35 who enjoyed a pint.

The plan is still in its infancy but they've hired a full-time marketing person, Warren Procter, and CCA General Manager Dave Parkes believes there are encouraging signs that the various provincial organizations will take the marketing push seriously. To help, the CCA has produced a video promoting the game for circulation to schools and clubs.

The new emphasis is on participating for fun and friendship. The CCA hopes to make sure that youngsters understand it isn't just an old man's game or a game for the unathletic. One of the clearest signals of that new direction came in the move away from traditional curling sweaters at the 1991 championships. The men replaced the sweaters with nylon pacesetter jackets in jazzy colours; the women, with spiffy track suits with neon accents.

But typically, there was an uproar over the change, especially from the women. The suits added bulk and made most of the competitors look larger than life on TV. The women complained the suits were uncomfortable and the Prince Edward Island team refused to wear them, opting instead for traditional kilts. This isn't a sport where change comes easily.

But trying to glamorize the heroes of the game is not really the goal of the CCA right now. For years they've concentrated on competitive curling. The result? The elite got better and the recreational curlers were left way behind. They've bubbled along on their own steam for years now but fewer seem to be dreaming the big dream and entering playdowns. In 1991, 40,000 curlers started the playdowns for the Labatt Brier. A decade ago it was 80,000.

It's hard to know exactly what those numbers mean.

Fewer curlers seek out intense competition but they still show up at the curling rink. They devote their leisure time to perfecting their slide or their rock delivery. They fret about strategy or admire the club champion's ability to draw to the button. But ask them why they do it and chances are they won't even talk about curling. They'll talk about the people, the jokes, the laughter, the sense of belonging.

The sport, the *competition*, comes way, way down on the list. The game is a jumping-off point. It's a world they all share at the bar afterwards, a point of connection strong enough to overcome the normal social barriers: education, wealth, ethnic background and even, occasionally, gender.

In curling rinks you see vivacious stay-at-home grandmothers in intense conversation with slick male accountants. On the street they inhabit different worlds but here, in the club, they are buddies. There's respect on both sides and a sense of fun that doesn't often spread thick enough in the real world to go beyond one's immediate social peers.

As more than one of the game's admirers has said, "This is curling; it doesn't have much to do with the real world."

Passion for this game not only cuts through social barriers but scoffs at pretension. Curling gives its devotees a highly exclusive private club and if they exercise full rights of membership they scarcely need an outside life. Barbara Crowe, an Ottawa curler, was told to quit by her doctor because the sport was causing lower-back problems. She obeyed and found her life significantly diminished. She'd go to the club, but without the game in common, the bond she had with her friends weakened. Finally she stayed away from the club for a year or two, trying to find a suitable substitute. Nothing worked and she felt herself slipping into depression.

Eventually she talked her doctor into giving her a back brace that enabled her to throw the rock and get back into the game. "I would never have believed I could have missed it so much," she says. "Sure the brace is uncomfortable, but it's worth it."

The bond between curlers is social but it doesn't make sense without the crisp edge of competition. One of the Ottawa group members commissioned a sculptor to make an alabaster trophy. At the first draw every year, they play for the trophy. Although many of them also golf, there's nothing at the golf club that gives them anything like the pleasure they get from their own curling bonspiel.

Much of the tone and etiquette of the curling world seems to have originated in an earlier, more sedate world where it was not considered appropriate to go into paroxysms of delight when you win. One should be sensitive to the feelings of the loser, shake hands, commiserate and buy the drinks. Only later, when you're alone, is it acceptable to dance around with delight. And if that convention is occasionally transgressed, people notice.

When Saskatchewan's Randy Woytowich lost the final of the 1991 Brier, the television interviewer tried to hand him an excuse about the rocks not being well matched. "Absolutely not," he insisted. "We chose the rocks ourselves. They were fine."

His performance won him plaudits everywhere. "He was perfect," said Rick Lang, who has been on three Northern Ontario Brier championship rinks.

The conventions are so strong, it is often difficult for athletes from another sport to find a comfortable niche in curling. Rick Lang remembers how four NHL hockey players from Thunder Bay all retired at the same time and eventually showed up at the curling rink, thinking they could find an outlet for their competitive drive.

"They lasted no more than a month and a half," he recalls. "It was total culture clash. There was no place to use their aggressiveness and they couldn't stand being beaten by 60-year-old men. They were looking for an outlet for their anger and frustration, but this wasn't it."

Morris Lukowich, Ed's brother and a veteran professional hockey player, had the same problems. He couldn't rein in his competitiveness enough to play on his brother's rink.

This is not, of course, to say that curlers don't get frustrated. There are examples of chair-throwing episodes in dressing rooms and name-calling, but, unlike hockey, these moments are so rare that no one ever forgets. If you cross a certain line, if you make too many excuses or complain too much, you're branded forever. After that, no matter what you win, your success is tainted.

Tears are by far the most common reaction to stress in curling— even for men. One Alberta curler who had tried all his adult life to get to the Brier lost the provincial final in 1990 when his last rock picked something and veered off into the boards.

"After everyone had left, he just sat there and cried and cried," says *Edmonton Journal* sportswriter Ray Turchansky. "It was one of the most poignant moments I've ever seen in sports."

Social curlers share the same strict rules of etiquette with competitive curlers. They also share the same mythology. For the Greeks, stories of fabulous supernatural creatures often gave form to their beliefs and perceptions of reality. For curlers, it's the exploits of Ken Watson, Matt Baldwin, Alfie Phillips and Ernie Richardson, Canada's greats.

One of the most famous Watson stories sets the record straight for curlers who dream of the perfect eight-ender. In his Brier history book, *The First Fifty*, Doug Maxwell describes Watson's brush with immortality. "With seven rocks in the house it looked good," writes Maxwell. "The sweepers were working his rock and a couple of feet before the house, the lead, Charlie Kerr, dropped an ash from his cigar. The rock ground to a halt inches from perfection."

Maxwell also tells the story of the heroics of Matt Baldwin. In the 1958 Brier in Victoria, Baldwin was laid low by a flu bug, but

Albertans are too tough to succumb; he won the Brier with the help of a chair into which he collapsed after every shot.

And just to make sure nobody gets the idea that curlers can't break out, there is the story of Alfie Phillips, Jr., stealing a bus to drive himself back to the hotel at the Perth, Scotland, world championship in 1967. It celebrates Canadian curlers as wild frontiersmen stepping around the rules of the staid Europeans.

And for magic, the one shot everybody remembers is Al Hackner's miracle in the 10th end of the Brier final in 1985 in Moncton, New Brunswick. The shot was so impossible no one in the arena or in the TV audience, except possibly the man himself, thought Hackner had a chance. Pat Ryan, who appeared to have buried his shot completely behind a long corner guard, was already signalling he'd won as Hackner stepped into the hack.

But Hackner's "Great Manitou" was on his shoulder as he threw a double takeout and stayed to tie the game. Some say Ryan was so demoralized he allowed Hackner to steal in the 11th end; suddenly the game was over.

Everybody who cares about the game knows these stories and reveres the heroes in them.

Curlers also share a language. Even the newest converts know instinctively what "shot," "steal," "wick" and "hammer" really mean. In Paul Savage's 1974 strategy guide, *Curling: Hack to House*, there is a glossary of 87 terms. Curlers know for example if they "burn the rock"—touch it with any part of their equipment, clothes or body—it must immediately be taken out of play. And no curler worth his salt would ever describe a curling shot— even one that was played 25 years ago—in anything but the present tense. Listen to Ed Werenich talk about a big shot he played in high school nearly 30 years ago.

"He's shot and three-quarters buried. I've got the hammer and I'm attempting a quiet tapback. I hair by the guard and with desperate sweeping, it taps four inches past for two points and we take control of the game."

Despite the CCA's innovation of athletic suits for competition, both competitive and social curlers prefer a very strict dress code. Sweaters are still favoured, especially among older adults, and kilts are always acceptable.

In the 1990 worlds, Canadian champion Ed Werenich, looking for somewhere to pounce, decided the Europeans looked scruffy in their

new-fangled athletic gear. "They look like they're going jogging," he
scoffed. But Eddie wasn't quite on the fine edge of the fashion scene.
Less than a year later, he was treated to seven days of the ultimate in
Canadian curling—the 1991 Brier—and there was not a sweater to
be seen. The age of the nylon pacesetter jacket had dawned. In fact,
Eddie himself was wearing one!

Finally, curlers everywhere, social, competitive and elite, are
bound together by one more thing: a common recognition of holy
places. When the names of certain curling clubs are mentioned,
curlers of every persuasion feel a rush of pleasure, tradition and
community. The Royal Montreal Curling Club, with its quaint
motto "How social the sport and how manly," was founded in 1807,
and is the oldest curling club in the nation.

The building on Maisonneuve is small, but full of pictures and
mementoes celebrating the past. Now, with only three sheets of ice
and a membership of just over 200, it's not likely to be a threat to the
Canadian competitive curling scene, but traditionalists love the dining room. The Saturday luncheons are probably unique in the country. Twice a month the club hosts a big luncheon with a guest
speaker. The turnout might be as high as 150 people but there's not
always curling afterwards. Sometimes members just sit around and
socialize, perhaps over a hand of cards.

The membership has a strong social bond. One group travels to
the Brier every year and makes a point of setting up what they call
"classes" at one of the official hotels. Every day class begins at
8 A.M. when they ring a bell to convene their party. Each person who
comes into "class" brings a bottle of gin. They mix it with Tom
Collins, lemon and sugar, and drink for exactly one hour, until
9 A.M., when the bell rings again and someone announces that class
will reconvene again the next day at 8 A.M.

"If you have a couple of those first thing in the morning," says Des
DesRoches, a long-time member of the Montreal club who makes a
point of attending "class," "it will really set you up for the day."

Des DesRoches hasn't curled for a couple of years, but his friendships still revolve around the club. "I'm a social member. I drop in
once a week for a drink, and I turn up for the Saturday luncheon
speakers once in a while."

Saskatoon's Nutana Curling Club is vastly different. The curling
is highly competitive and banners everywhere remind members of
the club's illustrious past. Rick Folk (Brier champion in 1980) and

Eugene Hritzuk (a finalist in 1985 and runner-up in 1988) are the two most recent hotshots, but the banners also celebrate women champions like Emily Farnham in 1974 and mixed teams like Bernie Yuzdepski's 1978 rink.

The club has 1,000 members and the curling sheets are always busy. The club also hosts a much-admired cashspiel, once called the Bessborough Classic and now known as the Canadian Airlines Bessborough Curling Classic. Elite curlers across the country have fond memories of losers' banquets in Saskatoon.

And finally, Avonlea Curling Club in an industrial park in Don Mills is another of the charmed spots. Eddie Werenich says he feels at home in the easygoing pay-as-you-play club that used to be run by Don Campbell. Campbell played in three Briers himself and won in 1955 playing third for his brother Garnett.

Both Werenich and Paul Savage play at the club, but the latest celebrity is Paul's 17-year-old son, Bradley. He represented Ontario in the 1991 Pepsi Juniors and finished with a record of 7-4, barely missing the playoffs.

Since Werenich and Savage are as close to curling royalty as the sport allows, their club has immediate resonance for curling aficionados. In 1990 they added to the cachet of the place by holding what turned out to be something akin to a huge house party. Officially, it was a charity funspiel, "Kurl for Kids," and it raised over $80,000. But that was only the official side.

Organizers Savage and Dream Team lead Neil Harrison are well known as princely guys at a party so people came expecting high times. Sixty-four celebrity skips from Kerry Burtnyk to Al Hackner couldn't wait to be part of an event that would give them a no-pressure opportunity to party with their friends in the name of a good cause. Even Hec Gervais and Ernie Richardson found the offer tempting enough to make the trip from the west to Toronto.

As for the Avonlea Curling Club, it certainly came up aces and immediately vaulted into the front ranks of clubs known for their parties. "Kurl for Kids" has since become an annual event.

It's tempting to stop there, to say that's what curling is all about—a great big Canadian bear-hug of traditions, parties and pleasure. But if you stop there, you leave out almost completely the subtle, intricate sport that is at the centre of that celebration.

For there's another group of curlers to describe, perhaps 25 percent of the curling population. They also love the social side of the game, and fully enjoy the lifestyle. They too talk glowingly of the conviviality. Like the first group, curling has them by the heartstrings. But it has also taken over their minds and it is what gives their lives meaning. This group would curl even if the social thermometer were at the freezing point. They want to win. In curling parlance, these are the competitive curlers.

These curlers—the CCA estimates there are nearly 200,000 of them—are in the game for the competition, and many of them take it excruciatingly seriously.

In 1991, 40,000 Canadian men entered playdowns to the Brier. Most of them knew when the team plunked down its $200 or so that the members were also depositing their store of late-winter creativity, their leisure time and probably most of their concentration for the six weeks of playdowns.

This is not an inconsiderable sacrifice.

The Scott Tournament of Hearts attracts 30,000 women. In every corner of the country, women pay approximately $150 and go out after the lovely diamond necklace and the red heart crest that are the prizes of the provincial champions.

The seniors' competition for curlers 50 and over attracts another 45,000 and grows every year. The promotion folks at CCA don't worry about this market of their sport. Its growth, they believe, is automatic. Many curlers find their competitive fires don't cool, but after 50 the outlets for competition, even in the workplace, narrow. Curling is a natural.

"It's my best sport," laughs Gord King, an active 52-year-old curling novice. At the 1991 Canada Life Bonspiel in Toronto he played lead on the second-place team in the senior division. He was astonished because he'd only curled a dozen games in his life.

Owner of a successful auto-parts business and used to flying south for weekends of golf, King found his first bonspiel an eye-opener. It had everything: he could play on a team, he didn't have to compete against himself and he could get lucky and win something others admired.

When I met him, King was basking in the admiration of a couple of tables of men who had curled all their lives and never got as close to winning as he had. But that was just a temporary treat. The real joy came from what he'd discovered about curling. His thoughts were already on next year. He'd love to get into the playdowns for the provincial seniors' title. And even if that were to elude him, there are bonspiels like the Canada Life that attract 700 teams and could obviously give his competitive spirit a serious workout. He feels a bit as if he is eight years old and discovering hockey for the first time.

Who knows? One day King may feel like Russ Lewis and be ready to focus most of his energy on curling. Russ was a supervisor at Toronto Hydro, nearing his 59th birthday, when he decided to opt for early retirement. Instead of facing the spectre of long, empty hours, he rejoiced, thinking of all the time he would have to curl. He is now 70, belongs to a couple of clubs and curls at least 10 hours a week. Retirement has been the best period of his life.

"Men have this real competitive drive," he explains. "This is my outlet. It's a good physical release, too. I come off the rink and my sweater's wet."

Lewis is still trying to win every time out. At the 1991 Canada Life Bonspiel, the oldest continuous bonspiel in the country, his team entered in the Ross Solomon event for men over 65. It was a 64-team draw and his team made it to the semi-finals. It was almost enough to satisfy him and certainly enough to bring him back next year.

And some keep a very strong competitive edge. They wouldn't dream of wintering in Florida and missing the bonspiel season. They keep hoping this will be the year they make it to seniors' play.

It's not unusual in this sport to find people—usually men—75 years old and still honing their competitive edge. The CCA is talking about developing a Skins Game for seniors on television. The idea is that fans would love to see heroes of the past, like 1977 Brier champion Jimmy Ursel, play again. The CCA believes it would have the same appeal that the Masters Tour in golf has.

They may be right. Certainly for the group of older competitive curlers who devote themselves more and more seriously to the game as the years go by, it would be one more avenue for dreams.

But the desire to be a competitive curler is rarely something that strikes late in life. Most often, despite the public image of the sport, the most passionate competitive curlers are quite young. Usually they are people who have grown up with the sport and the dream of winning. The game is so precise, so rich in subtlety, that they can watch themselves learn a little every year. Their ability to read the ice improves, their understanding of strategy deepens and experience helps them keep calm in tense situations.

And even if their physical skills diminish a little, there is no moment when a coach or manager arrives to say there will be no new contract. As a curler, it's easy to believe you're getting better year after year.

And so each year, as they enter the playdowns, they hope this will be the year when the promise is fulfilled—when the good club curler on the hottest of streaks finally cracks the charmed circle and makes it to the Brier. They can believe once again in the old homily, "on any given day, anybody can beat anybody." They can believe that this year the good club curler will actually slay the dragons and win the Brier.

Gerry Kent dreamed this dream. The 39-year-old British Columbia lawyer was 17 when he first started trying to get to the Brier. In 1991 he not only represented British Columbia at the Brier, he made it to the semi-finals.

"The Brier has always been my goal, but I never seriously thought I'd get this far," he said, after he'd been eliminated by eventual winner Kevin Martin. "I've never really been gifted in sports, but getting to the semi-finals proved to me if you have enough determination, dedication and faith in yourself and your team, anything is possible."

For 20 years Kent practised every day, curled several times a week and remained faithful to his passion. Along the way he also got a law degree, married and had five children. But curling remained a big item on his agenda.

And then, four years ago, he discovered mountaineering. He still threw 32 rocks a day at the curling rink, but now he had to channel his energy in two directions. "Mountain climbing relieves stress from work and home life," he explains. "In Europe, they understand the wonderful recuperative effects of the mountains, but not in North America."

Had he won the 1991 Brier and been going on to represent Canada in the world championships, he would have had to cancel a three-and-a-half week trip to Nepal to climb the Himalayas.

"I do it for spiritual renewal," he says. "If you take risks, you want the rewards to justify them. When I'm climbing I can set the priorities in my life. I think having this trip planned helped [my performance in the Brier]. It was a bit of reverse psychology."

So the dream almost came true and curlers everywhere will relish Kent's story. In 1989 they were a pick-up team trying the back-door route to regional playdowns when they suddenly jelled. The next year they shocked themselves by getting to the provincial final. The year after, they shocked everyone by contending for the Brier Tankard.

And what's next? The dream now is much harder-edged. "Next time, if we get to the semi-finals, we won't be congratulating ourselves for being there," Kent says with a smile.

Kent's new team, new chemistry and new attitude have made a huge difference. He's started to cross the chasm between recreational and competitive curlers, but only those who have made it safely to the other side can tell him how wide or how deep it is.

Here is where the crispness of the delivery of a John Kawaja stands out, as does the strategy of an Ed Werenich or the consistency of an Ed Lukowich. The rest of the curling world can only watch their televised heroics in delight.

Ask Phil Sagle, who manages the Tarentorus Sports Club in Sault Ste. Marie, what he watches for in curling and he'll tell you about the big shots of northern Ontario hero Al Hackner. "The greatest shot I ever saw was the one that won the Moncton Brier in 1985. He had no shot at all. It was fate; he was supposed to win that Brier."

Or ask Calgary's Dave Petursson, president of the Southern Alberta Curling Association, and he'll talk about Ed Lukowich's ability to know when a gamble will pay off. "How aggressive he is seems to depend on the ice and who the opposition is," observes Petursson. "He might be down but he can wait, and when he's got a half shot against the opposition, he can roar back and seize the opportunity."

Over at Avonlea Curling Club in Toronto, regular Brian Merriman loves to watch the aggressive, nerveless play of Eddie Werenich when he's really on. "The 1991 Skins Game, you don't get much more exciting than that. Eddie had to draw to the button to take home $38 grand. Now that's curling!"

The TSN Skins Game in Charlottetown excited everybody. Howard and Werenich were both in fine form. According to the Skins format, where money rides on every end, the ninth end of the contest should have been worth $4,000, but it was carried over to the tenth, making the final end worth $10,000 plus the $8,000 winner's bonus. Howard made a great shot and finished the end up one but, again according to the format, it wasn't enough to win.

The two skips were forced to a draw-off, which Eddie won by two centimetres. The Werenich team's total prize money? $38,000. The Howard rink carried home $15,000. No club curler, even on the finest day of his best year, would expect to move in this rarefied company.

Increasingly over the past decade the curlers of this tiny elite have come to inhabit another world—one with its own heroes and baboons, its own social mores, and its own—quite bitter—heartbreaks. Even its triumphs and joys are not exactly as the public perceives them.

Cashspiels, the Skins Games and the CCA's dalliance with a star system all pick away at the concept of amateurism that some say is the cornerstone of the sport.

Some believe curling is the ultimate participatory sport. A rock sliding down the ice toward the rings is not an object of beauty or excitement unless you've thrown hundreds of them yourself, the argument goes. But how then to explain the mushrooming TV audience? Since Labatt's took over the Brier in 1980, it has become a huge spectator sport. In 1991 over three million people tuned in to the Brier. Its audience share for the final game was an astonishing 24 percent. "It's one of the biggest sporting events we do all year," says CBC spokesman David Moorhead.

All of this leaves the marketing types drooling, and the curling fans scratching their heads. If only three-quarters of a million play their esoteric sport, how could three million want to watch it? The TV types have a neat explanation. First, the analysts can explain each end so that the viewer gets an insight into the strategy. But more important are the radio frequency mikes each skip wears. They put the viewer right on the ice at the skip's elbow. The viewer is privy to every little joke and every nuance of the intimate chat of curlers in the heat of battle.

No other sport gets into the minds of the competitors in the same way. The mikes can be dangerous, especially when you think of some of the minds that have been served up in this fashion. In one well-remembered incident in 1973, the flamboyant Orest Meleschuk was playing Vera Pezer in a Battle of the Sexes duel. After one shot he announced loud and clear into the radio frequency mike, "I've got her by the balls, now." The broadcast truck erupted in a huge guffaw and the snippers got busy editing.

The third reason why curling is so good on TV is that it has the right rhythm. The natural breaks come often and are almost totally predictable, so commercials can be inserted easily.

But for all that, some curlers are still sceptical. They insist it is not a spectator sport—especially the way it has developed in the last decade. There's not enough action, they complain. Now that ice conditions are so good, the very best curlers seem to be able to make the rock behave with boring predictability. There's not much of a kick, they say, in watching blank end after blank end, down to a big hot finish. And even if that finish is one final, magical shot, it's not enough.

"It's like watching a golf game with 18 holes-in-one," says Howard Neville, who manages a trust company in Burlington and worked on the Hamilton Brier. "It's perfect, but it's boring to watch." He understands why the spectators booed Kevin Martin when he got two up in the 1991 semi-final and immediately instructed his lead to throw through the house. "Spectators come to be entertained," he says. "We like high-scoring lopsided games."

Neville hints that Werenich wouldn't have blanked end after end if he got up in a final, but he's forgotten (mercifully) the world championship final Werenich won in Västerås, Sweden, in 1990. The final score was 3-1 and Eddie and his team later observed that winning the toss (and hence the hammer) was the key factor in their win. Scotland's David Smith never got a sniff of a chance.

Everywhere there seems to be a groundswell of support for something called the "Modified Moncton Rule" or Free Guard Zone. The rule is a refined version of one Russ Howard and his brother Glenn have used in practice for years. It prevents leads from playing take-outs on rocks in front of the rings. The idea is to generate more offence in a game where, at the elite level at least, perfect peels have become too easy.

But change—even a change that is very popular—does not come easily in curling. The CCA is worried about the uninformed forcing changes on the sport that might cause long-term harm. "We've been peeling rocks for 20 years," grumbles Warren Hansen, CCA director of competitions. "Suddenly everyone's complaining about it being boring. The TV numbers aren't telling us that [it's boring], nor is the fact that 7,100 people paid $30 or $40 a ticket to see the [1991 Brier] final."

But for all Hansen's brave words, the CCA is embroiled in a massive tussle over the rule change. Already the International Curling Federation, headed by Gunther Hummelt of Austria, has decided the 1992 world championships and the Olympics will be played according to the new rule. Canada so far has said no, and all across the country the debate rages.

While the CCA temporizes, the decibel level of the new rule's supporters rises steadily. At this time, the women's division of the CCA has flatly turned down the rule. The men plan to ask the ICF to reconsider its decision for 1992. If they can't persuade the Europeans, 1992 Canadian teams will be playing by one set of rules in their national championship and another in the worlds and the 1992 Olympics.

But the CCA had no trouble endorsing another change destined to please almost everyone from CCA Past President Ed Steeves to the youngest junior curler in Kelowna. The CCA is actively working to get curling medal status by the 1998 Winter Games in Nagano, Japan. "We're probably closer than we've been since the 1988 Olympics," says Parkes, general manager of the CCA. This time the curling boosters will be able to satisfy the Olympic requirements: the sport must be played on three continents and in 25 countries. Last time they were a few countries and a continent short.

Also new this time is a solid business plan, says Parkes, that will be enticing to an organization like the International Olympic Committee that keeps a firm eye on the bottom line.

Olympic status would do more than a hundred marketing plans to focus attention on curling and bring in competitive youngsters. But it would also change irrevocably the flavour of the sport, and that has some of the traditionalists worried.

And there are other changes in the wind. As the spectator side of the sport bulges, the curlers, who have always been thankful just to be allowed to show up at a championship, are suddenly getting restive. They hear some Briers, like the one in Saskatoon in 1989, make millions in profit and they begin to wonder if the time hasn't come for them to share in the bonanza. Should they not, at the very least, have their time and their expenses fully compensated? The traditionalists balk at this. The charm of curling, they say, lies in its amateur quality.

But the amateur argument is hard to accept when the best curlers, like Eddie Werenich's rink, have collected $500,000 in prize money over the last decade. Since that figure has to be split four ways, it's not a living, but it mars the appearance of pristine amateurism.

The curlers themselves see the next step in the evolution of their sport not as Olympic status or even a new rule that makes the game more entertaining to watch, but as the development of a pro tour.

As Dave Parkes points out, the idea is far from new. Both Parkes and Warren Hansen tried to get a pro tour going when they were competitive curlers in the 1970s. But the mantle has now passed to Ed Lukowich, aided and abetted by transplanted New Yorker and hotshot sports publicist Brian Cooper.

The dream as constituted by Cooper's firm, Hollis Communications of Toronto, is to get seven of the most prestigious cashspiels across the country to schedule their competitions sequentially. Each would be televised and an overall sponsor would provide continuity. The winners of each event would collect points toward a national cup or professional championship.

In return, the organizer would guarantee entries from at least seven of the country's top teams. By the spring of 1991, Cooper had collected assurances from Lukowich, Howard, Ryan, Werenich, Meleschuk, Hackner and Folk that they would be interested in signing on for the tour.

For the teams there would be (they hope) expense money, generous prizes and a good shot at a new "professional" championship. At this time no sponsor had signed on, but the rumour mill had both Rothman's and Labatt's impressed.

And if the CCA feared for its own amateur championships, they weren't letting on as the steam collected behind the idea of the pro tour.

"It's a good idea," said Parkes. "The way the cashspiels work now, they're like high-stakes poker games. You could win a lot or you could walk away with nothing in your pocket except a big bill for expenses. It's a hell of a position to be in."

He doesn't concede that a pro tour, however it is arranged, could hurt the Labatt Brier or the Scott Tournament of Hearts. "The strength of those competitions is in the provinces battling it out. People buy their tickets before they know who's going to appear. You never hear people saying they wish they could see a final with Russ Howard and Eddie Werenich."

From a distance, an interested observer can't help but see an amateur-pro split coming in the sport. The Canadian Curling Association pursues its Olympic dream, rejoicing in young national winners like Kevin Martin and Julie Sutton because they exude an athletic image. Meanwhile, the older guys, the wily foxes, the custodians of this ancient, subtle sport, are taking their marbles elsewhere.

Will a split follow golf, where the pro tour is everything and national championships are minor blips in the season, or will it be like figure skating, where the apex of a skater's life is reached on the amateur podium and the various pro championships are all an interesting but incidental sequel?

Anyone looking at the development of sport over the past 40 years must be struck by how curling needs a few stars. How much of the avalanche of interest in tennis was unleashed because of the exploits of a John McEnroe or the dash of a Bjorn Borg? What role did the Golden Bear play in gilding the image of golf?

Obviously, if curling wants to step into the limelight, it must shed its slightly dowdy, eccentric image. It must turn its heroes into glamorous princes and princesses of the game. And it will have to work hard at the change because, except for televised competitions, the sports media mafia largely ignores their efforts. In 1991 the *Toronto Sun*, the paper that boasts the country's largest, and arguably best, sports section, devoted a mere two percent of its vast editorial space to stories and pictures on the Scott Tournament of Hearts. High-school sports did far better that week in the space war.

The curlers are used to it and don't complain. They march to their own drum beat. Yet they are a colourful thread in the tapestry of Canadian life.

For men, the Labatt Tankard is the holy grail of curling. For those within touching distance, no sacrifice is too great, no prize more worthy than the distinctive two-foot-high gold trophy. The hardware is worth $50,000, but the price is paltry stacked against the hours of practice and the tears of anguish and frustration it has caused every curler with enough talent, drive and will to lust after it.

Every province and territory in the land has its own tales of the might-have-beens—of the great and nearly great curlers who came one end, one point, one horsehair from glory and the record books.

Some men's lives are on hold for years while they try again and again to get out of the club, the zone, the district, or maybe even the province to make their assault on the Brier. Again and again, in spots as far-flung as Corner Brook and Kelowna, you'll hear the same poignant tale: "He's the best curler in the province, but he never got to the Brier."

Sometimes perpetual disappointment cures the lust for the gold. Middle-aged men finally tell themselves it's time to start concentrating on their careers or their (nearly grown) families or the wives who have long ago learned to do without them.

Nobody knows when that moment will come, when a curler ceases to be "competitive." He could be 29, 39, even 49. The only sure thing is that a switch will one day click off in his head and he won't be able to take it any more. The pressure will be too great. He'll retire from the front ranks of Brier hopefuls.

He could do it in a glare of publicity, as did Harold Breckenridge, the 44-year-old Calgary transportation supervisor, at the 1990 Brier. As his team began to chalk up the worst record ever for an Alberta team, he cracked and sat out in despair, pleading "mental anguish." "We benched the worst player—me," he told the media. The team finished second last with a 4-7 record, and Breckenridge isn't sure he'll ever be back.

More likely though, after years of trying, our anonymous curler will wear out his hope and silently fade away. If anybody asks, he'll say that curling is becoming elitist, too expensive for the average Joe to cover expenses when he goes bonspieling. Or he'll point out how tough it is to find a good team these days.

Like the once-formidable Paul Gowsell, a two-time world junior champion, he'll blame ingratitude or restlessness, as one by one the up-and-comers move on to curl behind other, more competitive or more compatible skips.

Sometimes a father waits for his boys to graduate from junior to curl with him. Orest Meleschuk pulled it off when his son Sean joined his 1989 Brier team. But most often the young men are wary of tying themselves to their fathers. Like Jim Sullivan and Charlie, Jr., they feel the sentimental tug of their father's desire, but they need to know first if they could win with their hotshot boys' team.

The fathers (Jim's father Dave has represented New Brunswick six times in the Brier; his brother Charles, Sr., has been there five times) accept the verdict: their boys should be the ones in the front row now, they'll say. Theirs will be a gentler exit than most.

But often when his competitive days are done, the serious curler lives with a great dense cloud of regret as long as he hangs around the curling world. For all his faithful service, the Brier was never his. His friends commiserate, reflect on the fickle nature of the game. His wife and family (if they're still around) quietly prepare for his repatriation to family life. But no one can help him when he wakes in the night and replays that one rock, that one end, that changes everything.

And yet on the surface, curling has a vastly different face. A face that showed to perfection when its two media stars faced off in a Toronto horse palace a few years ago in a Battle of the Sexes that stood a world championship on its ear and made curling, briefly, front-page news everywhere.

In 1986 Marilyn Darte (née Bodogh) won the women's curling championship, the Scott Tournament of Hearts. The women had never had such a lively champion. One of her first acts was to challenge the men's champion to a grudge match.

Ed Lukowich excused himself, pleading that he had a world championship to win, but Eddie Werenich, Brier and world champion in 1983, knew a good thing when he saw one and promptly took up the challenge. The Battle of the Sexes rapidly became a PR extravaganza, a jokey send-up of a serious debate about women in sport. The feminists loathed it.

The irrepressible Darte hardly seemed a serious, never mind passionately dedicated, sportswoman. As her theme music blared, she exploded onto the ice doing cartwheels in her trademark red kilt. During the game she rode her broom up and down the sheet in her best witch imitation. In the end she lost abysmally.

Werenich entered as a king in royal robes, while Olympic silver medallist Sean O'Sullivan shadowboxed his way through a crêpe-paper heart to the dulcet strains of "Rocky." Behind them came the buxom barmaid from the Avonlea Curling Club. Her skimpy T-shirt had the word "Coach" emblazoned on it.

What would anyone think?

Certainly not that curling is a passion that dominates the lives of those who are best at it. Certainly not that elite curlers respect their game as a serious mental discipline steeped in history and governed by sometimes impenetrable traditions.

And certainly not that the high-jinks that spring evening were being provided by two teams racked by problems. In fact, Werenich's team had already split up before that April 5 spectacle. There had been a face-saving story explaining the split to the press in late February, but the four themselves had simply walked away, burying their pain and regret. There had been no discussion. This was the first time they had been together since they lost in the Ontario playdowns.

In the women's camp, the situation was equally grave. Darte's third, Kathy McEdwards, had told them she was pregnant and planning to take most of their championship year off. Darte was deeply disappointed and trying to come to grips with it. McEdwards had been battling morning sickness all week. Lead Jan Augustyn was continuing her battle with anorexia—a problem aggravated, if not caused, by her intense commitment to curling.

But none of that was revealed as the 6,000 fans in the Coliseum stomped and screamed as if they were watching a wrestling match. For the most part, the curling world took its trivialization with good grace, convinced that any exposure was "good for the game."

The Battle of the Sexes is typical of the attention curling usually gets. It is not surprising, then, that the popular view is that curling is a pastime, not a passion; a game, not a sport. The shock is that the people behind the masks of concentration in the televised game have strayed so far from general society's values of making money and being hip that they cherish a sport that often limits their careers and, in some circles, actually exposes them to scorn.

But the curling world has its own subculture. Safely inside this world, the elite curlers preside over their realm and must deal with both the adulation and the criticism of the fans. But unlike pro athletes, they have none of the buffers big money can buy. They can be wounded by the catcalls and overwhelmed by the attention, and ruined by the expense of competing.

And still they do it year after year. All but one of the skips described in this book are scheming to win big very soon. But first they must conquer their opponents, outmanoeuvre the other responsibilities in their lives and jump through the hoops and over hurdles set up by the country's various curling associations.

Every spring the odyssey toward the Labatt Brier and the Scott Tournament of Hearts is watched by millions of Canadians across the country. Some are ardent curlers who believe one day they too will take their place at the Brier or the Scott. They study the games, looking for a blueprint for their own success. Others, like icemaker Mike Warren, watch with less intensity: the dream of the Brier is not as personal with them. They watch and marvel at the skill, the precision and the dedication of the genuine article—a true Canadian champion.

1

EDDIE WERENICH
The Wrench Turns the Screws

EDDIE WERENICH HAS the most recognizable face in Canadian curling.

He'd be the first to tell you that it's not a beautiful face. The teeth
are slightly gapped and perhaps it shows a little too explicitly where
he's been in his 44 years on the planet. But it's a strong face, and
probably, in another age, those royal robes he wore in the Battle of
the Sexes with Marilyn Darte would not have looked outlandish.

But this king has a broad measure of the court jester in him. It
doesn't matter that his lofty accomplishments (world champion
twice over) mean that in some circles he is revered and treated as a
demi-god. Attention of that kind makes him rub the back of his neck
and squirm a bit. He's far happier in the role of scrappy underdog.

He loves his nickname. "The Wrench" has a solid, blue-collar,
meat-and-potatoes feel to it. But he's not so meat-and-potatoes that
you can't catch him in a black leather jacket, shades and a gold
chain. Two gold charms hang from that chain; one is a fireman's hat,
the other a wrench.

All his life Werenich has despised toadying. Growing up on the
wrong side of the tracks in tiny Benito, Manitoba (pop. 460), with
Ukrainian parents who spoke very little English, he loved to take on
what his brother calls the "snobs and big shots" of nearby Swan
River. "People looked down on us because we didn't have the best of
clothes or the newest car," remembers Tony, who is four years older.
"That really rubbed Ed and me the wrong way. The only way we
could get back at them was to beat them at curling. Maybe curling
gave him a feeling of power."

In the nearly 30 years since, nothing much has changed. Eddie is never as cranked up as he is when he sees himself as the little guy from Benito taking on the "rocket scientists."

For nearly 20 years he's been almost a legend in the Canadian curling world, but in his mind he's still the underdog. When he senses the time is right to make a move, he doesn't send for advisers or take a day to reflect, he shoots from the hip, or the lip—over-turning Christmas trees in the lobby of Toronto's posh Granite Club or skewering opponents with needle-sharp barbs.

And as the years go by, the point on Eddie's rapier seems to get sharper and his thrust more practised. There was a time when Eddie remembers himself as the "naive country boy" and Paul Savage used to walk along behind him to smooth things over. More than once Savage fired off a quick letter of apology over Eddie's name to get his buddy (and their team) off the hotseat. Doug Maxwell, executive director of the Ontario Curling Federation, describes Eddie's approach as "scattergun." He doesn't always have all the facts, says Maxwell, but his instincts are keen and he usually hits at least one worthwhile target.

Not surprisingly, the curling world Werenich adores is studded with enemies. That fact goes a long way to making him who he is, not only by some readings the best curling skip in the world, but also the most doggedly competitive man in the game and the sharpest thorn in the side of the curling establishment.

These qualities proved a potent combination in the spring of 1990.

On a Sunday afternoon, in the packed Sault Ste. Marie Memorial Gardens, Werenich crushed the hopes of Brier novice Jim Sullivan in a 5-4 battle that was never really in question after the second end. The victory gave Eddie his second championship and was unques-tionably the sweetest win of his life. "I honestly doubted if I'd ever get back. I was curling so bad for a couple of years there, I even considered giving up the game."

When he talks like that you can hear the emotion in his voice. And you can only guess what it would mean to Eddie Werenich not to curl.

But to preserve the sweetness of his Brier win, there was one more hoop to leap through. Much as the idea appalled him, as winners of the Brier, Eddie and his boys were going to have to go to Västerås, Sweden, and compete in a world championship for Canada.

Curling must be the only sport in the world in which it is generally believed to be more difficult to win the Canadian title than world honours. In Canada, among curling aficionados, the world title is almost held in disdain. They talk as if any club curler worth his salt could waltz in and snare the honour. They believe this, depite the fact that the cream of Canadian curling regularly loses the thing. In the 1970s, the men's world title was lost by Harvey Mazinke, Hec Gervais, Bill Tetley, Jack MacDuff, Jim Ursel, Ed Lukowich and Barry Fry in rapid sucession. And even in the 1980s, such hotshots as Kerry Burtnyk, Mike Riley and Pat Ryan have stubbed their toes in what is supposed to be a simple waltz.

But it was not merely the fear of losing that made Werenich dread Sweden. He knew in his bones he was not going to have fun. Since Air Canada backed out of the Silver Broom in 1985, the world event has been losing prestige. For three years it struggled under the patronage of Hexagon International, and when they signed off no other sponsor could be found. Without money, advertising or pizazz, the event has teetered at the brink of oblivion.

For Eddie, who confesses that he has never had much ambition in life but to win the Brier, chase curling glory, and have a little fun along the way, the world championship in Västerås, Sweden, had very little to recommend it. By 1990, he'd already won the Brier—twice. He'd won the world too, in Regina, in 1983. Nothing he could do in Sweden could add much to his glory.

As for fun, the Swedish sin tax practically rules it out. Like most curlers, Eddie and his team love to party. They look forward to the drinks and laughter after the game. It's an important team ritual: the way they let off steam after two and a half hours of intense concentration and precise moves.

But in Sweden, having a drink with friends in a pleasant watering hole is a prohibitively expensive luxury. The advance word was that draft beer would cost $8.50 a glass. For Werenich and company, weaned on the $3 beer at Avonlea Curling Club, this was an outrage.

There were other problems. Eddie is a nervous flyer. The eight-hour trip to Sweden was well past his tolerance level. Also, in order to get the time off work at firehall #1 in Scarborough, he'd have to use almost two weeks of his precious vacation time. He knew he would spend it under pressure in a cold, empty rink during the Swedish rainy season.

At the Brier, the VIP treatment by Labatt's, the adulation of thousands of fans and the conviviality of the Brier Patch make it a week of intense pleasure—at least if you're winning. Occasionally during Brier week Eddie thought of the stories he'd heard of the empty arenas in Europe where world championships were played. If the competition is held in Scotland or Switzerland, 1,000 or more North Americans can be counted on to fill at least some of the seats. But Sweden was too far and too expensive. Advance bookings showed that only about 300 of the usual crowd would make the trip.

After his first day of competition at the Soo Brier, Eddie was already fretting out loud about the prospect of this free trip to Sweden. He tried to be gracious, allowing that he had a way to go until his rink won the trip and the right to represent Canada. But if they did—"I'd love not to go," he told the media scrum. "If it [the world championship] was in Canada I'd be glad to go, but . . . ."

When Tom Slater, curling writer for the *Toronto Star*, reminded him about a blow-up he had with the Swedish team at the 1983 world championships, Werenich shrugged and admitted he wasn't "in love with the Swedes."

Of course, there were those who muttered that Werenich should wait until he'd actually won it before he complained about the prize. But as usual, most smiled at Eddie's candour and silently agreed that a world championship in some Viking stronghold halfway round the globe did lack allure.

Standing in the doorway, Eddie's team chuckled at their leader's antics. They knew he was the ultimate team player, that he would never stay home and scotch their shot at a world championship. But he would, they also knew, stir things up and use the media to make his point as often and as pointedly as he could. They delighted in the way controversy seemed to make Eddie's own fires burn a little hotter. And whatever it took, they wanted their skip cranked up.

"Cranked up" is exactly what Eddie was at the 1990 Brier. In the second end of the final game he came up with what the experts described as a "dramatic multi-rock double take-out," a shot that Werenich later allowed was probably the best of his career. Still, it wasn't over for another eight ends. The Sullivan rink from New Brunswick, the Cinderellas of the Soo, kept coming at them, hoping the master would make a mistake. They took Eddie into the 10th end tied 4-4. The Brier was won on the final rock.

Curlers speak with awe of the intense mental effort such a win requires. Most, after a game like that, would be limp with joy or relief or both.

Not Eddie. He was able to draw from some deep reservoir of

energy or bile, or both, and lunge out in a completely different direction to execute revenge on an old and bitter foe, Warren Hansen.

The instant Eddie won the national championship Hansen must have known he would be one of Eddie's targets. As the one identifiable face in the power elite of what was then Curl Canada, Hansen has exercised unwelcome control over Werenich many times.

Picture this. The Wrench is coming off the ice in what must have been a tidal wave of relief. He's back on top of his mountain after wandering in the wilderness for most of two years. But in the instant of triumph, his restless and exceedingly tough mind is bent on settling a score with an old enemy. As he slides down the sheet, hand in pocket, he looks down, trying to contain a sly grin.

"It was the most fun I'd had in a long time," he said later. He knew, of course, it would be virtually automatic that Warren Hansen would be assigned by the Canadian Curling Association to coach or manage the Brier winner at the world championship.

He also knew that being that winner would finally give him the upper hand with Hansen. "I don't want him as my coach," Eddie told the press. "I've worked 32 years for this moment. I don't want someone like him jumping in."

Later he told the *Toronto Sun*'s Perry Lefko he didn't want Hansen "portraying to kids across the country he's Eddie Werenich's coach. Even that bothers me after what he's tried to do to this game.

"I'd been planning that day for a long, long time," he explained the next day as he luxuriated in his triumph.

Within an hour of Werenich's broadside Hansen was history. He would go to Sweden but only as manager for the Canadian women's team, skipped by Alison Goring. "If Eddie's happy, we're happy," said Dr. Ed Steeves, the president of the CCA."

Eddie, doing his perfect little one-upmanship cackle, was most assuredly happy.

But that pleasure did not extend to the over 6,000 kilometres to Sweden. On balance, he wanted to be world champion, but he was having trouble taking the competition seriously. He knew that even though he'd already won the title in 1983 it would still be humiliating to lose in 1990. The image of Alfie Phillips played and replayed in his head. The cigar-chomping, irreverent Ontarian claims he never got over losing the world championship (then called the Scotch Cup) in Perth in 1967.

Even Warren Hansen has a similar story. He was on the Hec Gervais team that lost the world championship in the semi-finals in 1974. After that, Hansen said, he lost his desire to curl competitively.

It's not surprising, then, that in late March, as he watched "Lynnie," his wife of 18 years, pack his bag for Sweden, Eddie had a leaden feeling in his heart.

A feeling that only intensified when he got there.

The beer arrived just in time.

Afterwards Eddie would say: "I went to Sweden, drank beer in my room and came home with a bouquet of flowers and a $5 silver tray."

He wouldn't mention that he'd notched a second world championship. He wouldn't mention how much it meant to him to show his kids, Darren, then 13, and Ryan, 11, that he was *the man*, the best in the world in 1990. Flowery speeches aren't his style.

But he wouldn't forget the beer. It was, he joked, the "turning point of the week." Labatt's sent two 25-case shipments. The second arrived from London, England, on Tuesday, day four of the eight-day championship.

There's always Canadian beer at world curling championships. Labatt's likes the Canadians—players, spouses and officials—to remember the taste of home. Hence the first 25 cases.

But the second shipment, a gesture by Labatt's rep, Bob Klinck, was as expansive as the rest of the Swedish world championship canvas was limited. "We knew we had to subsidize Eddie," is the way Bob Walker, national promotions manager for Labatt's, explains it.

And so on Tuesday, in the precise middle of the championship, another 25 bright-blue cases of Labatt's Blue, specially addressed to The Wrench, appeared at the Scandic Hotel, complete with a bill of lading that told them that this contribution to Canadian good times had cost $1,000 to ship.

Eddie ordered his team to build a monument. The cases stacked very nicely into two pillars almost to the ceiling in what would have been fifth man Neil Harrison's bedroom, had this been any other sport. But this was curling and the room was the designated party room—especially now. The edifice of beer just inside the door of room 315 would play an important role in the unfolding of the world championship 1990.

Västerås, where the 1990 world curling championship was held in early April, is a Swedish commercial centre 1,000 years old. And as far as the spirited Canadians were concerned, the venerable old town was acting its age. No nightlife. No exuberant fans. The human factor consisted of 63 indigenous curlers stretched to the limit as they worked 20-hour days to stage a championship that, in Canada, would have taxed 10 times as many volunteers. Even their hardy Viking stamina couldn't disguise the fact that the Västerås committee was woefully understaffed. And the city itself was completely indifferent.

Afterwards, Axel Kamp, president of the Swedish Curling Association, would confide to his son Ragnar, who lives in Canada, "It was not very good, not very good at all."

Ragnar was not surprised. "Västerås is not a curling centre," he says. "I knew the spectators wouldn't come."

Even for the final game on a Saturday afternoon the arena was pitifully empty. The official estimate was 3,000 but it looked far sparser than that.

As the week drew to an end, Soren Brinkeborn, president of the local organizing committee, ruminated on why they had bid for the championship. "We organized the European championship in 1983," he said, watching as young men in shirt-sleeves with drained, pale faces rushed about shuffling paper and talking in staccato bursts. "Afterwards we said, 'Never again.' But it was a very big success and five years later we forgot the bad and said, 'Let's go for the worlds.' Now we again say, 'Never again.'"

Brinkeborn and his committee have scraped together 150 souls. Some are curlers from far-flung corners of Sweden, even Lapland; the rest are just generous burghers of Västerås hoping their city appeals to the visitors. Nobody's getting enough sleep. For the most part they are astonishingly good-tempered but, overworked as they are, they have no sizzle left over to make the event fun. And very little patience for criticism. None of the visitors tries very hard to disguise the general disappointment with the championship. Werenich, for example, repeats again and again, whenever he finds a willing ear, that the world championship is an anti-climax to the Brier. It is not a popular line with the Europeans.

Nor, to be honest, is the man who is about to be crowned champion exactly the toast of the Rocklunda Arena (the only corner of town that cares about curling). The Ukrainian peasant's son who represents Canada is too critical and too blunt.

The Swedish concession to humour in the opening ceremonies is a motorized curling rock with a mind of its own that lunges around the ice chasing King Frost, a human giant in a Viking's horned hat. More than one Canadian shivering in the near-empty stands chuckles at the prospect of the closing ceremonies if The Wrench wins. There will be no need for a rebel rock to chase the Viking then. The sharp-tongued 5'7" Mr. Werenich would take on any number of 7'6" King Frosts in any forum they chose.

But when Eddie has won and that scene is finally played, his speech is almost conciliatory. It virtually ignores the Swedes (fittingly, since most of them had ignored the tournament) and seems to hold out a short, frail olive branch to the Canadian Curling Association.

This is a new side to The Wrench and nobody quite believes it. Dave Parkes, general manager of the CCA, fumes later at the dance that it was unnecessary for Eddie to thank the CCA for "coaching" the team through the championship. He's right, of course, the word "coaching" carries a lot of freight between Eddie and the CCA.

Eddie scoffs at Parkes's interpretation. "If I wanted to hurt Warren again I would hurt him, not kiss him," he says.

He is equally direct about the Swedes. Coming so close on the heels of the raucously social Soo Brier, the Västerås world championship suffered mightily in comparison.

Sure, Västerås is old, beautiful even, with its medieval church, its footpaths and river, but this championship could never have the place in Eddie's heart that the Brier holds. When he was an eight-year-old Manitoba rink rat, lying on the floor listening to the radio announcer describe every shot of the Brier, he imagined a Valhalla populated by gods with names like Ernie Richardson and Matt Baldwin. As he grew up, the names changed but the magic remained.

In Västerås, the magic of tradition and the charm of childhood associations were missing. Eddie and his team were numbed by the silence in the arena and by the formal courtesy of their hosts, and deeply homesick for some good old Canadian hilarity.

In the home video Neil Harrison made for the team, he pans the Swedish equivalent of the Brier Patch. Gingham tablecloths, Swedish open-face sandwiches—and hundreds of empty chairs. Harrison's irony is never far from the surface. Calmly the voice-over announces, "As you see, we are barely able to squeeze into the Patch. You people over there [pan to empty chairs]—Keep the noise down!"

For the Canadians it was a joke that never wore thin.

If this was to be a memorable week they would have to make it so. Not surprisingly, the women partners of the Werenich team were more than equal to the task. Room 315 at the Scandic, where Eddie and the boys were preparing for world domination, was party central, and not just for the Canadians. "The beer allowed us to be good hosts," Kawaja explains with a grin.

Terry Kawaja, John's younger brother and a serious rival as a reveller, tried to bunk with Harrison the final few nights. He never made it. One morning Neil found him sleeping in the hall. The day they were leaving, he turned up in the shower, sound asleep, standing up against the wall.

Yes, the fun was a bit inbred they'll admit, but it certainly beat the alternatives. On Friday, the night before the finals, Eddie, John, Pat Perroud, Ian Tetley and Neil quietly celebrated their victory over Denmark in Harrison's room at the Scandic. Friends like Norway's Eigil Ramsfjell, who had already been eliminated, dropped in. It was, even by curlers' standards, a good party.

The Denmark game had been the toughest of the tournament. It ended on the brink of fisticuffs when Kawaja accused the Danish second Peter Andersen of "dumping" snow and debris in front of the skip's rock in the ninth end to slow it down. "In Canada that would probably have been a fight," said Kawaja afterwards.

And why not here?

"Did you see how big that guy was?"

Peter Andersen is listed in the fact book as 194 cm and 105 kg, Kawaja at 180 cm and 84 kg.

For Werenich and company, the party ended early Friday night, but for many of the Canadians it kept going as a consolation prize for Alison Goring and her rink. Their championship season had ended that night when they lost the semi-final to the eventual winner, the Dordi Nordby rink from Norway.

As for the men, they knew, even as they trundled off to bed, the ordeal was almost over. All that was left was the final against Scotland at 1 P.M. on Saturday. This was no time to get a little crazy.

Meanwhile, elsewhere in Västerås, there was another Canadian celebration going on. Gordon Craig, TSN vice-president, was taking his bunch out to celebrate a new contract with the International Curling Federation. Their choice was a hangout for local plutocrats called the Skybar, perched atop the two-month-old Grand Aros Hotel, the only skyscraper in Västerås.

The bar wouldn't have appealed to The Wrench. It was what hoteliers like to call "sophisticated continental" and that night was full of the wealthy "rocket scientist" types who make Eddie profoundly suspicious. The distaff side ran to bored blondes in high- end designer evening wear.

In one room Britt Ekland's father, a European curling enthusiast, leaned on the bar in earnest conversation with a bejewelled redhead. Two of the curlers from the Swedish team, which had been ousted by Scotland 5-3 in the afternoon's semi-final, cruised the room dejectedly. Once in a while they'd stop and glance up at one of the room's three TVs where their game was silently replaying. Aside from the TSN technicians occasionally discussing a camera angle, they were the only ones who showed the remotest interest in their on-screen misery.

The TSN celebration was a modest affair by curlers' standards. There was no dancing, no boisterous teasing, and very little laughter. They languished for an hour or two, had a couple of rounds of beer and wine and a little finger food. The dramatic chaser was a whopping bill, the Swedish krona equivalent of $1,200.

Gulp.

Laughter and Labatt's Blue in room 315 looked mighty good by comparison.

At the beginning of the championship, the on-ice performance was as flat as the party scene. Eddie kept talking about how he had to win or else "spend my summer explaining why I lost. You have to win or else it takes the pleasure away from the very real accomplishment of winning the Brier," he told everyone who asked.

It didn't sound much like the mindset of a champion shaving away all impediments but the pure desire to win.

His team-mates watched carefully. They knew if Eddie could only get up for it, the world crown was theirs. If not . . . well, they all knew that theirs is an unforgiving sport.

At first it seemed they might be allowed to sleepwalk through it. They were up 5-0 by the time they met Daniel Model of Switzerland in the 12th draw on Tuesday evening. It might have been another routine win coming up, except for the fire in Eddie's eye. Afterwards he would say this was the game where he finally felt "the adrenalin kicking in."

What made that happen? Was it the Model rink's reputation as near giant-killers because they almost upset Pat Ryan in the semi-finals in Lausanne in 1988? Or could it be their skip's fiery and unsportsmanlike conduct in flinging the broom about when he gets frustrated? (At one point Model nearly hit a rink attendant 10 metres away when he hurled his broom after losing. This is not curling etiquette, and next time Model played, the rink attendants showed up in crash helmets.)

But the truth was it was much more personal than that. Early Tuesday, Model and Eddie had passed in the corridor after practice. "Forty-two?" the Swiss curler was heard to mutter. "Looks more like 62 to me."

Interesting. A Swiss guy with a name like Model chooses to mutter about Werenich's age. He does it in English and within earshot of the Canadian team. Neil Harrison, who knows the precise value of Eddie's rage to his game, was quick to report back to The Wrench just in case Eddie hadn't heard.

When she heard about the comment, Linda Werenich chortled in delight. She knew that gamesmanship would come a cropper that night on Sheet A. "He wanted to beat Model real bad," was all she'd say afterwards. Her satisfied smile said much more.

But the Swiss curler had come to play. He took three points in the fourth end. Eddie, as is his custom, feigned not to notice. Like a cobra, he waited for his moment. In the end it was a gut-wrenching 5-4 win for the Canadians. Eddie curled 92 percent to Model's 70 percent.

Werenich loves a little gamesmanship of his own. At one point he woke from his somnambulant stroll through the early days of the tournament to observe that his fellow competitors looked as if they were going to a "pyjama party." Proper attire, according to Werenich, was a sweater and pleated slacks. Anything less, and the underdressed curler committed that most heinous of curling crimes: damaging the image of the game.

The chief offenders were the young teams from Sweden and Scotland, not coincidentally the two strongest teams at the tournament after the Canadians. "Eddie loves to wind everybody up," said Scotland's second, Peter Smith. "We just take it with a pinch of salt."

But Chuck Hay, a former world champion and the father of the third and the lead on the Scottish team, claimed his sons were upset by the clothes and unhappy with Werenich's drawing attention to them. "They just received the uniforms three days before they left. If they'd had time, they would have changed them," explained Hay. "The elastic [around the ankles of the pants] is sewn right in. They can't even take it out."

After Eddie's outburst the team's skip David Smith substituted pleated slacks for "jogging pants." When the press questioned him, he erupted, "We're here to curl and win this thing. Who cares about bloody trousers?" Eddie and the boys chuckled over one more skirmish won.

But later in the week, when the Canadians locked horns with the Danes over a sweeping problem, the tone was decidedly less playful. For someone like Eddie, with his intensely competitive nature and obsessive attention to detail, officiating will never be good enough. But usually he reins himself in. However, in the semi-final game against Denmark his whole team's composure was shattered.

The game was surprisingly hard fought. Since Werenich and company had dropped the final two games of the round robin, they were tied for first place with four others. A loss to the Danes would mean a quick plunge into ignominy. Tommy Stjerne's huge second, Peter Andersen, usually did pretty much as he wished both on the curling sheet and everywhere else. And in the ninth end when the Stjerne's rock was, according to Kawaja, "obviously heavy," what he wanted to do was dump some snow and debris in front to slow it down.

For the "Lebanese Lion," as Kawaja's team-mates call him, this was beyond bearing. While the officials continued to doze, John screamed at Andersen to get his broom off the ice. The adjective he used to describe the broom would never pass the test of curling etiquette.

The Danes later said Kawaja's verbal attack "confused" their second and caused him to sweep improperly. At any rate, dumping or no dumping, the rock which had seemed heavy ended up too short by several centimetres. The Canadians stole one to tie the game 4-4.

Andersen was not the only confused person. The officials appeared not to know what Kawaja was talking about. "No wonder," Kawaja laughed later, "if they take their rock off we're lying three. It would cause an international incident."

"I know the video looks illegal," Stjerne later told TSN'S Vic Rauter, "but it wasn't. I've been curling with Peter (Andersen) for 19 years and he just wouldn't do something like that."

Perhaps the incident unhinged Stjerne too. In the 10th he made a strategy mistake. Eddie pounced, and the game was over.

Afterwards Eddie explained that they didn't really like to "get into it" with the other team, but if the officials weren't going to do anything, they had to. If that's true, The Wrench has mellowed considerably since his blow-up with the Swedish team in the 1983 world championship in Regina. In that contretemps—which swirled around etiquette and corn broom chaff—Eddie very much wanted to "get into it" with the other team. He went so far as to tell the press the Swedes were "four real jerks."

The day his comments hit the papers Mikael Hasselborg, who played third for his brother Stefan, went out looking for Eddie. He found him having breakfast alone in a restaurant. "I wanted an explanation," says Hasselborg today. "I wanted to see if he stood by his comments."

Not surprisingly, Eddie saw the appearance of the tall, athletic, 29-year-old Swede—backed by his entire rink, including their fifth man—as an intimidation tactic. In the seven years since, relations have been barely cordial. There have been casual attempts at rapprochement, but no apologies have been, or probably ever will be, exchanged.

For a curler there are benefits in nursing bitterness. It can sharpen up his competitive edge. In 1985, at the world championship in Glasgow, Pat Perroud, then on Al Hackner's team and en route to his first world championship, asked to borrow some tape from the Hasselborgs. Inside their first-aid kit were 8x10 glossies of Eddie and the pugnacious Kawaja. "It was funny," says Perroud. "They said they were using those pictures to get up for games."

But today Hasselborg doesn't regret the corn brooms and denies Werenich's allegations about cheating by using corn to get an unfair advantage. "Now I've learned what a lot of Canadians do to corn, like wet it and dry it in the oven to leave more chaff on the ice. But we have never, never done that. It's not our way to play curling. And we have never changed brushes depending on the situation in the game."

Time has changed the two adversaries. In 1990 Mikael Hasselborg attended the world championship in the capacity of statistics supervisor. He no longer used the corn brooms but he missed them. "The main reason is we have a new team. Not everyone can handle a corn broom."

The Hasselborgs believed Werenich was playing mental games

with them in 1983 by taking so long to clean the ice after every rock. After a particularly scrupulous cleaning for what Hasselborg describes as a "simple" shot, he clapped as Eddie made his way to the hack.

The noise startled Werenich and caused him to walk over close to Hasselborg, show him the length of the broom, and threaten to impale him on it. For a moment the spectators in Regina held their collective breath, waiting for the first blow.

The moment passed and Eddie instead vented his fury in the press. Hasselborg insists he had clapped to attract the attention of the referee to what he believed was an unnecessary delaying of the game. "I realized the same second (that I clapped) that it was not right."

Werenich's mental tactics worked, Hasselborg says. "He had the benefit. He got us upset and we couldn't concentrate on curling as we should. We had a very, very rough game."

Sitting on his statistician's perch, Hasselborg had plenty of time to reflect on what makes a great curler. "Werenich has a very different way of meeting teams," he believes. "We've had no other experience like that in 23 years of curling. With others it's almost a friendly game."

But he takes inspiration from Eddie's ferocity and longevity. "Many top curlers leave the game too soon. There's so much to learn."

Whereas Mikael Hasselborg has obviously mellowed, it's not as easy to chart Eddie's change. For one thing, forgiveness doesn't spread itself very thickly on his soul.

"Yeah, I'll admit it, I'm a little vindictive," he says smiling over his latest swipe at the curling establishment. He's just as excitable as ever. In the past few years the highs and lows on his emotional rollercoaster seem to be steeper than ever. He's been through the embarrassment of the "Jellybellies" and the "Battle of the Bulge." He's seen days, he insists, when he's dreaded throwing even a simple takeout because he was sure he'd miss.

Sympathize with him, excoriate him, but don't count him out. Eddie is eight years wiser than when he skipped the 1983 championship team. He calls himself "mellower." Others would label him "shrewder." And if you look into those canny hooded eyes, don't expect to find pools of innocence. He wants to win as much as ever. But he's not as agile as he was at 34, and he's had a cataract removed from his left eye and it has affected his ability to read the ice. He has to find other ways to win.

He has claimed that losing 18 pounds as he was forced to do for the Olympic trials made him lose his touch. Unquestionably, after the debacle of the Calgary Olympic trials, he struggled as he never had before. But many of his opponents and friends dispute his assessment of the situation. "He's always very hard on himself," explains his wife, Linda. "In golf, he'll get onto the green in his first shot and complain it was a bad shot."

But whatever caused the change in The Wrench in his 41st and 42nd year, his championship rink of 1990 was quite a different proposition from the one of 1983.

Once Werenich was the undisputed master of the draw game. Every end was an adventure in tightening the screws and upping the ante. He oozed confidence as he set up ends which required him to make ever more difficult shots. Always the aggressor, always taking it to the opposition, he and his team went out to win it all in six ends.

"The way to beat us in those days," says Kawaja, who played second on what was universally described as the Dream Team because of the concentration of talent, "was to keep it close. If it was hit, hit, hit we'd get bored and make a mistake. The only game we knew was the aggressive game and we'd let teams back in the game after we were up four.

"This year [1989-90] we only lost one game after we were up by two points. With this team we just slam the door. But draw for draw the new team couldn't beat our old team."

Indeed, eight years later the edges of Eddie's game are flatter and the cockiness is gone. He takes a more conventional route to the same place. "You might see Eddie shoot more basic shots these days," agrees Harrison, who in many ways is Eddie's curling confidant. "In the old days, he would just dial it in. We never thought he'd miss."

Now instead of setting up the end so he has to make a triple, he relies on Kawaja's immense skill to keep it playable. He keeps saying he's in decline, but he never even thinks of quitting, according to his wife, Linda. And, as Harrison is fond of pointing out, "He did just win the world."

One of the ways he wins is by cleaning up every detail in his favour—on or off the ice—"shooting the angles," Harrison calls it.

Eddie loves to gossip about the curling world. He knows everything that's going on. That's another of the reasons why jetting into the unknown at Västerås, Sweden, was not an appealing proposition. Better than anybody else in the game, he uses information about opponents to help him control situations.

Mike Riley, the 1984 Brier winner from Winnipeg, can use his steel-trap engineer's mind to process information, figure the angles. But there's a limit to how much data he'll allow into the equation. Before the 1984 Brier semi-final, where Riley and Ed Lukowich met, Lukowich was worried that the TV lights were heating up the rocks and therefore affecting ice conditions. While Clare DeBlonde, Riley's coach, and Lukowich struggled to persuade CBC to cover the rocks with towels, Riley fidgeted. "Who cares?" he finally erupted. "Let's just get the game going."

If *he*'d believed the warmed rocks were melting the ice surface, The Wrench would still be arguing the point. Riley's attitude would be foolhardy and unthinkable for him.

In Sweden, Eddie and his team had carefully judged which were the best set of rocks at the tournament. Eddie was horrified when he heard that second Ian Tetley had casually mentioned which rocks they liked to Alison Goring's team. If the women were to get first pick of the rocks in the final and Alison snapped up the set they wanted, Tetley would have a lot of explaining to do.

After he lost Eddie, Paul Savage missed the edge Eddie's constant attention to such details gave him. He started taking notes after bonspiels or playdowns to remind himself which rocks were good on which sheet in which club. Eddie doesn't need a notepad. He can remember how a rock curled on a particular sheet of ice five years ago. Ask him how the playoff grid read in 1981 and he'll remember every detail. The same with that unimportant game they shouldn't have lost two years ago. But please don't ask him about opera or any of the myriad things he isn't interested in.

"When I'm on the curling ice, that's my office," he explains. "I'll challenge anybody in the world on certain things, like calling strategy. I know curling, O.K.? But I really don't know anything else, just curling and firefighting."

Nobody would have guessed the tack his life would take in 1957 when his grade five teacher got permission to take her class to the curling rink.

Even at nine or ten Eddie was already accomplished in the art of hanging out. And in Benito, the curling rink was the best hangout in town. He'd already fooled around enough with the rock to be able to throw it—with two hands and two feet in the hack. Miss Koroluk's curling league simply gave him a chance to excel.

"There wasn't much to do in the winters," Eddie has said. "You curled, played hockey or froze." Eddie opted for two of the three. But although he was competitive, he was never really big enough for hockey. Curling very quickly took over his life. By the end of the season in grade five he'd won a bonspiel and established a reputation.

In public school Eddie fed his desire to curl by playing in the ladies' league. By high school he was playing third for his brother Tony and zipping around Manitoba to play in bonspiels on the men's circuit. "We cleaned up pretty good until the principal called me in and said my grades weren't good enough to be taking days off to go curling," Eddie remembers with a chuckle.

At night he practised. His brother Tony remembers him throwing 200 rocks a night. He had the curler's fascination—obsession maybe—with getting it right. As the older brother, Tony skipped, but even then he remembers Eddie was the better shotmaker. "He was a hit man in those days. He didn't have the draw weight he has now. We laugh about that now."

Eddie remembers Benito as a "sensational" place for a kid to grow up, but at the time he and his brothers couldn't wait to finish school and set off for the big time: Toronto.

In 1966, with his high-school diploma burning a hole in his pocket, Eddie phoned his brother Al, who was already in Toronto. Sure he could come to try it out. Al even knew of a job at American Can that paid very good money—$125 to $130 a week.

So Eddie and a pal packed up and headed east. It was a classic case of bright lights, big city. "I couldn't believe it," Eddie says, trying to convey the impact Toronto had on the shy farm kid from the prairies.

He worked the summer at American Can but somehow, in a peculiar detour, he wound up that fall at Ryerson studying business administration. He insists he didn't believe they'd accept him, and when they did, he couldn't think of a good reason not to go.

Two semesters later a miserable "white-collar" student was sitting on the Queen Street streetcar. He'd just given a nightmarish presentation to his marketing class and he knew he had to get out of the course that was preparing him for a life he didn't want.

"I looked down at my brown corduroy jacket, the shirt and tie and said to myself, 'What am I doing in this monkey suit? I don't want to be a white-collar worker.'

"I got off the streetcar and never went back. I think that presentation had as much to do with it as anything. Can you imagine doing that for the rest of your life?"

Now Eddie's "presentations" reach millions via TV. But it's a long way from the Ryerson marketing class to the Rocklunda Arena. And in the era between the Beatles and Madonna, the Werenich psyche has travelled further than most.

Eddie went back to work in the can factory but the work was sporadic. He tried drywalling but it was only something that filled in the spaces between his pleasures. "In five weeks I quit four jobs because I needed time off to curl," he remembers.

In his Benito days he'd honed his skills with a pool cue too. Tony financed him as he gambled a bit on his ability. "He'd give me back $100 for my $50 and have some left over for himself too," remembers Tony. "I remember nine century breaks and I've seen him run the table."

In Toronto Eddie was carefully reassembling his own little corner of Benito. First he enticed Tony to come to Toronto. "We can curl together," Eddie said. Tony was on tap.

By 1969 he'd persuaded Linda Goulsbra, his high-school sweetheart, to join him too. "I came just to see what it was like," she remembers. "I fully expected to be going back."

Even though the Werenich boys were hotshot Manitoba curlers, it was far from certain that they'd be on one of Toronto's elite teams. With so much competition, it was easy for the self-effacing pair to get lost in the shuffle. But the Werenichs were about to acquire one ace in the hole. Eddie was about to meet Ontario curling's phenom, Paul Savage.

Paul had been out of circulation for a year in Montreal. One of the first things he did when he came back was look up his old teammates. Bruce Munro happened to be a classmate of Ed's from Ryerson. Munro and a couple of others had curled with Ed on the Ryerson team. They were dazzled by this rough farm kid's skill.

That slight connection was the beginning of the relationship between Eddie and Paul that has been central to both of their lives.

Paul Savage is two days older than Eddie, but that's about all in their backgrounds that is remotely similar.

Paul grew up in the Toronto suburb of Don Mills, Canada's first completely planned community and, in the 1960s, a bastion of middle-class WASP culture. He used to cut classes at Don Mills Collegiate to hang around the Parkway Curling Club, where Alfie Phillips, Jr. was king.

With the same knack he has now for knowing where the best party is, Savage enjoyed the curling club much more than the classroom. He stayed on the school rolls so he could curl on the high-school team (winning the Ontario title in 1965), but he lived for the afternoons at the curling club where an underage kid could finagle a beer, throw the rock and hobnob with curling heroes.

Werenich, whose parents emigrated from eastern Europe in 1939, just ahead of Hitler's invasion, has always had a strong anti-establishment bent but it is laced with respect for the institutions. His complaint is always that the people in authority botch the job, not that he wants more personal freedom.

Savage, on the other hand, was very much of the urban 1960s culture, mainlining on the "do your own thing" motto of the times. In those days he was the one who was wild, who ostentatiously bucked authority. But he also knew how to be successful. At 20 he was sent to Montreal to open up a new office for his company, Bowden Press Clipping Services. At 22 he was the youngest skip ever to represent Ontario in the Brier.

At 24 he hooked up with Ed Werenich. "Everybody was in awe of his ability," Paul remembers. By then Linda was established in Toronto and they were making plans to marry. Tony had gone back home. Life for Ed had settled into a routine of hustling pool, drywalling and a little UIC. Winters were largely reserved for curling.

Although Ed was an awesome shotmaker before he hooked up with Paul, both his temper and his teammates limited his success. "In those days if he made a bad shot, he couldn't forget it," remembers Tony. "It would affect how he threw the rest of the game."

Tony, too, was hobbled by his own intensity. It led to his giving up competitive curling and heading back to the farm in Benito. In Toronto, even in small bonspiels, he'd focus so ferociously he'd often wind up with a migraine headache. In one spiel in March 1970, he blacked out and was carried out on a stretcher to spend two weeks in the hospital. Finally, on doctor's orders, he agreed to cut back on his curling.

"I kinda regret it now," he says. "It was almost like I used the blackout as a crutch to get out of curling."

But he had lots of problems. He needed a knee operation, their diet of hamburgers and "tons of beer" was aggravating his headaches and their father, Mike, was having trouble managing the three-quarters-of-a-section farm back home. For Tony it was time to move on.

"I always kid Ed that I gave him the break he needed. When I left, the next year, or the year after, he caught on with Paul."

In those days, by many accounts, Eddie needed "saving." Paul and Linda teamed up for the task. Eddie remembers Paul "babysat me through my early years here. When I met him I didn't have a pot to piss in. He'd pick me up and take me home, feed me, pay my entry fees. I wasn't a bad person but I was too blunt. He'd walk behind me and apologize for the farm boy. He was wild too, but he knew how to smooth things over."

But even so, it was hardly a marriage made in heaven. At second stone Eddie wanted to consult on every shot. If he was overruled and Paul's shot didn't work, he was livid. "Watching Paul fight with his team was more fun than watching him curl," one reporter said of those early years.

Still, there was magic in that seething chemistry. A year later, 1973, they were in Edmonton playing in the Brier. Savage skipped, Bob Thompson played third, Eddie second, and Ron Green lead. Tony watched from the stands.

The team won its first two games and then lost three in a row. To Eddie, watching his dream slip away, the agony of the missed shots and failed strategy was beyond bearing. After the fifth game, Tony remembers Eddie shook hands with the opposition, crawled over the boards and said to his brother, "Let's get out of here."

As Werenich later told the story to the *Toronto Star*, he cooled down over a few beers but "when I got back to the hotel room, Paul tore me apart because I missed a luncheon hosted by the OCA [Ontario Curling Association]." Werenich, roused, let go his own tirade and "pretty soon we were standing face to face, yelling at each other with tears rolling down our faces."

They eventually finished the Brier tied for second place with a 6-4 record. The winning rink from Saskatchewan was skipped by Harvey Mazinke, who later would be another of Eddie's adversaries in the debacle of the 1988 Olympics.

The next year, 1974, they were back with the same team and finished with the same record. But this time they finished tied for third. Unaccountably, just as they had in 1973, they beat the tough rinks and choked against the easy ones. They beat Hec Gervais's Alberta rink, the ultimate Brier winners, but they lost to Newfoundland. It was the only game Newfoundland won.

This time it was Tony Werenich who got into trouble with Paul for criticizing his strategy. But clearly mental mistakes were costing them. The next year heading into the playdowns Savage admitted he had trouble focusing at the Brier. "In past years I was too distracted by the crowd and the other curlers," he told Mike Rutsey of the *Toronto Sun*. "I simply got psyched out. My concentration was bad and so was my strategy.

"Our rink plays a finesse game, a lot of draws and come-arounds. At the Brier you play on arena ice, not curling-rink ice, and in the past I just wasn't smart enough to adapt."

He intended to make 1975 different. Reporters were even talking about "The Brier or Bust" in January of that year. Savage himself joked about quitting if he didn't win the Brier.

As it turned out, 1975 was indeed different but not exactly in the way he intended. By Valentine's Day the team was mathematically eliminated in the Ontario playdowns. And in very hot water.

It happened in the third round of the British Consols at the Preston Arena. They had the afternoon off before the evening draw.

"We had this woman driver," Paul recalls. "We asked her if she would make a fast stop at the beer store and the liquor store before she took us back to the hotel.

"'I don't know if you boys should be doing this,' she said, but she made the stops. We got back to the hotel and we got into it. The driver's sitting there the whole time and she keeps saying, 'I don't know if you boys should be doing this.' We're giving her a few, too. Along about 4:30 or 5:00 we're pretty well-oiled and we decide we're going to go out for dinner—maybe a few glasses of wine."

But before they went Paul decided to terrorize the OCA executives a little. "The secretary at the time was a really serious guy named Leon Sykes. I phoned him and said, 'Listen, Leon, we've got a bit of a problem here. Ron Green's knee is really hurting him and he can't play and Chris Johnson's elbow's all swollen and he can't sweep. And Eddie's all pissed off and he's gone home.'

"There was about a 15-second pause on the line and he said very slowly and quietly, 'Holy Shit!'"

Savage told him to relax, that he was getting a couple of spares from Avonlea to come and play and that he'd get back to him. The driver then poured them into the car for the trip to the restaurant.

They made it back to the arena in time for the practice rocks but it would likely have been better for them had they defaulted.

"We show up at the rink and we're in fine shape. First of all Ron Green decides he's going to have a leak behind one of the scoreboards. That's how bad they were. Both Eddie and Ron fell down in their practice slide and it got worse. Eddie couldn't stop giggling through the whole thing. Our wives were crying in the stands. My mother was crying. The reporter from the *Toronto Star* went and sat with our wives and said, 'I really like these guys but this is disgusting and I've got to tell it like it is.' The stories were pretty nasty. The *Kitchener-Waterloo Record* called us 'knee-walking drunks.' The OCA. . . . I've still got the letter at home from the OCA.

"I'm going into a presentation last week [August 1990] at J.M. Schneider on this big hockey promotion we're doing. All these brand managers come walking in. This one guy says, 'Hey, I remember watching you curl loaded in the Cambridge tankard in 1975.'

"What's this, 15 years later and the guy still remembers? It wasn't that funny at the time. My mother was really embarrassed. I had a lot of family there."

Some spectators laughed, others were outraged. The press was generally censorious of the 9-4 loss. "Shoddy," one reporter huffed. "The Savage rink laughed and joked through 11 ends of play, showing total indifference by watching other games and at times not even bothering to sweep. In all, it was a shoddy exhibition by a three-time championship rink and it made a mockery of the tournament. For the many curling purists in the arena, it was agonizing to watch."

By the next day they were contrite and embarrassed. They went out to win any game they could. The performance netted them a disciplinary letter from the Ontario Curling Association and it's still something they'd rather not discuss.

Even without the spectacular blowouts, though, the brass ring seemed to be slipping from their grasp. There were team changes and another year with limited success.

But again in 1977 the phoenix rose from the ashes. They sailed through the playdowns 7-2 and tied once again for second place at the Brier. A month later they beat Brier winner Jim Ursel in the CBC curling championship and won $26,000—the largest bonspiel prize ever at that time.

Eddie was beginning to tire both of the on-ice battles with Paul and of the bridesmaid's role. In 1978, after a respectable bonspiel season, they lost the Ontario final in an extra end to Gerry Hodson. In 1979, after an undistinguished season capping their eight years together, Eddie jumped ship.

"It wasn't the best. When I told Paul I was quitting, he said, 'Good, we were going to fire you anyway, asshole.' We'd been really good friends but now we were avoiding each other at the club."

The quitting he now believes was overdue. "I had stopped believing we were ever going to do it," he remembers. "We were stale and sputtering." And although he doesn't like to admit it now, he wanted a little of the recognition that had been heaped on Paul for their joint effort.

"I wanted to prove that Paul didn't make the team go," he told a reporter in 1981.

Eddie was 32 and a much different person from the part-time drywaller Paul took under his wing in 1971. He was married with two infants. He'd worked steadily at the fire department for half a dozen years. In those years he'd skipped a team of firefighters to their national championship three times. There were even a few extra dollars in the pot. In the years of playing with Paul, the team had won over $100,000 (tax free).

"Now, looking back on my record, I can say I played second and third for Paul when I probably should have been skipping," he says. "But I can only say that based on the record. In those days I didn't believe I had the authority or the ability to recruit my own team. Paul was a nice guy; I was more than happy to play for him."

Splitting up wasn't an immediate success for either Eddie or Paul. Eddie and two members of his firefighters team, Neil Harrison and Jimmy McGrath, joined forces with Joe Gurowka, an old-style curler whose best showing had been in 1966 when he was runner-up in the Brier as skip for the Ontario champions. He'd gone back as Ontario's rep in 1976 and chalked up a dismal 3-8 record. Jimmy McGrath, Eddie's firefighting pal, had been lead on that team. Eddie blames McGrath for putting the team together.

From the beginning, it was clear Eddie and Gurowka were oil and water. "Joe wanted to hit everything," Harrison remembers. In those days Eddie was completely committed to the finesse game. After a couple of spiels McGrath was dispatched to tell Joe he was no longer skipping. By the end of the year Gurowka and Werenich had developed a deep and abiding enmity that underpinned their later skirmishes.

Even Paul was upset by that team. "I could understand Eddie leaving to skip, but what freaked me out was his leaving to play third for this old guy he didn't even like."

By 1981 Eddie was back on track. Gurowka was history, and although a young hotshot named John Kawaja had turned down a chance to play third, he made do with new third, Bob Widdis, and once again won the province. Eddie proved a much more fractious skip than Paul. At the playdowns they had problems with the draw. Eddie smelled nepotism, probably the human failing he has least sympathy for. At one point play was in the second end on every sheet but Eddie's.

"I refused to start until I knew what playoff rules I was playing under. They wanted to wait and see who won before they decided how to set up the playoffs." Finally Eddie launched a formal protest and began play. But partway through the first game Peter Krivel, the *Toronto Star*'s curling reporter, called him over to the boards and told him the OCA had refused to consider his protest because he hadn't made it in writing!

Eddie was hot. So hot that days later when he won the purple heart (the treasured crest of every provincial champion) he dropped his pants and mooned Leon Sykes, an OCA official. "I'm going to get you to sew that purple heart right here," he said.

Tempers were still running high from that confrontation when they got to the Halifax Brier two weeks later. It's customary for the provincial associations to take their championship teams out to dinner one evening during Brier week. But the night the Werenich rink was scheduled to break bread with the OCA turned out to be the low point of the tournament. In the morning they had dropped a tough one to Al Hackner. After outplaying their co-favourite for most of the game, Eddie missed a couple of key shots and the Ontario rink was suddenly down 2-3. That afternoon they came out flat against Quebec and lost another one.

"Right now I've got the yips," Eddie told a reporter. "Every time I go to grab the rock I start shaking."

To another journalist he went even further. "I've blown three games personally. I might have to drop back to third to give myself time to heal."

It was against this backdrop that they set out, in extremely grim spirits, to Fat Albert's in downtown Halifax to celebrate with the OCA. Their record was an abysmal 2-4.

Eddie was drinking wine. "He should never even look at wine," says Linda, who remembers the night with a laugh and a shudder.

"You'd have to see this scene to believe it," adds Harrison. "The only good thing was that we were upstairs in one of those ex-bedrooms, so we were a little private.

"Eddie always blames me for starting it," Harrison begins. The first round began with Harrison and an OCA official in an abstract discussion about the relative merits of toe sliding. Not the sort of topic that usually brings the house down. But the subtext of the argument was whether or not Curl Canada really was the revealed word on every subject related to curling.

"I got hot," Harrison admits. "You have to remember we were two and four and not real happy. Suddenly down at the other end of the table Mount Vesuvius erupts. Eddie's standing on the table—or at least the chair—screaming."

Jimmy McGrath scurries around telling Neil he'll have to settle Eddie down. Eddie shouts irrelevantly that McGrath and Widdis are fired from the team. Somehow in the ensuing fracas Eddie also manages to hijack the abandoned steak from one of the OCA wives' plates.

"Mr. Werenich, you have atrocious table manners," she hisses.

Linda and Neil decide a strategic retreat is the best salvation. They hustle Eddie downstairs to a cab.

But the tirade continues inside the car. When Linda reminds him of the driver's presence, he offers the cabbie a quarter so he can keep swearing. Lynnie protests the insult and she gets fired too.

"He was just boxcars. The last I saw of him that night he was headed off to the press party—alone," laughs Harrison. "The next morning he had to phone everybody's room to see if he still had a team."

But, as so often happens with Werenich, the deeper the trouble, the clearer the head, and the fiercer the concentration. After that night they didn't lose another game until the playoffs, when they lost to Saskatchewan in an extra end.

The team had done well enough to warrant another year together but insiders knew trouble was looming. Partway through the 1981-82 year Bob Widdis was demoted to second. "Bob and I were a problem on the team," remembers Harrison, "Basically both of us wanted to play the same position—third. Obviously we were going to have to make some hard decisions. It was almost a relief that year when we lost."

But the hard decision Eddie was about to make was one Harrison had never dreamed of. Sometime in mid-January he called Paul Savage and asked him to play third.

It wasn't a new topic for the friendly rivals. They'd talked casually through the year about playing together once again. Paul had had a mediocre couple of years and was on the brink of chucking competitive curling. Eddie was having trouble with his legs, trouble with his team and very little fun. Both were nostalgic for the old tough-nosed, bickering, hard-partying style they'd lived through during the 1970s.

"I'd been to the Brier three times [1973, 1974, 1977] with teams I thought I had a good chance to win with," says Savage. "I don't know if it's a rationalization but there always seemed to be a good excuse for not winning—horrendous ice conditions or sudden changes in ice. You began to lose the confidence you had in winning. Not because of the talent but because of outside things you couldn't control."

The bright spot in Paul's 1982 season had been John Kawaja. After the 19-year-old junior star had turned down Eddie's offer in 1981 and watched that team go on to the Brier, he was determined not to make the same mistake again.

"In 1980 Eddie was an unproven skip," Kawaja explains. "I'd skipped all through junior [finishing second in the country]. I wanted to try skipping in men's."

After one season he'd had enough. "We got our asses kicked the whole year and I couldn't help but think I'd just blown a purple heart."

The next year (1982) Paul asked him to play third and John jumped at the chance. "It was a big thrill," he says. "Paul had been my idol when I was growing up. Every weekend I used to get my dad to drive me to Avonlea to watch them play. Paul was the big guy."

The team made money, even made it to the zone finals. But where he had once skipped the dominant team in the province, now on the list of the top 10 teams in Ontario in the February 1982 issue of the *Ontario Curling Report*, Savage was in third spot behind Al Hackner and—horrors—Joe Gurowka. Werenich was fourth.

"When Eddie phoned," Paul remembers, "I didn't have to think about it. I recognized Eddie was a great skip."

Paul's only stipulation was that John play second.

That left only lead spot open for Harrison and Eddie knew he would have a tough sell on his hands. "I basically asked him to give me one year," says Eddie. "And after that I said he could pick the team. If he wanted me on the team I'd play any position he wanted."

(The favour wasn't called in until 1988, five years later, when Eddie once again played third for Paul.)

"We were driving to some spiel on the 401," Harrison remembers. "Eddie turned to me and said, 'What would you think of Paul at third?' Paul had been the premier skip in Ontario for years; I'd never even thought of him as a third."

Neil was hurt. "The basic message was the lead was mine. I was reluctant; it was a demotion. Here I am, 33 years old. I'd been to the Brier at second and, I thought, handled it OK. And now they're bringing in a 22-year-old kid and I get to play lead?

"I gave Eddie a lot of grief and he said it was up to me. But basically the bottom line was: take it or leave it."

Talking about it eight years later in his comfortable Pickering home, Harrison can look at the tankards cluttering his mantle, prizes he's collected for winning. He unconsciously grimaces when he thinks of how close he came to leaving and thereby missing (as he says) the best fun he's ever had.

"My goal in curling, and I guess in life, has been to win a Brier. You start to realize it might happen. If I hadn't joined the team they would have had to put a suicide watch on me," he jokes.

Right from the beginning the Dream Team, as Eddie labelled it, was everything they hoped for and more. At first the smart money was giving low odds on their surviving the season. The voltage on their collective egos was far too high, the pundits declared.

Eddie loved that line of argument. Even though he was amalgamating the two strongest teams in southern Ontario, the predictions of disaster meant he could still think of himself as the underdog with something to prove.

Asked about the team's compatibility, Fast Eddie had a swift answer: "That's right, we fight. In fact, we fought our way to three Briers and $150,000."

Everybody on the team seems to remember the same miracle moment, early in the 1982-83 season, when they knew they really were a team of dreams. They began with a losing spiel in Ottawa and shook it off, investing a tidy pile of cash in airfare to zip themselves to B.C. for the Vernon and Kamloops carspiels. Things were not going well. They'd lost the A side; then with only a simple draw to qualify out of B, Eddie failed them. "He sent it 100 mph into the kitchen," laughs Savage.

"It's probably still going," chuckles Kawaja.

Eddie was miserable. "Maybe you should skip," he said to Paul plaintively.

"No way, skipper," was Savage's reply. "This is the way we started and this is the way we're going to play."

"That was the smartest decision I ever made," he says now, thinking back. Forty minutes later they had moved down two sheets and were out for the C round facing Lukowich. "We played the best game of our lives," says Kawaja, "and after that everybody knew."

By Monday night they were walking away jingling keys to four brand-new cars. The local radio station told its listeners if they wanted a deal on a car to get down to the bar at the Vernon Motor Lodge and talk to Eddie and the boys.

"The later in the day they came, the better the deal they got," says Kawaja. Ultimately the last car went for $4,500. "By then we were in no shape to negotiate."

Savage picked up another $5,000 in the Calcutta. The Dream Team was virtually unknown beyond Ontario's boundaries and the $700 he spent to buy his own team paid handsome odds. "We'd won the cars and I had an extra $5,000 in my jeans. We had a great time celebrating that Tuesday. We pissed away $1,200 in bars and restaurants. I spent most of it."

It was a perfect year. Paul and Eddie were 35 years old and they'd been dreaming this dream since they were 16. Even now when they talk about it, they break off in wonder and say something like, "Geez we had a great time."

Two weeks after the B.C. win, they won the Molson Classic at the Royals in Toronto and they were fully launched on their great year. It's still the highlight of all of their curling careers. They'd glide into tournaments, clean up on the ice and have more fun at the parties than anyone else. They loved being together. The money (they won $55,000 that year) was a bonus and the Brier and the world championship were no more than the icing on the cake.

"I was in third-year economics at York University," says Kawaja, "but my focus was entirely curling. That was the first time my parents ever started to worry about my school."

He never did finish his degree. "It's stupid really," he says now. "I think I'm only one course short."

But university life was dull and flat compared to the excitement of the cashspiel trail. "I couldn't wait to get out on the ice and beat the shit out of everybody," Kawaja remembers. "Paul was the catalyst of that team. Everyone was at the top of their game, but Paul played so well at third, Eddie had an easy year.

"I was absolutely convinced we would win the Brier and the world championship. We were such overwhelming favourites, our big concern was what would we say if we lost."

"We did unbelievable things," Eddie remembers. "We partied all the time. The only rule we had was that if we had a morning game we had to go hard early. There had to be a certain number of hours between the last drink and the game."

In mid-February Eddie was telling the press: "You won't find a keener bunch of guys anywhere. We're on a roll and we're just going to enjoy the ride, hopefully into the Brier."

But by early March 1983 when they headed up to Sudbury for the Brier, Eddie's tone had changed. Their cockiness was starting to evaporate. He was up against an opponent of vast experience. Bernie Sparkes was making his tenth Brier appearance; he'd won three times at second. For Ed Lukowich, it was only his second appearance, but the first time he'd walked away the winner.

Eddie felt the pressure. He knew this team should win, but so much depended on him.

Going in he was fidgety and nervous, and as usual he and Paul were bickering. Paul grumbled that Eddie was "trying to watch the other games" when he was supposed to be playing his own. But they soon settled down and in the early going lost only one game—to Ed Lukowich.

Halfway through the week Eddie was described as "slap-happy" over his best-ever Brier record. Paul seized the occasion to celebrate. For one very long evening he was missing in action. Paul laughs about the search party that finally returned him to his team. "There was a minister, a funeral director from Kingston and a wife (his own, Barbara)."

He has witnessed the Brier change from the casual, hard-partying atmosphere of the 1950s and 1960s to a more competitive, professional event under the tutelage of Labatt's. He accepts the reasons for the change, but can't help but feel the old way had more style and spirit. "Personally, I've always been more like those 1950s and 1960s guys. There are legendary stories. Those guys like Alfie Phillips, the Richardsons and Lyall Dagg would really enjoy the social aspect and still show up for their morning games and play extremely well."

Style and spirit, though, weren't exactly uppermost in the skip's and third's minds on a sunny Saturday afternoon in March as they prepared for the semi-final against Bernie Sparkes. Both were having problems with their stomachs. Savage was throwing up in the wash-room while Eddie gobbled antacid tablets in the dressing room. The front end wasn't much better. Kawaja was pacing, talking faster than ever and champing at the bit to get started. Harrison, sitting quietly in the corner, could feel the dampness under his collar and on his palms. Nobody was comfortable.

The Sudbury Arena was packed to the rafters with an SRO crowd of almost 5,000. They weren't to be disappointed. For Eddie's game-winning triple takeout in the sixth end, they were on their feet roaring their approval. Eddie turned it up a notch and played, as he would later explain, "over my head."

The shotmaking was brilliant, the experts agreed. Some said never before had there been such a display. Bill Good, a veteran of 36 Briers, wasn't so easy to impress. He remembered his own B.C. Brier champion of 1948, Frenchy D'Amour. At any rate, nobody had seen the like for 35 years and Eddie's show was more than enough to retire a wilted Bernie Sparkes.

The next day The Wrench expected to have to do it all again. He tuned up by playing his beloved video games. "It helps my reactions, keeping track of three or four buttons at a time," he explained.

But the final against Alberta's Ed Lukowich was such a tame affair he might have managed it even without the help of PacMan. Eddie won the toss as he had 11 of the 13 times he'd had to toss in the Brier. While mere mortals cried foul, the gods continued to sit on his bench. In the first end Alberta's second, Neil Houston, ticked a guard set up by Kawaja and buried it deep in the house. The Ontario rink took two and never looked back.

Television fans got one small glimpse into the depth of feeling under the calm exterior when Eddie forgot he was wired for sound for national TV. Talking a shot over with Savage, he opined they should just throw it in and "sweep the piss out of it."

CBC's Don Duguid nearly swallowed his teeth. On balance the television folks were probably very lucky the game was sedate and went Werenich's way.

As the SRO crowd assembled for the 2:30 P.M. draw, there were plenty of yellow buttons proclaiming COOL HAND LUKE. Outside, Eddie's fans were a little more raucous. They were tearing up and down the Sunday-quiet streets of Sudbury in an antique fire truck, whooping it up for the Scarborough firemen who made up half of the southern Ontario squad.

Who could blame the Alberta partisans if they had slightly superior grins on their faces? Their man had sailed through the round robin with only one loss and won a bye into the final by defeating both Werenich and Sparkes.

Lukowich went in calmly, a slight favourite. He came out rattled and deeply disappointed. "We were playing well but everything was going 100 percent their way," he griped.

He did have one squeaker of a chance to tie it in the final end but he missed the triple. Later he dismissed it as a "horribly impossible shot."

But it was the kind of shot that The Wrench, "playing over his head" though he may have been, was making in the 1983 Brier. And so, as the crowd of 5,000 filed out of the Sudbury Arena late that Sunday afternoon, there was a general feeling that justice had been done. The right man had won. After years of standing in the wings Eddie Werenich was centre stage. And his life would never be the same again.

The next day, in bright red headlines, in big-deal newspapers, there would be headlines like: "They Swept The Nation."

"I was always really shy and a little bit like Moe Norman," the little guy from Benito remembers. "I was afraid to win a bonspiel because I'd have to make a speech."

After the Sudbury Brier speeches and interviews were, for the moment at least, his business in life. The glare of publicity was astonishing and Linda is still surprised at how well her husband coped. "He didn't like it at all, but he got to be really good at it. It got to the point that I'd say, 'Don't give Ed the mike, he won't shut up.' Yes, I think that was the part that surprised me most."

Nobody was prepared for the avalanche of invitations. "The phone never stopped ringing from the minute we walked in the door," Linda says. "We're still getting calls [even after the 1990 triumph] because of 1983."

For Linda, this was a part of the Brier dream she had never imagined when she was a young bride hanging out at Humber Highlands' old 16-sheeter in west-end Toronto. "Back then I used to daydream about when we could go to the Brier, what it would be like, how it would feel."

But Eddie? Eddie was euphoric. "I can remember when I was in grade five or six and the teachers used to say, 'What's your ambition?' All I could ever talk about was curling," he babbled to reporters.

"I used to play hookey to watch curling. I used to sneak out on the ice and curl in the dark when they wouldn't let me play. This is just a dream."

Three weeks later, "drained mentally and physically" from the post-Brier high, they showed up in Regina to take on the world.

The biggest fight was with the Hasselborgs but generally Eddie was unimpressed with the Europeans' sportsmanship and skill. His first game against the Dane Tommy Stjerne was a bit of a ho-hum affair. The Canadians won 6-3. But when he heard later that Stjerne had said he wasn't too impressed with the Canadian rink, Eddie did his best fox-terrier-for-the-throat imitation.

"Yeah? Well they threw them pretty badly, they deserved to miss. There were a couple of in-turns they threw where they were lucky they went down the same sheet of ice."

About the Hasselborgs' corn brooms and intimidation tactics he said: "Those guys know nothing about sportsmanship or etiquette. I can't believe the stunts they pull. . . . It'd be easy for us to say nothing, but I've chastised these guys and I think they deserve it."

Paul didn't mince words either. "I don't think a lot of people wanted to hear that today. But I'll tell you this, what goes on out here and what's allowed to go on is bullshit."

Paul and Eddie still at it. Except this time it was Eddie and

Paul. To be sure, Paul was still a visible presence on the team but by spring of 1983 the focus had shifted to Eddie. His outspokenness and his penchant for dashing off for hotdogs after the fifth end earned him the reputation as a "character" in the curling pantheon, right alongside the Richardsons, Alfie Phillips, Jr. and Paul Gowsell.

By the time he'd beaten Keith Wendorf, who represented West Germany, in the final of the Silver Broom, Regina and most of Canada was at his feet.

Eddie was uniquely positioned to become a media star. First, he was talkative and the words meant something. For sportswriters weaned on the "one game at a time" non- speak of most professional athletes, this world champion was heaven-sent. Second, he had no coach or PR department screening his calls, just Linda. If you called the Scarborough townhouse, you'd often hear Eddie chirping, "Home of the World Champions." He liked that line. And third, he lived not in some tiny outpost but in Toronto, the media capital of the country.

Interest would not die quickly. Eddie might be starting to long for the golf links but he had hundreds of PR functions to wade through first.

"There were so many banquets. The eight of us were together all the time," remembers Linda. Like everyone else involved she also remembers that it was a blast.

There were dinners, receptions, celebrity golf tournaments and speeches for Eddie to give. "He did an awful lot of it in 1983 and '84, but he doesn't really like it," Linda explains. "After the 1990 win he didn't accept nearly as many invitations. It takes a lot of time."

In a life that had been casual, spontaneous, and oriented toward pleasure, time was becoming a major issue. He didn't, doesn't, won't keep an appointment book, so there were foul-ups and double bookings.

"I never write anything down. Guys line me up for things and I completely forget about them. I don't know what I'm doing this afternoon but they want to tie me down for 11 A.M. next Thursday," he complained to the *Star*'s Tom Slater.

Among the great times was a wild trip to Grindelwald, Switzerland, in early January 1984. The Swiss have a bonspiel—the winner takes home a prize bull—and they love to have the world's best as part of the festivities.

Linda remembers it not for the curling but for the spirit and the socializing. "We were together all week," says Linda. "We took over a tiny bar on the main street, just the eight of us." She pauses and grins before adding, "We were crazy."

They took the train from Zurich to Interlaken, where their hosts met them in a 4X4 and took them for a hair-raising ride into the mountains. At the hotel they weren't allowed out of the vehicle. "They just dumped our luggage and screamed up the mountain through a horrendous snowstorm for these special coffees," Linda says ruefully. "They kept telling us, 'Ah, you guys are nothing. We had Hackner's team here last year.'

"I don't think any of us drank Scotch—oh, maybe Ed did then— but on the way down the mountain the villagers came out with trays of Scotch. We drank it quickly, just to be polite."

When they fell into bed that night they'd been "going hard," as Eddie calls it, for 30 hours.

"We kept going like that the whole week because it was so much fun," Linda says. "We didn't even notice jet lag. But when we got home it took two weeks to get over it."

The party continued in the plane on the way home. Paul remembers they were looking for a capper to appropriately end what had been the best holiday they'd ever had. Sitting at the back of a DC10, 37,000 feet above the ocean, they decided to make love in the airplane washroom and join the "Mile High Club."

John was there with a girl who was just a friend, so they passed, but the three wives agreed. "Barb and I went first. Then Neil and Jane. Then it was the Skipper's turn," Paul says.

"They'd just taken away the trays for dinner and everybody's starting to get up and line up for the washrooms. They're in there for about 20 minutes. About 12 people are lined up waiting when finally the door opens. Out comes the Skipper with a big grin on his face. We all stand up and start clapping. Lynnie comes out behind him with a really red face."

Although the celebrations went well into the next year, the Dream Team was still battling the disbelievers. After winning the world championship Eddie said, "I hope we can last [together] another five years. I know it won't last forever but this is a lot of fun."

Some of those who knew the Toronto curling scene best scoffed at the idea. Dream Team maybe, but dreams are brief and so would be the lifespan of this team.

But Eddie and the boys loved to surprise people, and nobody more than the pundits. As the season began in the fall of 1983, they weren't perfect. They lost the cars in the Kelowna spiel on Hallowe'en, but not until the final, and only after a huge verbal showdown with Ed Lukowich over what they claimed were his illegal sweeping practices.

Perhaps The Wrench was saving himself for the World Challenge Invitational Bonspiel in Calgary two weeks later. There he was all-star skip and the team won $60,000, at that time the largest cash prize ever in a bonspiel.

By December, when the playdowns started, the team had won an unheard-of—east of Manitoba—$83,000, and the critics had stopped carping about break-up and were now harping about money.

Alison Goring's father, Barry, dumped them from the A side in the double-knockout playdowns, but Eddie was patient and steady and focused on a repeat performance at the Brier.

It would not happen easily. As 1984 began, observers could see the team at the top of their game with $90,000-plus in winnings and a spot in the up-coming Tankard. On the face of it Eddie was having the time of his life, enjoying the high times like Grindelwald and TV appearances on CTV's "Thrill of a Lifetime." (A Stayner, Ontario, farmer wrote in to say his thrill would be curling with Eddie Werenich, and the network—and Eddie—obliged.)

But dig a little deeper and the pressure was razor-sharp. The main reason they'd accepted the all-expenses-paid trip to Grindelwald was that it gave them a holiday, a chance to let off steam and get themselves together. They worried they'd been running on adrenalin for so long there wouldn't be enough left for a hard-fought playdown.

Eddie was well aware no team had repeated a Brier championship since 1971. Then, as everybody knew, life was simpler, the Brier less intense and Donny Duguid, obviously, the class of the field.

Eddie badly wanted to win. And when he decided the OCA was trying to thwart that desire, he "flipped," as Savage recalls.

When they got back from Grindelwald there was a registered letter waiting for Werenich. It detailed a revision of the playoff format, and it had been sent to all of the skips who had made the Tankard. Obviously the letter was attempting to head off the problems they'd had in the 1981 Blue Lite Tankard in Markham, where the playoff structure in the rulebook had read differently from the one in the program. In that situation they'd tried to thrash out a compromise during the competition.

In 1981 Eddie identified Leon Sykes, "an old warlord from Brigadoon," as the enemy. But in 1984 the stakes were much higher and the enemy much better known. Joe Gurowka, whom Eddie had played with, fought with and ultimately split with in 1980, had gone on to the provincial finals in 1982 and by 1984 was president of the Ontario Curling Association.

By early 1984 the rivalry between Ed Werenich and Russ Howard was percolating. Eddie saw in the scheme that Gurowka and his cronies had dreamed up an advantage to Howard.

"Before the Tankard in February I spent hours on the phone with the Ontario Curling Association, but I didn't get anywhere," Paul remembers. "Gurowka hated Eddie and he didn't have any time for our team."

Basically the OCA's system would make it advantageous for a first or second place team, under some circumstances, to lose a game late in the round robin to protect their bye into the final.

"At the skips' meeting [before play began] I pleaded with them," Eddie remembers. "No team should ever be put in that position. I said 'We haven't thrown a single rock yet. Make it right before it happens.'"

Gurowka was not about to cave in. He argued that the scenario Eddie was sketching was highly unlikely. "Our objective was to drop one tie-breaker draw," he says now. "We felt we could accommodate two but not three because it would mean a Sunday night final. People travelling from Toronto wouldn't want to have a final in Peterborough on Sunday night."

This had already happened in 1982 in Brantford, he said. "And on Sunday night they, of course, played a nothing final."

In the end it was as Eddie predicted. In the final game of the round robin against Russ Howard, Werenich's rink played at a snail's pace, waiting to see how the other games would turn out, waiting to see if they had to lose. Eddie excused himself to go to the washroom several times. Once, in the men's washroom deep in the bowels of the Peterborough arena, a voice Eddie recognized as belonging to one of the local officials floated in from behind the door. "Eddeeeeee," it said in ghost-like tones, "it would beeeee in your best iiiiiinterests to loooooose the game."

Eddie went back to his game laughing uproariously. He called his team together and they too started howling, making rude associations with the Watergate informant "Deep Throat." "It was bad," he says now, chuckling. "There we were in this very serious situation and we couldn't stop laughing."

Gurowka had left for a nearby hotel for lunch with his cronies. By the time he got back, it was all over but the recriminations. It had ended in a five-way tie for third. Chief Umpire Jimmy Waite had already decreed that since a five-way tie had not been discussed in the contingencies, they would revert to three tie-breaker games and first and second place would be in the finals and semi-finals.

"In the last end, Eddie hogged his final shot and I flashed mine," Paul remembers. "But we've never said we threw that game. It was a horrible spot to be in."

His teammates remember Paul in the dressing room afterwards crying over it all. The spirit of curling, the game he loves, had definitely taken a beating.

Now he says, "I felt proud of the way we handled the whole situation. It was the worst example I've ever seen of somebody making an asinine decision."

Later, in a letter to the editor of the OCR, Paul criticized Gurowka's "win-at-all-costs attitude," which he claimed had been proven when Gurowka resorted to straw brooms against opponent Jim Dyas, littering the ice when he was three points down at the 1983 Ontario Challenge Round in Owen Sound.

"We believe the playoff format in Peterborough was established to make it more difficult for our team to win. That's not a lot different from making it more difficult for Jim Dyas's rink to hang on to their three-point lead."

Certainly the whole Tankard had left an unpleasant taste in their mouths—especially for Neil Harrison, who was playing in his hometown. But their eventual triumph dispelled the unpleasantness. Eddie and Paul were, for the sixth time in 14 years, Brier bound. Neil was about to make his third appearance; John, his second. With a little help from their friends, they'd made it over what they believed was the toughest obstacle, the Ontario playdowns.

En route to Victoria, basking in their success, they developed an elaborate practical joke, to unhinge, they hoped, their new and toughest foe, Ed Lukowich. Luke had just published his second book, *The Curling Book*, and joked to Paul that he'd plagiarized Paul's *Curling: Hack to House*. With the help of a lawyer friend they'd drawn up a letter on the letterhead of a big downtown Toronto law firm, threatening to sue for the allegedly stolen words.

"I don't know if he plagiarized or not," Paul laughs. "I never read his book." But they did know, at least by reputation, that Lukowich was a little naive about the world of business.

"We saw Ed eating breakfast with his team in the restaurant of the hotel the first day. We called over the bell captain and asked him to deliver the letter."

Then they sat back behind the potted palms and howled with laughter as Lukowich opened the letter while he ate his toast. They watched in delight as he stopped dead and read it again before passing it gravely over to his team.

He heard them laughing and their ruse was up. But that joke was just about the end of the good times for that week.

"We were really rolling," remembers Kawaja about that year. "We had been in at least the semi-final of every bonspiel we entered. We'd won \$95,000 and the provincial final, and we got to the Brier and all of a sudden everything fell apart. We weren't used to losing, and here we are one and three after the first four draws. Everyone was struggling."

They decided to try a little R&R on the golf course. Even there the TV crews followed them.

"You have to picture this scene," Kawaja recounts. "We're on the first tee, the cameras are rolling and Eddie steps up. 'I don't know whether to try a fade or a draw,' he says. 'You'd better go for a fade,' Neil pipes up. 'You haven't made a draw all week.'

"The cameras are going, everybody's laughing and Eddie shanks one right into the clubhouse window," Kawaja, the scratch golfer, laughs at the memory. "It wasn't our week."

In Victoria they were back where they—at least Eddie—liked to be, the underdog with something to prove. "We went into this thinking we needed 8-3 to get into the playoffs," he told reporters. "We've got the easy three over with. Now we have to go after the eight hard ones."

They roared back into contention. As it turned out, they could lose four and make the playoff round. Their only loss in the last part of the week was a prophetic one to unheralded Mike Riley of Winnipeg.

"I bet 95 percent of the people here have forgotten about us. It would be nice to remind them that we're still world champions," Eddie said as he turned the corner on the week.

In retrospect, the words are packed with irony. Not nearly as many people had forgotten about the 1983 Brier winner as had failed to notice the soon-to-be 1984 winner. In solid, unspectacular fashion, the Manitoba investor was carefully building his lead. He ended the week tied for first with Ed Lukowich.

To say Riley was a dark horse is to understate. He was practically a non-horse. Outside of Manitoba no one had heard of him. "Mike who?" even the Manitoba journalists were delighted to say. He was dismissed as a fluke whose bubble would burst long before the final game of the Brier.

But when the smoke cleared on the 11th of March it was Riley who was hoisting the tankard. And a subdued and slightly ungracious Werenich was discounting the whole Brier experience. "We didn't even deserve to be in the final," he said. "No way. We played only marginally all during the Brier—myself in particular. We never got serious and didn't give it an honest effort."

Maybe they were feeling something of Linda's vibrations from the stands. She remembers watching the big show with butterflies in her stomach. And yes, somewhere in there, a slightly sinking feeling. She knew this phenomenal come-from-behind act. They were the sudden-death specialists and she'd seen it a hundred times before. But this time as she watched, she knew exactly what a win would mean and she doesn't mind telling you that she asked herself, "Could I take it again?"

They didn't win and it would be seven years before she would have to answer that difficult question.

For those who like to chart such things, the final that Sunday afternoon, when they all felt whacked out and unmotivated, is as good a place as any to fix as the beginning of the end for the Dream Team. Not that it was obvious. No door was slammed. Taps was not sung. In fact, it would take two years before everyone, even Eddie, could see the writing on the wall.

*

Complacency in curling is a fatal disease. No team can survive it. It doesn't matter how old or venerable the friendships, how deep the family ties, the slow rot of complacency has no respect.

They weren't winning as often on the cashspiel circuit. Their total for 1985 was only $50,000, half of 1984's take, and in the playdowns they lost out in the finals of the Challenge Round.

"I guess the complacency had started to kick in," Kawaja says, looking back.

1986 wasn't much different. "It was a half-decent year by anyone else's standards, but we started to get on each other a bit," says Kawaja. "All four of us were guilty of not having the hunger and desire, of taking the odd weekend off. We'd show up at the bonspiel and want to get the curling over with and get to the party."

"Eddie was the most competitive. Paul and I were more guilty of being complacent."

Harrison agrees. "The cracks were starting to show." What the Dream Team themselves saw as "cracks" everyone else was describing as a chasm. In part, it was the inevitable gap between married men in their late thirties and an exuberant, cocky 23-year-old.

Paul Savage was the bridge. But he too was having trouble balancing the demands of career, family, curling and the bonspiel party scene. Now he concedes—without regret—that they might have done better over the years if he and the team had been abstainers or "more focused on the health aspects. For sure, in certain situations, our social activities had a negative effect on how we did.

"There were some legendary losers' banquets," he says. "Every weekend after you're out of it [the competition] all hell breaks loose. In fact that's the single most important reason why I might one day give up competitive curling. At my age [44] I find I can't be competent at work on Monday and Tuesday after a weekend like that."

Meanwhile Kawaja, single, dark, handsome and in his early twenties, was just hitting his stride as curling's version of a matinee idol. In many of the bonspiel towns, the 1983 world champions were the closest thing to professional athletes the burghers were likely to see. There were always plenty of women interested in making an impression.

There were flowers sent to the room, letters slipped under the door, late-night phone calls. Kawaja, who married Laura Barker in June 1991, smiles thinking over those years. "There are always women interested in meeting you [the competitive curler]. It's just that then I was interested in meeting them too."

For Savage, who was Kawaja's roommate over those years, it was an education—and an exercise in humility. He remembers being at a disco in Digby, Nova Scotia, where he was playing in a celebrity golf tournament, when he was pounced on by a pretty young student. She planted a huge kiss and said, "Ooooooh I just looooooove John Kawaja. Will you give him that for me?"

"If there were cracks in '86, our last year together, they were between Kawaja and Werenich," explains Harrison. "John was partying it up at the spiels and not performing up to snuff. It still all boils down to performance on the ice and John wasn't showing as much responsibility to the team [as he had]. The feeling was gone."

In January 1986 the OCR still ranked the Dream Team second in the province, behind defending world champion Al Hackner, but with the ranking it ran the cryptic note, "Some people have challenged this rating. Won Sarnia and Whitby SunLife. Amen."

Elsewhere in the issue Eddie continued to defend his rink. "Everyone figures we're not playing well but with six more wins it would be a tremendous year for us. We've been in three semi-finals and won Sarnia [as well as Whitby].

"In my opinion anything over $20,000 is a good year. Sometimes winning a game is just breaks."

But behind Eddie's happyspeak an OCR reporter caught Paul muttering, "Eddie practises PacMan 20 hours a week and his curling 10 minutes. I guess he's only got so many shots left. He could be an outstanding skip if he just practised. Now he's just great."

And after an early-round win Paul fumed, "Ed's too fat, John's hung over and I had to win the game for these guys."

A weakening of commitment showed up in other ways too. Unlike their super-confident 1983 selves, they had trouble deciding if they were playing well enough to risk big-time expenses on the western bonspiel circuit.

"We're on again, off again every 10 minutes," complained Paul. "One moment Ed's decided we're not going to Saskatoon [the Bessborough Classic], the next moment we're in the Brier."

But later that month, in the zone and regional playdowns, they lost two straight and were forced into the Challenge Round. They lost two straight again and were out on their ear.

It was the second time in two years they hadn't made the Ontario Tankard and a reassessment was overdue.

Watching them, people had come to expect style in the Dream Team's every move. Even breaking up would be a big party, the prediction went. But when it came, the break-up was smaller, slower and sadder than that. Like a painful, uncontested divorce.

The first sign was Eddie's trial balloon to the press saying that Kawaja was impatient to skip his own team. John, who had never said a word about skipping his own team, read Eddie's remarks and wondered.

"I didn't really want to skip, that was just an excuse," he said. "Nothing was ever said. We played our last game and that was it. We didn't really talk to each other for two months. I was the one who made other arrangements."

Paul had some fences to mend with his work and his family after four years of intensive curling.

"The first time Paul and I broke up we'd been together for eight years and toward the end we were getting so stale it affected our friendship," Eddie explains. "I didn't want that to happen again; [this time] I wanted us to walk away with our heads held high." No eulogy for a marriage was ever spoken with deeper feeling.

Two months after they split up, three of them were back together (with Rick Lang filling in on third for Paul) to answer Marilyn Darte's challenge in the Battle of the Sexes. They squashed her and ended up on the front page of all three Toronto dailies.

The next year Eddie and Neil stuck together, but although they went to the final in February 1987 with a new front end, the feeling was gone. Reporters remember Eddie partying it up with abandon on the eve of the 1987 final against Russ Howard. "I've never seen him go so hard, dancing and drinking," says Perry Lefko of the *Toronto Sun*. "The next day he looked like porridge—and his play wasn't much firmer."

Lefko was puzzled, but a colleague of his at the *Sun* might have been the reason Eddie was treating himself to a little celebration that Valentine's Saturday night. The Wrench (new and slightly improved) had been named by Christie Blatchford to her annual list of the 10 sexiest men on the planet. What's a guy to do?

Eddie insists Kawaja wouldn't speak to him for weeks afterwards and Lynnie still laughs when she remembers the hoots of disbelief and hilarity that came out of the dressing room that morning when Neil read *The Sun*.

After the final on Sunday, Eddie sounded like he might be having his old problems with motivation. "It hurts. I'm disappointed, but not as much as I thought, maybe I'm mellowing. It's a major disappointment to the other guys though, to lose the heart."

Another factor that eased the pain of losing was that the main prize that year was still up for grabs. The country was caught up in Olympic fever and winning the right to represent Canada in 1988 had, at least in the eyes of the media, eclipsed the usual spring curling competitions. By the time the Tankard took place, Eddie had already dieted himself into a spot in the Olympic trial playdowns scheduled for Calgary in April.

The Brier winner would also get a spot in Calgary. But Russ Howard, the purple heart winner that year, had first to undergo a gruelling Brier and an intense world championship in Vancouver.

Savage, despite his insistence that he was easing into semi-retirement with his curling, was also one of the 10 teams at the Chatham Tankard. But for Paul, without the Blatchford endorsement—and with very little sleep because of other revellers—the Tankard was a bitter disappointment. In the crucial semi-final with Howard, he was called in the eighth end for a hog-line violation. Everyone was taken aback. Calls are rarely made at such a critical juncture and this one was made by a fledgling official "who hadn't pulled a rock all week." But for all the raised eyebrows, and even the video that Savage insists proves his innocence, his season—as a skip—ended that morning.

"Three members of my team went to the officials room afterward and threatened serious violence," Paul recalls with a grudging laugh. "They should have done it on the ice; it would have made great press."

Kawaja wasn't at all happy with the new spin on his curling life either. "I played like a bum for two years," he says. He didn't travel to the big bonspiels because he knew he didn't have a winning team and he had trouble adjusting to a less skilled level of play.

"Sewage told me I still wasn't ready to skip," he says, agreeing that the game he called as skip was too difficult for the team he had. ("Sewage" was the name Paul Gowsell gave Savage when the witty Alberta curler thought Paul was taking inordinate pleasure in his "macho" surname. To balance the insult he turned the nickname Werenich loved into "The Stench".) Looking back on that low point in his career he shrugs and adds ruefully, "It was the only game I knew."

Ironically, the greatest success any members of the busted-up Dream Team had in 1987, they had together. Earlier in the season they'd fulfilled two commitments to play together, won both bonspiels, and pocketed $46,000.

Now they were once again together and headed for the big show, the Olympic trials. By the time that fiasco was well and truly over, they would have bonded together as they never had before—and Eddie's game would be in ruins.

2

THE DREAM TEAM
Courting Disaster

ED WERENICH IS far from being the only competitive curler in the country to have difficulty with curling's director of competitions, Warren Hansen. But, because in 1987 Hansen and the Curl Canada crew seemed to own the prize of representing Canada in the Olympics—a prize Eddie dearly wanted—their battle turned into a comic opera, played out in front of the whole country.

In fairness it must be said that Hansen did not act alone in devising the $600,000 scheme for picking the Olympic representatives. But Eddie and many others believed they saw Warren's philosophy and style running through the whole rigmarole.

Warren and Eddie go back eons. In the 1974 London Brier, they played second opposite each other for Hec Gervais and Paul Savage respectively. For Hansen, that Brier was his most triumphant moment in curling. For Eddie it was humiliating. Although his team placed third, they were psyched out, made far too many mistakes and lost to the worst team at the Brier.

Werenich, for all his apparent insouciance, hates to lose and this was assuredly not his finest hour. In the same Brier, Hansen, curling in front of living legend Hec Gervais, won the competition and the right to represent Canada in the Silver Broom in Berne, Switzerland. But it was to be the end for Hansen as a fiercely competitive curler.

Hansen remembers how central Gervais was to their success. "A lot depended on him," Hansen explains, "but he'd already won so much that a lot of the time he just didn't have the killer desire. When he had it, though, he was unbeatable."

In Berne the roof caved in for the Alberta rink. Even now, 16 years later, Hansen remembers it in aching detail. "We were using European stones, the dullest rocks I've ever seen. You couldn't finesse anything. Some got the feel of it, but we never did. If we'd played those teams under any other conditions we would have won. But after all the battles and wars we'd gone through to get there, we had these impossible conditions to deal with. It was total frustration. We lost in the semis to Sweden 8-7. After that my heart wasn't in it any more."

But he made mental notes of what went wrong.

"It was the same thing [as many curlers face]," he explains. "Gervais was overweight [280 pounds, his friends estimate], and out of shape. By the time the Brier was over he was hurting. It [intense competition] takes a toll mentally and physically."

Thirteen years later Olympic hopeful Eddie Werenich would pay a steep price for the lesson Hansen learned in Switzerland.

Meanwhile, in the fall of 1974, Hansen with his perfectly coiffed hair, trim jogger's build, and teetotaller image was recruited to set up Curl Canada. It was to be the training arm of the Canadian Curling Association. Twelve years later the tentacles of this organization would reach so far that Eddie, by then a world champion, would not be officially allowed to coach his own children because he didn't have the right paper qualifications.

If you want to see steam rise, ask Werenich about the bureaucracy of officials who run the sport. In the 16 years since its inception Curl Canada has, by Hansen's own admission, "blossomed to include instructor training, coaching certification, ice-technician development, officiating, club management seminars, etcetera—almost everything common to the CCA and the CLCA." (In 1990, after a nudge from the government, Curl Canada and the Canadian Ladies' Curling Association amalgamated with the CCA.)

In 1974 the two men were just beginning their ascent to the twin peaks of Canadian curling. By 1987 Warren would be the most powerful curling bureaucrat in the country, and hence the world, while Eddie—four years his junior—would be, by many tallies, the supreme competitor.

Both men care passionately about the game, but in style and personality they are diametrically opposed—for years they have been locked in a dialectical dance. Every time their paths cross, animosity has crackled between them and occasionally lit up the sports pages of newspapers across the country. In 1987 it was a full-scale conflagration that hit the front pages and even found a place on TV news-magazine shows like W5.

To Eddie, Hansen epitomizes everything that is wrong with the game he loves. The poobahs and empire builders have taken over the sport and have set out to wreck it, he believes. He still smarts over the letter he received from Hansen in the mid-1980s when his team adopted the new, angled push broom first introduced by Al Hackner.

It seems Hansen, who was a strong corn broom sweeper, was offended by the innovation. Eddie sensed an implication that the new brooms were a fancy form of cheating. There was nothing in the rules to prohibit the new brushes but Hansen, whom one fiery curling columnist has dubbed "the little general," sent out letters saying he wouldn't change the rule but he would, henceforth, interpret it differently.

The arbitrariness of the letter still makes Eddie's blood boil. His response to the Hansen missive was inflammatory enough to get Hansen talking about lawsuits. Or at least that's how Eddie interprets a vaguely worded reply to his critics Hansen wrote in *Curling Canada Magazine*.

But Eddie's problem doesn't end with the way the rules are devised. The officiating drives him crazy too. Officials are crawling all over every big competition but "they would never pull a rock in the last end of the Brier," Eddie maintains. "They've told me that. And if they won't do that, what are they doing there?"

So the air between Warren and Eddie didn't exactly sparkle with congeniality when Curl Canada was dealt the big hand of picking the Olympic competitors. This war was to be about power, nothing more and nothing less.

Hansen and Werenich were bizarre combatants in a war of exceptional nerve. By 1987 they had to swoop in from radically different planes to engage in battle. But in 1974, when Warren was settling down to write curling manuals and Eddie was trying to learn the ropes in his new job as a Scarborough firefighter, they were just two curlers trying to make their way.

"Firefighting was the first good job I ever had," Eddie says. Before that all his jobs had been mere meal tickets to get him from curling season to curling season. Recently he asked Linda why she used to get up and make him breakfast but wouldn't do it any more.

"In the old days, I kept hoping you'd keep a job for more than a week," she replied.

But even at the fire department he has had no hankering to get promoted or to make the correct political moves to get himself bumped up the ladder. In fact, he's even refused to write promotion exams. "I could care less," he says. "I have no ambition whatsoever."

So while Eddie has remained an entry-level fireman in a one-truck Scarborough firehall which he laughingly refers to as "purgatory," Hansen has toured the world as a curling ambassador. He is deeply ambitious for the sport, longing to get it out of the backwoods of amateurism into the glitzy ranks of professional sports like tennis and golf. As he sees it, the first step in the process is to achieve Olympic status.

In such a campaign appearance is extremely important. The competitors can't haphazardly police the game themselves. The officials—in outfits— have to have a firm, professional presence, but not be too intrusive. And the athletes? Well they have to look like athletes. They can't be overweight, out of shape, middle-aged and obstreperous. Look at tennis. They have to be slender, fit, young and—if at all possible—obedient. Whatever would the venerable old IOC poobahs think?

To Eddie this point of view was a sellout, trashed the spirit of curling and, most important, gave Warren and his cronies like Ron Anton and Vera Pezer too much power over him.

The exercise of that power started in late 1986 when the Olympic trial camps were held. There were all kinds of problems regarding the selections for the camps. In the end Al Hackner boycotted the process, as did Kerry Burtnyk and Rick Folk because they didn't approve of the selection criteria.

In his first interview with Dr. Garry DeBlonde, national coach for the Olympic program, Eddie remembers scoffing at his offer of help in motivation. "The only way you can motivate me, pal, is to have the beer cold when I come off the ice."

DeBlonde, as technical director of the CCA, was another of the chief architects of the Olympic program, so it looked like a long trial week. Still, thinking back, The Wrench dons his cloak of innocence and says earnestly: "I had decided to play the game their way."

His resolution cracked a little when he sat in a classroom submitting to the psychological testing for Vera Pezer, a three-time Canadian champion and now a sports psychologist in Saskatoon.

"We had this questionnaire and I swear to God the fifth question was: Do you peek at Christmas? This is how they are going to pick their superhuman-Arnold-Schwarzenegger team?"

When Savage got to the question, "Did you do illicit drugs as a teenager?" he put up his hand and asked if that included marijuana. "I'm not asking for myself," he quipped, "John Base wants to know."

There was plenty of machismo in that room of hard-bitten, tough competitors. There was also a strong sense of unreality.

However, for Eddie and Paul it got much worse. As part of the fitness requirement each competitor had to do 20 curl-ups. Neither of them could do one.

But Eddie, for all his brusqueness and torpedo-the-establishment style, does have a few friends in high places. "I knew we were in anyway," he says. "I got a call from Calgary."

Paul wasn't quite so sure. He remembers that at the time the selections were to be announced he was at a restaurant in Montreal with a client. "I excused myself and called Ottawa. Garry DeBlonde said: 'I have some good news and I have some bad. The good news is you're in. The bad news is Eddie has to lose 22 pounds and you have to lose 16.'"

This would be the nastiest skirmish of the battle and the one Eddie will probably never forget. First, they made no attempt to protect anyone's feelings. Later, the hierarchy said they had not intended to release names but somehow Hansen, as director of public relations, got his wires crossed and the names were released anyway. Secondly, there were public statements by officials unfavourably comparing the two "fatboys," as they came to be called in irreverent media outlets, with the proverbial 70-year-old Swede.

And, finally, the time limit meant that they had to do this wondrous renovation of their bodies in two months. As the critics were quick to point out, such rapid weight loss would be deemed dangerous by medical authorities.

Eddie and Paul vehemently disagreed with the principle that slim curlers were inherently better. "They don't want the best team, they want the prettiest team," Eddie argued. And when it turned out he was going to have to do aerobics too, he added, "Now, they not only want me to look pretty, they want me to be able to dance too. I just hope they don't ask me to use Grecian Formula and get my teeth fixed."

Although he was delighting the country with his stand, it was his defence mechanism against the humiliation. "It really hurt him," his brother says. Eddie admits he still smarts and feels some vindictiveness because he had to go through with such farcical demands and eat odious amounts of crow to be allowed to play.

"It was funny and all that, but it had to have humiliated him," says Neil Harrison, Eddie's close friend and fifth man. "It didn't bother Paul as much."

"Eddie was more offended and affected by it than I was," remembers Paul. "I found it a unique experience and a lot of fun."

Like many others, Al Hackner saw the demands as an abuse of power. "Obviously it's a move to intimidate him. Clearly they're looking for a way to keep him out," he told reporters.

The irony is that under all the protest Eddie and Paul both believed they needed to lose weight. "But when I saw how the media was reacting, I threw another log on," Eddie says now chuckling his best rabble-rouser's chuckle.

Over the years Paul had sporadically worried about his weight. Worried enough, that is, that he'd bought himself the array of "yuppie dust collectors" (as his wife Barbara calls them) that grace his basement. There are cartons of Fibre Trim, a weird rubber suit for jogging on the spot while plugged into the family vacuum and a number of other, more conventional apparatuses.

Eddie, too, had thought about his weight enough to mention to Linda occasionally that he'd have to go on a diet. "But that's just about all you'd hear about it," Linda reflects. "He's still talking about it."

But he never really got motivated until December 1986 when he was 39 years old, when the stakes were impossibly high and the whole country was suddenly taking notice.

He did, as he promised, "find a way to compete" in the Olympic trials but on February 6, the morning of their weigh-in, Paul found himself wondering if the "Skipper" might have paid too high a price. "He looked terrible. He was weak and he had big rolls on his neck. He definitely needed a lift."

As events unfolded in the next couple of months, it appeared Paul's fears were well founded.

But that morning, at least, The Wrench triumphed. Although he still couldn't do a single curl-up, he had lost 18 pounds. Paul, who had worked out daily at the Fitness Institute, had lost 11 and improved his cardio-vascular fitness 30 percent. He could even manage a few curl-ups.

The weigh-in was a huge media event just like the mini-heavyweight title bout it really was. "They wouldn't let anybody in the room but Eddie and I," remembers Savage. "But somebody was trying to open the curtains so he could sell tickets at $15 a crack to watch Eddie do the sit-ups. It was amazing, the interest and the specific questions."

Along with others, like Ed Lukowich, they were also battling about the contract. The proposal was that the two teams selected would be funded by the Olympic program for the whole next year leading up to February in Calgary. They would sign a contract to formalize the arrangement.

The contract devised by the CCA and its president, Harvey Mazinke, gave almost complete control of the teams' schedule to the bureaucrats. One contentious clause even decreed that the team couldn't enter the playdowns to the Brier in 1988. The curlers screamed so loudly the CCA withdrew the contract, but the dark hints remained: they wanted plenty of control over the Olympic representatives.

"I don't mean this as a threat," the OCR quoted Mazinke, "but if we can't get agreement with the teams, and they say we're not the people they want to run the program, then maybe they're not the type of team we want representing our country."

If Werenich had won the Olympic playdowns, 1988 would have been an extremely interesting year.

He didn't. For the first time in any of his friends' memories Eddie cracked a bit under the pressure that April. "Eddie's solid and very muscular," Paul says. "He sleeps a lot anyway, but I think he was physically tired from the dieting. Over the years he's played some of his best games when he's been involved in controversy. We thought it would work in our favour, that Eddie would perform miracles."

Not this time. By the semi-final against Lukowich, Eddie had retreated to third in disgust and the once-invincible Dream Team was demolished 7-2 in eight ends.

That's what you saw on the surface; behind the scenes it was nastier. "The nastiest we've probably ever been involved in," says Savage. "Before we had thrown a single rock they had already threatened suspension—twice."

*

To get the full flavour of the story you have to go back to a North Bay bonspiel in early April 1987. It's Saturday night and the boys have finished playing and are sitting around having a few—swapping stories. Marina, 22, magnificently statuesque, dressed in black leather, slips in and sits tentatively at the end of the table.

As Savage tells the story, it takes the boys half an hour to get around to asking her what she's doing there. It turns out she's a stripper and happens to have a couple of outfits in her purse.

"One thing leads to another," Paul explains, and before long she's putting on a private show at $10 a head for the enthusiastic crowd. As the night wears on, the Dream Team suddenly has an epiphany. Here before their eyes—blonde hair and rhinestones—is the answer to their coaching problems.

The next week they are supposed to report in Calgary for the playdowns with a coach—all expenses paid. Curl Canada has thoughtfully sent them a two-page list of the potential coach candidates (Level 11 Curl Canada graduates).

"I know maybe 60 percent of them—club curlers. It's a joke," says The Wrench. However, looking up at Marina, the canny, media-wise protagonist in the next round of the Olympic battle sees opportunity staring him in the face.

Savage is excitedly babbling in his ear. "Fabulous! Getting off the plane, press, TV exposure . . . "

Marina likes the idea. She's free that week anyhow. These guys are fun, and an all-expense-paid trip to Calgary would sure beat another week in North Bay. Besides, a little national media exposure never hurt an entertainer's career.

They make a deal and exchange phone numbers.

The next morning cooler heads prevail. John's not sure Laura would like the idea. Neil doesn't know if Jane would understand. The argument see-saws all the way back to Toronto, but in the end they decide to drop the plan.

Paul is assigned to call Marina. "I couldn't get in touch with her," he explains, "but the Thursday night before we are supposed to leave, Eddie gets a call at home. 'Mr. Werenich,' the woman's voice says, 'This is Marina. When are you going to pick me up for Calgary?'"

Reluctantly Eddie explains their change of heart. "I wish we had had the balls to go through with that," he says now, three years later. "If I have one regret about that whole thing . . . " his voice trails off.

In fact, having Marina with them might have headed off a much more serious problem that surfaced on the first day.

Since they had not been able to find a coach acceptable to the CCA, a friend, Steve Clement, had volunteered to pay his own way and just go along for the fun. He'd do the management chores and enjoy the social side of the tournament.

Eddie estimated the trip would cost Clement $2,000. "That's OK with him, so off we go. After many, many beers on the plane we land in Calgary and head for the accreditation room where they are sizing us for jackets." Eddie was not exactly at his most jovial, and when they balked at giving Clement a jacket because he wasn't on their coach list, Vesuvius once again erupted. Most of the lava fell on poor Fred Storey, a Curling Hall of Famer who played lead on Ron Northcott's three-time Brier winning team. He's curling's equivalent to a national treasure. And in this wrangle he was far more observer than antagonist.

"I was abusive," Eddie admits, "but Fred handled it pretty well. They were going to give jackets only to their monkeys, so I called them F---ing Baboons.

"Garry DeBlonde was sitting in the corner, not drinking or anything. Just waiting for me to say something about the CCA."

The next morning, Saturday, as Eddie prepared to throw his first practice rock, Warren Hansen appeared and, without a word, shoved a piece of paper in his hand. It was a summons to appear in front of a specially convened committee of the CCA that afternoon to explain his behaviour.

Eddie crumpled up the paper in fury. He was certainly not going to show up at any "kangaroo court" to explain anything. He'd really had enough. Since he'd lost the weight he was having a terrible time with his delivery. He seemed to get down lower and his release point had changed. "I can't explain it. I was hooking everything," he says now.

"I told the guys, 'Look, there's Paul Gowsell sitting in the stands. You could win this thing with him as skip.'"

But by the appointed time he knew, first, that they were on the brink of suspending him and, second, that in at least one legal opinion they didn't have the jurisdiction to do that. He went to the meeting flanked by his team and a Labatt's ally. He didn't go in willing to eat crow, but knowing he still had one trump card to play seemed to make him less confrontational.

They thrashed out their complaints and "Eddie basically apologized," says Neil. An agreement was made to talk out their future differences rather than sounding off in the papers.

"After we leave the room, I remember I'd done an interview from Toronto with the *Calgary Sun*," says Eddie. "I expect, the way they do these things, it's going to be in the paper the next day, Sunday."

Later that night he met Harvey Mazinke, president of the CCA, and explained the situation. "It was nothing new, just what I'd been saying all year, I told him. Harvey said: 'No problem, I'll handle it.'"

The next day Eddie slept in as usual. Neil, Paul and John were in the hotel dining room chuckling at breakfast over the full-page story, "The Wrench." Instead of a subtitle the paper opted for a quote in large print: "They've been shooting themselves in the foot all along. I can't believe their stupidity."

Another headline quote read: "If we win, I won't be the picture of co-operation."

"It was unbelievable," Paul says. "Eddie did a number on everybody: other curlers, the CCA, everybody."

In the middle of their slightly guilty mirth, in walked Mazinke with a rolled-up paper under his arm. "His feet aren't touching the ground," Neil says. "He wants a retraction. He wants an apology. He wants a press conference. He's talking about suspension again."

"I can't remember his exact words," says Paul, "but it was something about this being the most gut-wrenching experience of his life."

When they woke The Wrench, he was puzzled. "I told him. He said he'd handle it," he kept repeating. He read the Al Ruckaber story and chuckled too. "It was nothing that I hadn't said all year but it was all on one page. I thought it was pretty well done, actually."

Competition was beginning that afternoon, but before they could gear up for that they had some fences to mend. Jeff Timson of Labatt's helped them frame their retraction in a press release. But it turned out to be an exercise in futility. Nobody printed it. Nobody even asked about it.

"Nobody cared," Eddie laughs.

The only fallout from the article was that Bernie Sparkes whom he had called "the old guy" showed up with a cane. And Eugene Hritzuk's wife never spoke to Eddie again after he trashed her husband's character.

"Now take Hritzuk," the article quoted Eddie, "there's a beauty.

He loves being on an all-star team because he couldn't get three other guys to play with him. He told everybody he was taking the year off to prepare for the trials. In reality he didn't have anybody who would play for him."

When Eddie lost in the semi-finals, the CCA and Curl Canada probably were not alone in their glee—or their relief.

"I don't think the Olympics mattered that much to Eddie," says Paul. "I think from talking to him then and afterwards what really bothered him was that the rest of us, Neil and John particularly (because I was in the same boat as him), might miss the opportunity to play in the Olympics because of him."

The *Sun* article had ended on a prophetic note. "If we don't win," it said, "a number of combinations could arise. One might be that I'll step down from skipping for a year and let Paul Savage skip. I don't mind playing third. Maybe one year out of the house would be good for me."

Before summer arrived they'd made that deal.

Eddie tells the story this way. He was worried. His skill, his touch on the rock, seemed to have evaporated with the excess poundage.

"I didn't know what to do. It even crossed my mind to quit curling. I never ever thought such a thing would cross my mind. But I couldn't make a shot. You have no idea how frustrating it is to be on the top of the world one minute, making everything—I didn't care where the guy put the shot because I knew I could make a better one—and all of sudden I couldn't make a wide-open takeout or a free draw, shots a D-club curler would make."

In the middle of this period of angst, Harrison called. "As soon as I heard who it was I said, 'Yeah, I'll play third for Paul.'" Harrison, who hadn't yet got the question framed, was amazed. "I'd already thought of it. I knew you'd call," Eddie explained.

But beyond that, Eddie remembered a promise he'd made to Harrison when he was putting together the Dream Team in 1982 and forcing Neil to play lead.

"Give me one year," Eddie had said, "and next year you can pick the team. I'll play any position you want."

As Eddie saw it, Neil was calling in that favour. Neil sees it differently. "You know Eddie makes his own decisions. I can suggest but . . . "

Whatever—Eddie was going back to sweeping. But as it turned out, very little sweeping. He'd been away from it for five years and now his hips bothered him. There were times he sat on the bench and watched when he felt he should have been sweeping. "It hurt his pride, I think," Paul mused.

They started out the year winning the Royals Classic as they had many times before. "We formed this team with the idea that if Eddie got hot he would move up to skip, and I would drop down," Savage said at that spiel.

But as the year wore on, that possibility became more and more remote. So did Eddie. His shotmaking didn't improve dramatically and Paul was happy skipping. By November Eddie had decided he would leave the team the next year. "He didn't have the same intensity at third," Paul remembers, "but he still contributed an awful lot. He's still the smartest skip ever to play the game. In his perception of shots, his foresight, his ability to read the weaknesses of the opposition, there's nobody like him."

Paul marvels at Eddie's ability to focus and concentrate when his back is against the wall, but more amazing to Paul is the way he remembers critical games and shots from years ago. "One of the secrets to strategy and reading the ice," says Paul, "is that certain shots and situations register as important and you remember. For Eddie a lot of it is unconscious."

The natural talent that makes him exceptional at curling shows up in other things too, says Savage. Although he doesn't play much bridge, he could easily win master points if he wanted to. In pool, which he once considered as a profession, he can still go several years without playing, pick up a cue and beat all comers. In golf he shoots in the 70s mainly because he's a "fabulous putter," says Savage. His secret lies in his ability to read the greens.

"It all seems to come naturally to him," marvels Paul. "We know it's important to know the rocks in the various clubs we play in, but I can't put the same thought process into it that he can. I can't remember didley squat from a game three weeks ago. I write all this shit down now."

Eddie laughs as Paul struggles with things that to him seem tediously obvious. "It amazes me. He's a really intelligent guy. He does really well in business. He's organized and everything. But years ago Ronnie Green and I would tell him how to play his shots and what shots to play. Now 15 years later he's still very good at executing, but he still doesn't know what shot to play. I can't understand that. Now Neil tells him. Neil controls the whole team. He's the skip on that team."

Whether or not Eddie was indulging in his habit of hyperbole, the fact is Paul doesn't read the game the way he does. In fact, the general consensus among elite curlers is that few in the world read the game the way Eddie does.

"I know more about the game now," Eddie says, trying not to sound immodest. "I can tell you 10 little things about an end that the average curler will never see. That's why curling is in trouble as a spectator sport."

And why it's more attractive on TV, with analysts reading the play.

But for all that, in 1988, with Eddie at his side, Paul looked as if he might finally—in his fifth attempt—win the Brier as skip. He led the province in money won, and with $80,000 was second in the country to Lukowich. He got to the Brier by fighting through a spectacular provincial final. He talked about being calmer and wiser than he had been as a skip in the 1970s. "Having been on a team that has won the Brier and the Silver Broom helped tremendously," he told the *Toronto Sun*'s Perry Lefko on the eve of the 59th Brier. "I can approach every shot or competition with much more peace of mind because of that achievement."

The stage was set for Chicoutimi.

The round robin began well. They were solid and ready, and before Paul knew it his fondest dream was knocking at the door. But on Wednesday, sitting with a record of 7-0, Paul began to unravel. "We really started losing it in the game against New Brunswick [a game they won on Tuesday]," Neil remembered afterwards. "We all could feel it slipping away."

In the end they faced Eddie's pal Eugene Hritzuk in the semi and Paul pulled down his own house of cards curling a mere 67 percent.

"I can't really explain what happened to Paul," Eddie told reporters afterward. "Sometimes you just go cold."

But Paul didn't consider dropping back to third. "I probably had just had the best year of my life skipping; I wasn't willing to play third next year."

He thought it might be easier to renovate his mental toughness. "I'll have to address those difficulties," he said. "I may talk to a professional psychologist."

It seems hard to believe that one of the irreverent, mocking,

supremely self-confident Dream Team could be talking about con-
sulting a sports psychologist, but by the spring of 1988 it was clear to
anyone with eyes that Paul and Eddie were adrift in separate row-
boats and caught in very different tides. Now in their forties, they
were reverting to the type they'd been programmed for at birth. Paul,
the conservative insider, was a businessman with a view to the big
picture and the bottom line. Eddie, for all his success, insisted on
being the feisty outsider with his nose pushed up against the glass.
"Compromise" still hadn't made its way into his vocabulary.

The Hall of Fame issue was a case in point. In fact, the way that
spun out it may have had more than a little to do with Paul's dete-
riorating play in the Brier.

On the Tuesday—the day Neil said they could feel it "slipping
away"—it was announced Paul and Eddie would be inducted into
the Curling Hall of Fame on Thursday.

Eddie exploded and refused point-blank. In fact he'd already told
power-brokers at the Olympic trials he wanted no part of their Hall
of Fame, which he said was full of "social butterflies" he'd never
heard of. He was also angry that John and Neil were being left out.

On the surface it looked as if Eddie had left his skip very little
ground to manoeuvre. But Paul didn't act as if a grenade had just
gone off at his elbow. "I was appreciative and thrilled," he says. "I
didn't necessarily share Eddie's opinions. As far as Neil and John
were concerned, I know they felt it was a non-issue. I hope I didn't let
that affect my play. I'd gone through stuff like that with Eddie for so
long—you get used to it." Paul says his lack of "mental preparedness" in the crucial game against Hritzuk had more to do with being
out "till 1:00 A.M. at the Fifth Man Party."

On the Thursday morning Paul dutifully accepted the pin on
Eddie's behalf and gave it to Linda. "She put it away somewhere,"
says Paul. "Maybe years from now when he's mellowed out? . . .
Well maybe not. But at least his boys know he has it."

(Two years later at the 1990 summer seminars, when CCA president Ed Steeves was explaining the decision to send the Brier team to
Sweden without a coach, he reviewed some of the history. The decision to induct Eddie into the Hall of Fame against his will was
probably a mistake, he said.)

Another complication at the 1988 Brier had to do with fifth man
John Kawaja. It had pained him that the Dream Team had essentially reunited in 1988 without him. But he'd started to make his way

out of the desert in 1988 when he hooked up with Al Hackner's front
end from 1985, Pat Perroud and Ian Tetley. However, the third, Russ
Mellerup (the Caveman, as his Thunder Bay friends like to call him),
hadn't worked as well. "I knew I wasn't going to be skipping forever," John explains now. "I was putting in time. I knew with Ian
and Pat I had the nucleus of a very good team. I also knew that third
wasn't really Eddie's spot—that he had done it basically to repay
Paul for playing third for him.

"But I had no reason at all to believe he'd come to my team. In
fact I spent the week before they broke up talking to other players—
Reid Ferguson, Todd Tsukamoto." He did this in full view of Eddie,
because he too was at the Brier—as fifth man on Savage's rink.

Eddie was watching that action with a not-altogether-
disinterested eye. He'd known since November that playing third was
a mistake. He wanted to help his old friend win the Brier but he'd
outgrown the third's role. He'd had problems with motivation even as
a skip; at third it was much worse. Besides, the sweeping continued
to make his arthritic hip act up. "I don't enjoy watching the rocks
going by [when he should have been sweeping]," he said. "I was the
deadbeat on that team.

"To tell the truth I was kinda hoping John would save me a spot,"
he confesses.

They hadn't spoken about it, and John denies he was "saving a
spot," but it was an ideal match—three world champions, all keen,
all under 30, and the wily fox with the seven purple hearts on his
sweater, who had things to teach them about the game they had
never yet guessed at.

"I ran into Eddie at the club. I'd heard he wasn't going back with
Paul. I told him to consider it an open invitation to move in and skip
my team," says John. "Within a day, we had a team.

"Later that night Neil phoned and offered the second stone spot
on Paul's team. The next day Paul phoned and asked if I wanted to
play lead."

How many angels can dance on the head of the pin(nacle) of
Ontario curling?

Not many.

Eddie had talked about wanting to cut back on competitive curling, but he was hardly dropping back to club competition. This
team, an amalgam of four world champs, looked formidable—at
least on paper. But insiders knew. "Eddie hadn't played well in 18

months," John recalls. Still, he refused to worry. History was on his side, he said. Anytime Eddie had made a change he came back the next year and "shot the lights out."

For John, the change could only be positive. He'd had a moderately good year in 1988. A disastrous ninth end in the regionals ended his season. He'd lost to Savage who went on to win the province, and for the first time since junior he felt comfortable skipping. Still he hadn't travelled out of the province and was clearly not in the main show the way he'd been for almost all his years in men's. With Eddie as his new skip, that was about to change.

They didn't immediately sweep to the top of the charts. "Eddie still wasn't the player he was in 1983-84," John remembers. "He'd miss shots." They hung around Toronto doing local bonspiels because Eddie wanted to spend more time with his growing sons, who were then 10 and 12.

But there was something percolating on that team. Everybody had something to prove: Eddie, that he could still play; John, that he'd grown up a bit from the cocky, success-soaked days of complacency on the Dream Team; and Ian and Pat, that they weren't just handsome passengers on the Hackner-Lang train to glory in 1985.

In November they trounced Russ Howard 7-2 and won $10,500 at the Standard Trust Classic cashspiel. In December Eddie cracked up his car and wound up in the hospital. A piece of guardrail pierced the front of the sportscar. "An inch closer and we wouldn't be having this conversation," Eddie told well-wishers.

But by the playdowns Eddie was hot—undefeated in both the zone and the region. Onlookers were describing him as "rock solid."

"This is really a nice feeling," said the grateful and newly confident Wrench. Although they weren't travelling, they were doing all right in money too. By February they'd won $19,000 in just the Toronto and area spiels.

They steamed into Trenton for the playdowns and rolled up an 8-1 record. But the gods were neither crazy nor smiling. For the second year in a row Howard got Eddie in the final. This team still had dues to pay.

"We're one of the most superstitious teams around," says Tetley. "Eddie was up dancing the night before that game. He never dances." The next day they went down in flames, in part at least, Ian believes, because of one error in strategy and one serious throwing mistake—both Eddie's. The shot was "brutal," "disastrous"—so bad Eddie almost fell on his face delivering it.

"You wonder if he was being punished for dancing," laughs Tetley.

Asked if he was disappointed about not getting the eighth purple heart for his sweater, Eddie was succinct. "It's nice to win anytime," he said, and then added with a twinkle, "to hell with history."

He wasn't in much of a mood to talk. Asked if he would be quitting his team again because he lost in the final, he grimaced at the question and said something about being too old to shuffle teams.

This team most assuredly would be heard of again, they all vowed. By the end of the 1989 season, Eddie's hair seemed a lot greyer but his smile and confidence were back. It had happened by accident, but no tactician could have positioned Eddie better. The 41-year-old Wrench now wanted to win as much as ever, and he had three youngsters in their twenties with formidable talents to mould. At third, John was steadily improving, becoming "a more complete curler," he says. "The best in the world," his admirers insist.

Tetley says he always believed Al Hackner to be the best curler because of the variety of shots he could make. Now he sees Kawaja edging forward to snap away the informal crown. "John played so well in 1990 that Eddie never had to make a tough shot."

For Paul Savage, watching from the sidelines, it wasn't much of a surprise. "Eddie had a lot to prove that year [1989]. He needs that. With a new team to show off to and not let down, he started to practise and put a bit of effort into it."

But the changes in Eddie's game went deeper than macho histrionics. Werenich, once the master of the draw game, has now almost abandoned it for the running game. The old "Kamikaze Kurling" that Savage loves simply didn't work as well any more. Other teams had closed the gap on strategy. The mental gaffes the Dream Team used to be able to capitalize on just didn't occur as often. And as Eddie's touch seemed to fade, others came on very strong. It was time for a new strategy.

After watching Pat Ryan's back-to-back Brier wins in 1988 and 1989, Eddie started asking himself tough questions like: "Why should I go out and pass the ball when I can run with it and win? I've got to play by the rules they give."

So gradually over the past few years Werenich has edged his game

in a new direction. He sometimes refers to his new team as the
"peeler healers," a reference to their great ability to keep it clean
after they've rolled up a solid lead in the first few ends.

"With our old team we used to let our opponents back into the
game all the time," says Kawaja. "With this team we like to grab an
early advantage and then slam the door.

"The way to beat our old team was to keep it close and clean,"
explains Kawaja. "We'd start daydreaming in the hack and before
you know it the game would be over. In those days the harder the
shot, the more we'd get into it. You could see the fire in Paul's eyes, as
he went into the hack."

He hesitates for a moment, considering before he adds, "And I'm
not going to say how to beat the new team."

Werenich, along with many others, hopes the low-scoring peeling
game is just an aberration, not the wave of the future. New rules and
formats like the TSN Skins Games and the Moncton 100 rule try to
tip the scales in favour of more rocks in play and fewer blank ends.
But when a world championship is on the line and you've won the
toss; when your opposition wouldn't think twice about "peeling you
out" if they got the upper hand—well it's not a hard decision to
make. Trouble is, everyone acknowledges that style of play is bad for
the game because it's boring to watch.

So will the curling establishment change the rules to force more
rocks into play? Don't hold your breath, says Eddie. "The curling
executive doesn't care. They'll mention it at their meetings and that's
it. They're old traditionalists who don't really care about the game as
long as they're looked after."

There is a growing sense among bonspiel organizers and TV pro-
ducers that something has to be done to liven up the game. When the
Moncton city fathers were putting together their $250,000 bonspiel
to publicize the city's centennial, they tried the "leads can't peel"
rule change suggested by Russ Howard.

So, just after New Year's Day 1990, when the 16 invited teams
assembled for the richest bonspiel in the history of the sport, it was
expected that Eddie and the Dream Team would carry home most of
the cash. (The invitations went to specific teams and everyone still
remembered the magic of the Werenich rink from 1983 and 1984.)

Leading up to Moncton they were excited. Ed even practised a bit.
By the Saturday morning game against Hackner, Neil would later

write in his column in the OCR, "The Dream Team has that old feeling and the fat brothers are playing as well as ever."

"Eddie was amazing," remembers Kawaja. "When they turned the page on the calendar it was like the rebirth of the old curler."

The Dream Team's feeling of invincibility was in fact so strong that in the semi-final against Howard they were incredulous when Eddie's angle raise take-out didn't score.

"That was our bonspiel to win," remembers Savage. "Eddie threw the last rock exactly as he should have. I raised my broom to signal a great shot—and when the smoke cleared Howard's team was doing a $50,000 jig, John's sitting with his head in his hands, and I'm saying, 'Who cheated?'"

Writing about it later, Harrison quipped, "We still think David Copperfield created the illusion that our last shot missed."

"When rocks are between one-quarter and three-quarters of an inch apart they go the opposite way to what you expect," explains Paul. "Eddie was the first one to let me in on that well-kept secret."

They went home sobered—well, at least chastened—lugging $26,500 and a new determination. The confidence was there too—quieter than it had been in 1983, but just as sustaining. Eddie was happier than he'd been in years about curling.

Both Savage and Werenich's rinks had banner years. Although Savage's crew "passed out" in the provincial final, he says, they led the province in winnings at $85,000. Across the country only Ed Lukowich with his $140,000 did better.

And Eddie, after going through the club, the zone and the regions side by side with his old pal Savage, suddenly, at the provincials, stepped ahead of the pack and displayed his new, world championship form.

Most of the sparkle at the Tankard belonged to Kawaja. The knee that had been bothering him sporadically for 18 months suddenly felt fine. He was helped by the fact he didn't have to play every game. He missed one meaningless game at the end of the round robin for a business meeting and came back a little fresher for the final.

"He shot the lights out," says Linda Werenich, who was extremely grateful to see some of the pressure ease off her husband.

The "Control Master," as they called Kawaja for his impeccable shooting, was in fine form for the final, a game that seemed to leave opponent Bob Fedosa in awe. "There were no weaknesses," he told reporters afterwards. "It was gut-wrenching calls—sweeping—a grindout game. I'm drained."

Eddie was no slouch either. "He wasn't pretty," mused Harrison afterward, "but he showed his usual bulldoggedness and patience."

While the Wrench was pulling out all the stops on the curling sheet, he was also battling the officials. "If they're trying to intimidate us, it's working," said Eddie bitterly, partway through the tournament after officials had called a couple of hogline violations on Pat Perroud.

Aficionados of the Werenich act nodded sagely—the old, now completely grey fox stirring things up, playing the game the best way he knew how.

At home Linda remembers the mood was more jubilant. "We'll win this year. We're going all the way this time," he'd say. She knows this refrain; he always uses it, even in losing years. But the tone was something new and she loved the sound of the conviction in his voice. The half-mocking note was missing. Eddie, she knew, believed this was the year. In fact they all seemed to believe it.

And by the time the Chatham Tankard was over, so did Linda. "They were curling so well—especially John. He wanted it so badly this time. He really wanted to win at third."

Eight weeks later, sitting in the Västerås community auditorium idly watching fire-eaters and jugglers assembled to celebrate the world championship that her husband's team had won, Linda Werenich sighed. It was over: they'd done it again. She listened and smiled in agreement as Eddie told the people who came up to his table to shake his hand and kiss his cheek, "Now none of our summer parties will be ruined." She, too, had hated the prospect of spending a summer explaining why they couldn't, or didn't, win in Sweden.

The four champions and their relieved and delighted fifth man were clearly ready to party. The thermos of vodka was close at hand under the table. So was the beer. They'd loosened their ties, pushed back the brown fedoras which were the *pièces de résistance* of their Mafioso-style dress uniform. They were laughing a little louder and a little more frequently than they had all week.

Linda knew this act too: the release when the monkey is finally shrugged off the back for at least another season. Eddie had proven everything there was to prove in the arena of his choice (not literally).

Now they could go back to normal, back to life in their comfortable—not quite fully furnished—new home on a third of an acre in Newmarket, back to bringing up their sons, Darren and Ryan, back to friendly barbeques on the patio, back to training the new dog not to destroy the screens in the sunroom.

Or could they? The world championship has a dynamic all its own and Linda knew she couldn't really predict what would be waiting for them back home in Canada. Nor, she suddenly realized with a jolt, could she predict what her interesting mate might do next. Eddie's partying had stepped up its tempo a little, Linda felt a quiver of foreboding. The place was too full of media and curling establishment for Eddie to start sounding off. It was getting close to the time to leave.

A few minutes before, she'd noticed Ian Tetley and his wife Sherry leave abruptly. Around the table the women had exchanged glances. One more chapter in a difficult week.

They wondered if it was more fallout from the Marina episode at the Brier. Seems that one afternoon "team meeting" had been held at the strip club in the Soo where Marina (their would-be Olympic coach) was working. Not all of the women had seen this as an unmissable opportunity for a reunion. But both Laura Barker and Jane Hooper had grown up in curling families. They knew and accepted the tone of this world. Sherry was new.

Linda had kissed off the situation, telling Eddie not to bring back any diseases. But Ian knew his career-minded new wife would not see the situation in quite the same light. He'd put off telling her where they'd held that particular meeting. In Sweden Sherry heard about it from the other women. It hadn't been the high point of anybody's week.

But if it hadn't been Marina it would have been something else. The styles of Sherry and Eddie were on a collision course. The others watched helplessly as Ian struggled with his double loyalties.

Eddie and Linda have an excellent relationship, the envy of many curlers. But it was forged 20 years ago in a small Manitoba farming community and it hasn't changed much since. Linda says curling has been a great asset to their lives. "Financially, first," she explains, "instead of me working it was Ed curling." She now works part-time but arranges her hours around her husband's schedules and spends her weekends driving her boys to their curling games or watching Ed curl.

It's been a great life, she says, lots of friends, lots of good times. She remembers, as a new bride, dreaming about going to the Brier and she still picks the Brier as the highlight of her year. She looked forward to the almost-hometown Brier in Hamilton more than any of the others.

When Eddie offered to take her to Winston's, an expensive power hangout in downtown Toronto, to celebrate their 18th wedding anniversary, she opted for supper and a few drinks at Avonlea Curling Club with their friends.

The relationships of the next generation are never as simple or as clearly defined. Ian and Sherry met at a Dale Carnegie course. They both have university degrees and strong career plans. Sherry is a product manager for a large pharmaceutical firm. She's used to making decisions, handling responsibility and travelling for business. She's efficient and likes to plan her time and work to a schedule.

As an equestrian she competed nationally in show jumping until her final year of university. "I'm not a spectator," she confesses. "I'd rather be out there doing."

"I haven't had the experience of the others either with the game or the [curling] world, but I've come to appreciate the sport and the strategy," she says.

Chances are it will take much longer for her to appreciate a world that has yet to completely shed attitudes based on an assumption of male supremacy.

"We're still newlyweds," she says. "We're so busy and independent, we really appreciate our time together. That was the hardest part of the trips, like the one to the worlds in Sweden: the men spent a lot of time together playing cards. It was so expensive there, we [the women] couldn't afford to do anything. We spent our time lounging around, eating, and waiting for them to come back."

Eddie sees no end in sight for his competitive curling. "Not yet anyhow," says Linda.

Ian is different. He was under 30 and had just won the world championship for the second time when he made this sanguine comment: "I look at it [curling] from a financial standpoint right now. It's supplemental tax-free income. We want to buy a house and it's a big help. But it takes up a lot of time and I'm definitely ready to give up curling."

A year later Ian, 14 years younger than Eddie, had already stepped out of the intensely competitive arena. In 1991-92 he signed on to play with Paul Savage, instead of Werenich, because the Savage rink had planned to curl in only five or six big bonspiels.

The resignation surprised no one. The team had had three incredibly successful years together. In 1989 they went to the Ontario final. In 1990 they won the world, and in 1991 they were on course in the Ontario Tankard, steaming to a bye to the final, when Eddie's last rock caught a hair. Abruptly it was all over for Werenich.

"I wasn't there in the next game against Kirk [Ziola]. I was drained emotionally. I lost it on a routine shot that I've made a thousand times. I misread the ice and overthrew the rock. Still it was one of the top two or three years we've ever had, moneywise." (The Werenich team topped the country's Gold List at $61,350.)

Yet for all the success of those three years, Ian's resignation was almost expected. The situation came to a head during Brier week, when there was speculation in the *Toronto Sun* that Neil Harrison would replace Tetley on the Werenich team.

"At that point no one had talked to me," insists Harrison. Nevertheless it was an open secret that Neil was leaving Savage because he felt that team had run its course. And in January of 1991 when the world champions took their much-appreciated reward trip to Grindelwald, Neil was along as fifth man. (Kawaja, once again, had business commitments.) The inference was there for anyone to draw.

The year before, when the idea of Ian's leaving had surfaced for the first time, Eddie was upset. "Yeah, it would be a blow to me," he said. "Nobody's irreplaceable but I know how much the game means to Ian. If his wife made him quit, I wouldn't be able to understand it."

But a year later when it happened, he was resigned to the inevitable. "I'm angry in a sense, I guess. They broke up a great curling team."

But none of that diminishes his anticipation for the coming season. He and Neil are looking forward to curling together again. "We've got a really heavy (cashspiel) schedule planned for next year," Eddie says, with a glint in his eye that men 20 years younger can't muster. "I'm 44 years old. Five years from now I might not be able to do this any more. I want to have some fun now while I still can."

Sherry Tetley is the first woman to challenge the Werenich team philosophy. Undoubtedly she won't be the last. Besides there are already other cracks showing in their approach to the game.

As the 1992 season opened, Paul Savage talked about the changes he's seen. Keener ice, he said, "has made the touch part of the game so much more important. You have to be in much better mental shape today. Our heroes of the 1950s and 1960s like the Richardsons, Matt Baldwin, Hec Gervais were out at all hours enjoying the social life, and would still get up and curl extremely well in the morning. But it's different today, mental preparedness is so important. We often talk about how much more successful we would have been if we'd behaved ourselves.

"Eddie and I are sort of the end of the line for a certain type of successful curler. I don't think guys like us will make it in the future."

3

JIM SULLIVAN
New Kids on the Brier Block

AS THE 1990s began, Paul Savage and Eddie Werenich were sadly contemplating the passing of the championship curler as *bon vivant*. Meanwhile, 1,000 kilometres east of their Toronto Avonlea home club, two youngsters were plotting the arrival of the next generation's champion. The "Arnold Schwarzenegger superchampion" Werenich likes to call the type.

The casual observer of the 1990 Brier final certainly would never describe either skip, Jim Sullivan, or his third stone and cousin, Charlie Sullivan, as Schwarzenegger clones. But it wasn't their muscles they had relentlessly prepared for this competition; it was their minds and their rock delivery. When they arrived in Sault Ste. Marie, Ontario, in early March 1990, for their very first Brier appearance, they were as scientifically close to perfection as Warren Hansen and Curl Canada could have hoped.

The final of that championship, on the cusp of a new decade, showcased the future of the sport. And in doing so moved the game a little further away from art, intuition and revelry, into science, athleticism and sobriety.

But by the end of 1991 the Sullivan team was finished. Jim and Charlie were heading in opposite directions and their lead had left the province. The small time-window they'd allowed for curling success had slammed shut and the painful rebuilding process had begun.

But in the Soo in 1990 that was all in the future and curling fans were watching an interesting clash of styles as Jim Sullivan, tall, slender and perpetually easygoing, lined up at the T-line at the Labatt Brier final beside a short, roly-poly spark plug named Ed Werenich.

Jim's cousin Charlie knew what was coming: "He's a drone out there. The more excited he gets the quieter he becomes."

The fans were calling Jim and his team the New Kids on the Block, but that too was only a skin-deep observation. The Sullivan rink from the Capital Winter Club in Fredericton, New Brunswick, might have been kids but they hadn't come just to play. They had come to win.

The odds-makers put them at 20-to-1 as the week began. By the final everyone conceded that Eddie Werenich, if he wanted to win, would have to be at the top of his game. The kids (average age 21) were coming on strong.

They were shaky on the first game, losing to Werenich 8-3. After that they battled every game, advancing through the Brier with a relentlessly even record—2-2, 4-4 and 5-5. Jim Sullivan, slow and easy before the TV cameras, told Brier fans that was fine with him. They just wanted to win a few—not embarrass themselves. But Craig Burgess, second stone, admits they were very unhappy with that record.

For them their last round-robin game with Prince Edward Island was the biggest game of the tournament, the point at which they served notice of their intentions and took charge of their destiny.

They beat P.E.I. in the lowest-scoring game in Brier history, 2-1, and finished with a 6-5 record good enough for the playoffs.

In the sudden-death games at the end of the week, the Schwarzenegger heroics began to peek through; they curled with the confidence and aggressiveness of seasoned pros. Jim still boyishly twisted a lock of his hair with his index finger and Charlie still leaned impassively on his broom. But the game was on—the Kids were tough and aggressive. They wanted no giveaways, no mistakes. Everybody had to make every shot and in the end Jim had to draw to the four-foot to win.

For three games in a row, as they moved through a tie-breaker to the final, Jim was called on for last-rock heroics. And three times in a row he pulled it off. The crowd loved it. Even when they beat hometown hero Al Harnden there were shouts of "New Kids on the Block" from the crowd. Everybody knew they were watching the future of the game.

These young men, already world champions at the junior level and runners-up in their province in 1989, were curling with the kind of confidence and precision that would not be denied. Some were dismissing their burgeoning strength as the result of a fluke. "They're on a roll," said one reporter. "Curling above themselves," another competitor sniffed.

But from the Maritimes, where curling fans had watched the improvement over the nearly five years they'd been together, there was no such talk. The Sullivan boys were simply taking the next logical step in what was beginning to seem an inexorable sweep to the top.

To understand what propelled this motion it's necessary to go back five years to the beginning.

At 17, cousins Charlie and Jim Sullivan, both grade 12 high school students in New Brunswick, were intensely aware of how tough it is to win curling's biggest prizes. Only four months apart, they'd grown up in a family where competitive curling was as natural as walking.

Before they were born, their fathers had curled together in the Brier. By 1990 Charlie, Sr., and his brother had made 11 Brier appearances—eight of them together.

But their fathers had never been close enough to smell victory. Not even in junior competition where Charlie, Sr., had skipped the New Brunswick entry in 1958 and Dave had done the same two years later.

By 1986 their sons, both skips too, had started to repeat what was beginning to look like an "also-ran" pattern. Both Charlie and Jim had played in juniors but never quite made the big show. In fact they hadn't done as well as their fathers: neither had ever won the province.

"I always finished second or third," explains Charlie, who now plays third on their men's team and is 114 days younger than Jim. "I'd never won anything serious."

Jim, playing out of Fredericton, had been no luckier. He was a very good curler, solid and steady, but he'd had trouble getting out of the zone. In grade 11 it was his younger brother Evan, a grade 9 kid, who had beaten him in zone play. For Jim that was a particularly tough loss. He knew he needed an infusion of talent on his rink to dramatically improve his curling fortunes. It would take another year and another loss in the zones before he could pull it off.

"Halfway through grade 12 we decided to curl together in university," explains Charlie. First-year university would be their last year of eligibility as Canadian juniors. If they wanted to make their mark, this would be their moment.

The commitment they made to each other was no casual school-boy kind of thing. At the time they were living in different cities. Curling together meant that Charlie, who is an extremely good student and could have gone anywhere to study, was committing to the University of New Brunswick in Fredericton.

"He went to university to curl," his father Charlie, Sr., says shaking his head ruefully. Charlie, Jr., doesn't deny the allegation. He even picked business, he admits, because it gave him enough free time for curling.

The Sullivans attacked the game with the dedication of any athlete preparing for competition. Every afternoon they were at the rink for a couple of hours throwing rocks. Several evenings a week they curled in Superleague games. In the season they travelled to cash-spiels for three days every weekend.

Of course their studies suffered, but they were convinced that they had only a few short years to improve their game. They had to practise and improve now. Later (after 30 or so), a curler keeps sharp with practice, they say, but the opportunity for dramatic improvement has passed.

Charlie, who is passionate about winning in curling, is strangely neutral about his career. He has no interest in even lining up for the race for the fanciest job and biggest paycheque. Even though he has now graduated with honours in business, he's not interested in pursuing it. He'd thought about being an accountant but he found the field too confining. "I'm going to study education for a couple of years. I'm interested in control. Teaching gives you lots of control."

Making money doesn't seem to enter his calculations. "I want to do something I like," he says.

Still he was by far the best student on the team. "He has the closest thing I've seen to a photographic memory," marvels Burgess. "He gets 85 percent by reading the text over once. Jim will study all weekend for 73 percent."

In high school Charlie had already established this pattern of fierce practice and commitment. He swam competitively, practising both at lunchtime and after school. But even then—feeling physically depleted from the exertion in the pool—he'd head for the curling rink and throw rocks for another hour.

It wasn't cool to show up at school with a broom under your arm, but Charlie dismissed the teasing. "I really liked curling. I liked the practice; there was always something competitive you could do. And it wasn't something that took just physical skill, the mental skill is a big part of the game—the best part. You can outthink the best people in the country. In curling, every shot has an outcome."

Swimming was more frustrating. The boring, repetitive drills against the clock offered no intellectual stimulation.

"Besides I didn't get anywhere swimming," Charlie says. "At 14 I was five feet tall. Others were six feet. Because of physical limitations you can only get so good no matter what you do."

So at 17, Charlie was more than ready to see how far he could go with curling. He quickly agreed to drop back to third in the interests of their new team. "Jim's a lot [six inches] taller and I was told he wanted to skip," Charlie chuckles.

"I wanted to skip," Jim confirms. "I'm just lazy I guess. I don't like sweeping and I'm not the world's best."

He likes to take his time in everything. The rest of his family regularly make the one-hour trip from Fredericton to their summer camp near Saint John. Not Jim. His 18-year-old brother Brian goes down on the weekends, and at least once during the week for sailing races. Jim isn't interested. He prefers to play golf closer to home.

Even for curling he won't make the trip. In Saint John the ice goes in two weeks earlier than it does in Fredericton. But even though he's anxious to practise, he would never drive down to throw rocks with Charlie. "I'd rather wait until they put in the ice here," he explains, moving slightly in the comfortable rocking chair he has set up in front of the TV. "I don't like to rush around."

Charlie is vastly different. Jim has worked in an office in the summer; Charlie lifeguards. Jim loves to watch TV sports; Charlie likes to windsurf and race under sail.

They had been friends as youngsters primarily because they were cousins, not because they had a natural affinity. But by 1986 Jim had wound up in the same place as his cousin—ready to commit totally to curling for at least one year—even though his route had been radically different.

When they were 14 their fathers competed in the Brandon Brier and went back in 1983 to Sudbury. Charlie, Jr., remembers resolving that he, too, would represent his province in that magical event—at least five times. Jim recalls little about it. At the time he was too busy being a high-school basketball star to dream about the Brier. Yes, he played with his father in the Superleague and he loved the competition, but other sports took priority.

"He was on his way to being the best basketball player that New Brunswick ever produced," explains Burgess, "but he injured his back and had to quit."

At Albert Street Junior High in Fredericton, when Jim was named Outstanding Athlete of the Year, it was for his prowess on the basketball court and the hockey rink. Nobody knew he curled.

In the thick of that kind of mainstream sports life, curling seemed no more than an arcane family pastime. Even today he admits he'd watch the World Series over the Brier if they were on TV at the same time.

Like so many champion curlers, Jim was loaded with natural athletic talent. Every sport seemed to come easily and he loved the environment and the team dynamics. He reached his full height of 6'2" by the time he was in grade 11. By then his family was well acquainted with his coolness under pressure.

His father Dave remembers when Jim was 10 and one of the youngest kids on his grade-school mini-basketball team. That was the moment he first noticed his son's icy nerve. In the championship game their opponents were up one with less than a minute to go when someone fouled Jim and he was given two free throws.

"He made both shots," his father remembers, "and they won the tournament."

It was the first time he had ever seen his son perform in a clutch situation. But it certainly wouldn't be the last. In fact his own 1990 curling season ended when Jim drew to the four-foot in the New Brunswick provincial quarter-finals and eliminated him.

"We were tied in the ninth end and I thought I had the four-foot pretty well guarded but . . . " Dave's voice trails off. It wasn't an easy loss.

Nobody had looked for that game: the father and his 20-year-old second son facing his oldest son and favourite nephew in a winner-take-all elimination round. It was a nightmare of mixed loyalties for everyone concerned, especially Dave's wife, and Jim's and Evan's mother, Carol. "Whatever happened I knew it would be a Sullivan winning," she says brightly trying to deflect the talk.

"I can tell you this, it wasn't me she was cheering for," Dave adds with a smile.

But given the boys' (as their family calls them) record no one was surprised at the way it turned out. Back in high school when he was putting this team together, Jim would never have dreamed of eliminating his father from the provincial finals. He'd always planned on playing with his father on a very competitive New Brunswick Brier entry.

But that was before the triumphs of his final year of junior.

For 1987, their first year together, the goal was simple in the extreme. They wanted to represent the province in the Pepsi Junior just as their fathers had. Charlie and Jim were shopping for junior curlers with desire and talent enough to help them do it. Todd Burgess, who had beaten Jim in the zone playdowns in 1986, suggested his brother Craig who was thinking of coming to New Brunswick to study forestry. "He's a better curler than I am," Todd said.

That endorsement was more than enough for Jim and Charlie. They wrote to him in Truro, Nova Scotia, and offered him a spot on their team without meeting him or seeing him curl. "We knew Todd; he was a nice guy and a very good curler," Jim explained. "And if Craig was better than Todd that would be great."

At the time the letter arrived Craig was 17, living at home and deliberating about his future. He too was planning to enter university in the fall and he too was wondering how to make the most of his final year of junior eligibility in curling.

Should he go to Halifax to study at Dalhousie University? The team that was courting him there were great guys, but he knew playing with them would mean more good times than good curling. "I didn't think they had it. And I didn't think I did either," he says, remembering.

It was exceedingly tough to get out of Nova Scotia on the junior circuit. His 1985 team had done it, played in the Pepsi Junior nationals, but they'd moved on to men's and he wasn't sure he'd ever see their like again.

Maybe New Brunswick was the answer. Todd had finished his junior play in that province and didn't think the curling was as competitive. He'd beaten Jim Sullivan in zone play. But next year, he told Craig, Jim would be a powerhouse with his intense cousin Charlie at third.

It sounded like the ticket he needed. He sent in his application for forestry to the University of New Brunswick and let Todd know he

was coming. But there's a rhythm to these things and it wouldn't do
to seem overeager. So it happened that Craig was already installed in
residence by the time Jim and Charlie came calling.

"It was really funny," Charlie remembers of their first meeting.
"We knew he was here and then we heard another team was after
him. We scurried over to residence to pin down our team right then."

It was a perfect match. Charlie and Jim were a little "quieter"
than most of Craig's friends but they were easy to be around and he
felt comfortable right away. All three had an abundance of drive and
Craig added the vital ingredient of knowing how to win. The Sullivans, for all their dedication and skill, had nothing like the experience of winning that Craig had.

The year 1985 had been very big for him: in track, running in the
400-metre event, he had represented Nova Scotia in the Canada
Summer Games; in football, he'd played on the team that won the
provincial championship; and in curling, he'd been to the national
junior championships representing Nova Scotia.

Neither of the Sullivans had been that far in any sport—never
mind three sports in the same year.

With Craig signed on at second and another solid player, Danny
Alderman, at lead, they settled in with the secret, exhilarating
knowledge that they were poised on the lip of the big time.

They practised maniacally, sharing what they knew about the
game and helping each other achieve the elusive perfect delivery.

Curling aficionados, like Al Garcelon, who was running the New
Brunswick junior program, watched with delight and a little awe as
they practised. "One, two, three hours a day, seven days a week," he
remembers. "I've never seen that kind of dedication before. Other
teams practised—that's what makes the difference between a very
good team and an outstanding team—but not like that."

But in the fall of 1986 there was more to get used to than curling
with a new team. Charlie was adjusting to both university life and
living away from home for the first time.

Jim, although he was still living at home, was finding university a
tough grind. He'd enrolled in engineering (both his father and uncle
are professional engineers), but the workload was killing. By Christmas he'd decided academic challenge and serious curling were incompatible. Next semester he would enrol in business with Charlie.

"When I went to university I went to study," his father Dave
teases. He carefully neglects to add that by the time he got to univer-

sity he'd already had his kick at the can of junior curling. Besides, when he and Charlie, Sr., were studying engineering they competed in the less demanding college circuit and won the Maritime intercollegiate title.

But 30 years later when their sons enrolled in first year the climate had changed dramatically. Sports had become such big business that pursuing even an amateur sport like curling is considered as significant a career move as taking a challenging course in university.

So although their fathers gently chide Jim and Charlie, both are backed solidly by their families in their all-out assault on curling's biggest prizes.

In the Sullivan clan the curling mania has endured for three generations. In 1958 Herman E. Sullivan skipped his two sons, Charlie, Sr., and Dave, and a friend, Murray Carson, to victory in the Saint John city bonspiel. In fun, Carson complained to the media that as lead and the only non-Sullivan on the team he didn't get enough attention. When their accomplishment was written up in the local paper the story read, "Murray Carson and three others have captured the city bonspiel."

"I don't think we ever quite got over it," laughs Herman. In 1990 Herman was 94 and lived in a veterans' retirement home, but he was still the spirit and spark of the clan. When the boys were interviewed on TV before the Brier final, both said they'd like to win it all for Herman who had played for half a century and then watched and encouraged their development.

In the summer, when curling was the subject of the lazy speculative talk on the verandah of the family's "summer camp" overlooking the Saint John River, Herman was part of every discussion. When they told each other the old curling stories, it was Herman they consulted as the authority on what had happened in which year, just as he was the authority on exactly how many weeks ago the first great-grandson was born.

It's easy to imagine how much pleasure the family got watching the Sullivan junior team jell. Everybody knew they were good. The question of how good would have to wait until the provincial finals in 1987.

Jim believes that final was "the toughest win ever." Three teams finished tied for first. "We just happened to win. They were all close games—a lot came down to the last rock."

Charlie remembers that the ice was very bad but it turned into a great tournament for the curling Sullivans. Half an hour before the boys won, Lisa, Charlie's bubbly younger sister, skipped her rink to the provincial title for junior women.

With his children both representing the province Charlie, Sr., had little choice. His own team had qualified for men's provincials but he was heading off to Prince Albert with the youngsters. Dave, who was third on that team, had already booked off. He was going to Prince Albert in the quasi-official position of coach.

The Sullivans were among the very few junior teams that didn't have a serious CCA coach working with them. They preferred instead to self-coach. Charlie, Jr., remembers how surprised some of the coaches were that Dave didn't scurry down to consult at the fifth-end breaks. He believes the dominating presence of some junior coaches inhibits the growth of young teams.

"Some of the big national coaches *are* the team," he says . "They don't really teach them anything—they tell them what to play. I think that's why it's so hard for some junior teams to make the transition to men's. They aren't used to thinking for themselves."

For Craig, who'd worked a great deal with junior coaches in Nova Scotia, the difference was that the Sullivan team seemed much more "mature" than the teams he'd seen at home.

For Charlie, Sr., the difference lay in the boys. Some people are more "coachable" than others, he says. His son falls in the "less coachable" camp.

At any rate, Dave was coach in name only. "More like a 'gofer,'" he laughs ruefully.

"Jim thinks it gives him confidence to have his father there," explains Charlie. But they both know, when it gets down to the heat of the battle, it really doesn't matter who's there; Jim will scarcely notice.

Just as they did later in the 1990 Brier, they announced that their goal was not to embarrass themselves. But just as in Sault Ste. Marie, that goal could easily be adapted to fit a new situation.

Jim remembers how excited they were making their first big trip out west to play on a 12-sheeter. It was the biggest curling rink he'd ever seen, but as the novelty wore off, they gradually noticed they were far from the worst players at the tournament. "We watched a few games and we realized we had a half-decent chance to do well," Jim says.

"Half-decent" is typical Sullivan understatement. They rolled over all comers and were 9-0 near the end of the week. They lost their last two but ended with a bye to the final and were the odds-on favourites to win. They faced Ontario's Wayne Middaugh and won 6-4 when Jim hit and stuck for two in the final end.

Back home in Fredericton the local curlers faced them with new respect. No more were they the painfully quiet, reserved Sullivans with a family tradition of being teetotallers and fine curlers. Now they were that rarity in New Brunswick curling—national champions. The first New Brunswick national champions since 1970.

In 1987, Canadian junior champions had to wait until the next April before they could try for the junior world championship. For the New Brunswick rink of 18-year-olds this meant 13 months of marking time practising, before heading for Füssen in Bavaria and the junior worlds.

Since they were now too old to compete against Canadian juniors, they had to spend their second university year searching out men's teams who would play them. There was no opportunity to go into the provincial playdowns, because the time overlapped too closely with the Uniroyal junior world championship.

With Jim only taking a half load of courses and the experience of one European bonspiel—in Glasgow, Scotland—they were doing everything they could to improve their chances at Füssen.

One of the things they did was establish a team policy about drinking. "When I go away to a bonspiel, I go to compete, not to drink," says Charlie. "We treat it like an athletic meet. In junior I used to have to tell them, 'No drinking, guys.' Now [in men's] they're telling me, 'We're not going to drink.'"

He claims their biggest bonspiel win so far came in part at least because everyone else let their partying get out of hand.

For the myriad of competitive curlers who periodically regret over- indulging, Charlie's sombre words pound another nail into the coffin of the *bon vivant* curler. Most of Canada's competitors still remember with affection the days before the money got semi-serious and the curlers got solemn, when your score as a partyer was almost as important as your score in the spiel.

In those days if you didn't drink, as Charlie, Sr., and Dave didn't, you certainly didn't talk about it. Charlie's plainspoken opinions are another signal of the arrival of the athletic superchampion.

But the "abstainer's edge" is only the ribbon on the package. Inside is solid hard work, clear thinking and practice. As the boys prepared for the West German world championship the practices got more and more intense.

Charlie and Jim discussed strategy interminably. "We were known as a very slow team in 1987," Charlie chuckles. "We discussed every shot. In 1988 it got a little better. Now our strategy is pretty well set." They've struck a compromise between Charlie's gambling style and Jim's more conservative approach.

After Christmas in 1987 they began to see big dividends from their hard work. As a team they could feel they were dramatically improved from the foursome who won the Canadian junior national championship the year before. They had one workshop on sports psychology, although none of them really took it to heart. "The little we did do really helped," says Burgess. They ended their preparation by winning $3,000 and the Moncton men's bonspiel. Look out Europe!

Füssen is a little town in Bavaria near mad King Ludwig's Hohenschwangau castle. This castle, the one Walt Disney appropriated for his "When You Wish upon a Star" theme, was an apt symbol to loom over their fortunes that spring. It was a dream, something that a year before had been beyond their imagining. In the flower-decked Bavarian town it could all come true.

As usual, Canada was considered the team to beat. But Jim, Charlie, Craig, and Danny all knew there would be nothing automatic about winning. They knew the Europeans would be gunning for them, and they also knew that the teams they were about to face had prepared as carefully as they had.

They curled brilliantly. "The best they've ever played," says Dave. Equally at ease with both corn and push brooms, they showed the world that curling was alive and very well in Canada. To celebrate they toured the fantastic chateau Ludwig had built to celebrate the operas of Wagner.

When they came home there was an open-car parade for a few blocks along the main street of Fredericton before the blustery winds and gusting snow drove them inside. They were presented in the legislature, mentioned in the throne speech, and honoured at a reception in the mayor's office.

Quite a line-up for a group of teenagers who savour the predictability and control that curling offers. Jim, especially, was the centre of a small maelstrom of media attention. He confesses it unnerved him at first. In Prince Albert, the year before, he'd been very nervous. What on earth would he say when they shoved the microphones in his face and asked for a comment?

But the knack he'd learned over years of facing clutch situations in curling came in handy in media scrums too. He settled down, took charge of his own space, and answered at his own pace. The jumpy, frenetic style of the live 30-second TV clip would have to adjust to Jim.

Now he claims the media aspect of the skip's job is "no problem." And if some interviewers still tear their hair in despair at his leisurely style and carefully neutral comments, that's their problem, not his.

In the spring of 1988, with a Canadian and a world championship under their belts, it might have seemed they could rest on their ample laurels. But there were two problems looming before they could launch themselves into men's competition. First the Sullivans had to deal with their fathers, Charlie and Dave.

The Sullivan families had always talked of the day when fathers and sons could play together. Grandfather Herman and his sons had won bonspiels together. Now Dave and Charlie, Sr., might be able to build on that tradition.

"When we won the province in 1987 I was still looking forward to curling with my father," says Charlie. "But then we won the nationals and had to stay together for the worlds, and then we won that, too, and we wanted to see how we'd do with our junior team in men's."

In the 1989 New Brunswick provincial final they went down to the last rock before they were beaten by Gary Mitchell. They also won the biggest bonspiel they entered, and finished the year with winnings of $10,750. It was enough to make them thirsty to try again in 1990.

Everybody understood, and when 1990 turned into their greatest success nobody even thought of breaking their team up. But there's a vein of poignancy running through the success. Their fathers are 50 and 52, and the years when they can play competitively together are quickly evaporating.

"I tried to get on the team but they just laughed at me," says Dave with a grin.

"We thought of them at skip and third," says Charlie, "but they might not make all the shots. Then we thought of front end, but they'd have to sweep. They haven't made the switch to push brooms real well. They look really funny—Dave, especially, looks like he's using a vacuum."

Charlie, Sr., laughs too, taking the rejection in stride like his brother. "David and I got older and got put aside," he says.

Both Charlie, Jr., and Jim insist they will, one day, play with their fathers. But the accepted subtext is that the foursome will never be good enough to get to the Brier.

The other looming problem was what to do about their lead Danny Alderman. This was another emotionally difficult situation. Danny had been with them from the beginning, but the other three agreed he should be replaced. It was a "personality problem" more than anything related to curling ability. Alderman's intensity made it difficult for him to fit into the resolutely positive and controlled tone of the team. "With Danny on the team he'd curse and swear if you missed," explains Craig. "Our new lead, Paul Power, just says, 'Don't worry, you'll make it next time.'"

Jim was faced with the unenviable task of cutting a friend who'd helped them win the world junior championship. To complicate matters, everyone knew that Danny was the one who had neglected his studies for curling. The others all either graduated or were very close. Danny, in the fall of 1990, started over in a new course.

But despite the potential for destruction, Jim managed the difficult task with aplomb. Older, more experienced skips have had old friends disappear from town and drop out of competitive curling for years after they deliver this lethal *coup de grâce*. Others have quit their own team rather than face doing it.

But Jim's emotional stamina was more than equal to the task. Alderman accepted it well. He ended up playing with Jim's father in 1990 on the team that almost derailed the boys' glory train in the New Brunswick quarter-finals. And when the boys went to the Brier, Danny went along as fifth man.

But the rough patches weren't over. In the weeks leading up to the Moncton 100 they had their first taste of the trouble the media sometimes kicks up for athletes.

When the list of the 16 teams invited to the world's richest bonspiel was made public, the only New Brunswick team was Jack MacDuff.

Jim and Charlie shrugged and passed on, thinking nothing of it.

They knew people still thought of them as juniors. MacDuff had won the city's qualifying playdowns. There was no route for anyone else in the province to qualify.

But the list was heavy with unknown European rinks. And even MacDuff was born in Newfoundland and had won the Brier in 1976 as a Newfoundlander. Almost immediately there was a public outcry that the homegrown Sullivans had not been invited. They were the only curling world champions the province had ever produced and the only national champions in 20 years. The organizers, forced to justify the exclusion, trampled on the Sullivans' feelings.

"I wasn't upset or anything, until people started giving reasons why we weren't included," says Jim. "They said things like, 'What have they done lately?' and that got me."

They had never complained, but as the uproar in the press continued, fuelled by a Moncton columnist, some inferred they had orchestrated the whole campaign. "We didn't say anything," explains a still-angry Burgess. They said we couldn't compete with the men, we weren't in their class. It felt so good to get to the Brier, stick the knife in and turn it."

In Fredericton the call to boycott the bonspiel met a favourable response. The Sullivans are well known and well liked in the town's curling community and the snub was nasty and unjustified.

"There was a boycott in Truro too," says Burgess, who comes from a prominent Nova Scotia curling family. Paul Power had similar support in Prince Edward Island. Since the Moncton 100 was a disappointment at the box office the Fredericton curlers felt vindicated.

For Jim, Charlie, Craig and Paul the controversy was a big help in focusing and digging deep for the real prize—the Brier tankard. It's the same kind of hassle that Werenich thrives on.

If the boys needed any more incentive, it came in the mail shortly after they won the province. In their information package they saw the draw as already arranged. They would meet the old fox Werenich, the most dreaded of their opponents, in their very first game.

They'd been to major championships before, but nothing has the pizazz of the Brier. At the opening banquet on Saturday night the Sullivan team watches the Werenich crew make a grand entrance when their name is called. Everyone else had trundled in self-consciously in their blazers or tartans. Werenich et al. strutted in, grinning broadly and wearing spectator shoes, double-breasted zoot suits and fedoras.

A little later in the evening, as the fans delightedly mingled with the curlers, two-time Brier champion Pat Ryan brought the house down with his Elvis routine, liberally spiced with hip gyrations and rich baritone coloratura.

Their own lead, Paul Power, the only guy on the team who hadn't brought a girlfriend from New Brunswick, was suddenly squiring a local beauty queen.

Many older, more mature curlers get distracted in this atmosphere, but not the Sullivans. They kept focused, stayed only briefly at the banquet and told themselves over and over Werenich was a foe like any other they'd faced.

But they knew it wasn't really true. And if they needed proof they got it the next day right after opening ceremonies, when they were plunged unceremoniously into one of the biggest games of their lives. Jim admits he was "very nervous inside" with the living legend standing beside him on the curling sheet. "The boys" held their own for five ends but then "crashed to earth," says Craig. The game ended 8-3.

Throughout the week they battled to stay in the middle of the pack, but by the time they got to their last round-robin game against P.E.I. they knew they hadn't really shown their stuff. And they didn't quite know why. Beating the Island might get them into the tie-breakers and give them a second kick at the can.

Heading into that game early Friday morning, they were looking for a new formula for success, some way to make their mark. "We didn't exactly decide to shoot for the record of the lowest score but we knew they were a peeling team and we joked about it," explains Charlie.

P.E.I. was their best game so far. They were confident, strong, and by the end, nerveless. They broke both the record and P.E.I.'s will in their 2-1 game. The game resparked their confidence and put them into the tie-breaker ready to attack. "We noticed other teams started to try to keep it clean against us," remembers Charlie. "They weren't too sure what we were going to do."

Charlie and Jim usually play two or three games in the course of one as they discuss shots. Charlie likes the unusual, the aggressive stance. Craig who curls on the mixed team that Charlie skipped to a provincial championship in 1990 describes his approach as occasionally "outrageous." Jim prefers the conservative "wait and see" approach.

"He hardly ever listens to me," Charlie says of his constant suggestions to Jim. But once in a while something Charlie says strikes a chord and Jim tries a shot that surprises everyone. One of those, earlier in the week, a "takeout raise takeout" in the ninth end against the Northwest Territories, made "Shot of the Day" in the *Tankard Times*, the Brier daily newsletter.

Charlie even tried to get Jim to play some psych games on their opponents. "We tried, but we got our signals crossed and it didn't work out," says Charlie.

Later, as he listens to his son talk about it, Charlie, Sr., is aghast. "You have to be careful. It could backfire and if it was your idea you would never be speaking to Jimmy again."

"Yeah," says Charlie with a small laugh. "I usually get the blame because I'm the one thinking these things up."

But his skip's displeasure doesn't seem to restrain him particularly. He's excitable and he loves the idea of faking out his opponent. In one classic case against an old family friend, Richard Belyea, in the 1988 New Brunswick playdowns, they forced him to take one by pretending they were upset with a shot they had placed exactly where they wanted it. Belyea pounced on what he assumed was a mistake and played into their hands.

"He'd just never think we'd do anything like that," Charlie says with a delighted grin.

The Sullivans are well aware that Eddie Werenich is a master of this brand of manipulation. When he rubs his nose in a certain way his front end is supposed to understand that the shot he's apparently calling for is not the one he wants. The signal is so subtle, even the front end has to watch carefully or they'll miss it.

Although the Sullivans don't have that polish yet, Charlie, for one, is eager to develop that part of their game.

But it wasn't psych games that got the youngsters to the final of the 1990 Brier. Nor was it creative circus shots to throw their opponents off balance. No, they got to the final on Jim's coolness under pressure.

At the end of the Brier in three consecutive sudden-death games he sent the final rock exactly where it had to go to win the game. His teeth did not chatter. His hand did not tremble. He bore down and blocked out everything except the rocks at the other end of the sheet.

In the semi-final game, as he started into his delivery, there was a lone hoarse shout from high up in the crowd of 5,000. He stopped, looked down for 20 seconds, and then started back into his delivery.

"I always like to take my time in the hack," he said later with a little shrug.

It's his strongest suit and he knows it. He's a master at controlling his mind and emotions. But he's got his own Achilles' heel. He can't remember what happened in earlier games. "He reads the ice, but I've got the record," says Charlie tapping his temple.

It was this symbiosis that Charlie believes made their team special. "I don't think I'll ever curl on a team like this again," he says.

Being cousins added another dimension to their relationship. It was not quite the tie that brothers like Glenn and Russ Howard have, but it was stronger than most friendships. Charlie had a bad game in the Brier final, curling 68 percent to Kawaja's 86 percent. Jim ("they-should-call-him-the-Iceman") curled 94 percent.

In his TV interview after the fifth end, Jim talked about Charlie's hogged rock in the second end being an obstacle they were going to have trouble leaping over. That hogged rock quickly became the story of the final game, a theme that was repeated and repeated by commentators and players alike.

Charlie doesn't accept that one rock in the second end changed everything. He points to other misses, and especially errors in strategy that hurt them. He also points out contributions he made, like the "perfect freeze in the ninth end to give us two."

"I get letters and everything about that hogged rock, but it doesn't bother me," he says. "I know what my contribution was and what it wasn't."

And that's the end of it. In a less resilient relationship the inevitable recriminations and resentments might cause irreconcilable damage. Not here, not between cousins who grew up sailing together and who eventually joined forces in the deepest commitment so far in their young lives.

But the commitment always had a time limit. They knew before the 1990-91 season began it would be their last. Jim, Charlie and Craig had been together for four years and the end was coming. But before they graduated and started into the world of work and responsibility they had one more chance.

"It just didn't work out," says Charlie a little ruefully about their disappointing year in 1990-91. "Maybe if we'd done less well at the Brier [in 1990] this year wouldn't have been so bad. We needed a break from each other but I'm hoping that we'll get together again in four or five years."

Up on New Brunswick's Acamac Road, a couple of miles off the highway from Saint John to Fredericton, sits the 200-year-old Loyalist homestead that the Sullivans call their summer camp. Except for electricity, the old farmhouse is pretty much as it was in the eighteenth century—no running water, no time-saving gadgets, no neighbours.

Sitting on the verandah looking down as the tide comes in on the river and the sailboats flutter, it's easy to lose track of time. There's no trace of the urgency that dominates contemporary city life. Nobody frets as time evaporates in casual chitchat. Up here the hours flow together as they always have, and curling glories past and present are a large part of the family history. Last year it was Jim and Charlie's Brier they talked about. This year it's 18-year-old Brian Sullivan's appearance in the Pepsi Junior. Even though his team finished 4-7 he came home with the Ken Watson Award as the most sportsmanlike player. The family likes that.

Both Jim and Charlie grew up spending summers here. But a couple of years ago Jim found golf and summer work in the city and left Acamac Road and endless summers behind.

In the summer of 1991 Charlie is back for his seventh year of lifeguarding on the river. In the evenings he stokes his competitive fires by sailing in the Grand Bay races against his uncles, aunts and cousins. But even as he repeats the familiar pattern, Charlie is acutely aware that things have changed.

Last Christmas Herman E., their 94-year-old grandfather, the symbol of the Sullivan strength and perseverance, quietly passed away, and this summer everything is different.

The curling team had been the heart of Charlie's life for five years. Now it too is broken and scattered. Jim and Craig have graduated and left university. Jim is working for a real estate appraisal firm in Fredericton and Craig has a job in physical education in Dartmouth, Nova Scotia. Paul is back home in P.E.I. and plans to finish his degree there.

Although Jim and Charlie could technically still curl together they have chosen not to. Neither knows exactly what he will do about curling next year but they won't be in the same city. Charlie will spend the first four months of school practice teaching in Saint John.

Charlie has always found it relatively easy to dedicate himself to curling. "Charlie's life is curling," Craig marvels. "He was always at the rink, always the first one there. Jim and I had other things, not Charlie."

But in the 1990-91 season that dedication weighed on them all. They had worn out each other's will to compromise. Charlie watched as his three teammates relaxed a little at the last few bonspiels they entered.

"I expected too much," he says. "The others weren't into it as much as I was. It wasn't as if we could go to the Brier to try to improve on a ninth-place finish. We had to win it to better our record."

After a frustrating year in which they didn't qualify for the provincial finals, Charlie has decided he should either skip and take all of the responsibility or play second and take none of it. As third he was always conscious that he could mess things up for Jim and he found that pressure uncomfortable.

And so the learning and the adjusting continues. But curling, at least for Charlie, is still front and centre in his life. He's sad about the break-up and he knows how difficult it will be to find a similarly talented new team. Jim is, as always, more low-key. There's plenty of time to think about curling in the fall. Right now it's golf. He shrugs off the bad season. Next year he will definitely have another run at the competitive circuit, as long as it doesn't interfere with his new job. At a time and place where jobs are extremely scarce he's landed one with a future—and one that allows him to come home for lunch. For a young man who doesn't like to rush around, it's perfect and he won't do anything to compromise it.

Charlie's approach is, not surprisingly, quite different. The education course he enrolled in at the University of New Brunswick will buy him one more year of competitive curling. After that, if he takes a teaching job, he won't be able to take Fridays off to travel to bonspiels or weeks off to play in the Brier, should he make it that far.

And so he feels the sand trickling through the hourglass more acutely than Jim does. But they all know, as they head into adult responsibilities, that none of their lives will ever again be as uncluttered. And Charlie wonders if the karma will ever again be so right for winning.

So it's here on the Acamac Road, in the middle of this apparent timelessness, that Charlie Sullivan, a boyish 23-year-old, makes an odd statement: "I believe I've only got one more serious year of curling left."

And then, like many young men across the country who struggle with the same career-or-curling dilemma, he presents the compromise position. "In some ways I don't really want a job after next year. Maybe I could substitute teach for a year ... "

For the Sullivans the prologue is over, and the hard part is just beginning.

4

FAST EDDY LUKOWICH
Still Hungry After All These Years

IF CHARLIE SULLIVAN feels time evaporating for him at 23, what about Ed Lukowich at 46?

Fast Eddy is the oldest of Canada's active curling heroes, but numbers can deceive. In some ways he seems as timeless as life up on the Acamac Road. Watch him sitting at the Calgary Winter Club in his whites waiting for a squash game with his brother Morris, a professional hockey player 10 years his junior. He doesn't look his age. He doesn't act his age. He doesn't think his age. So what makes him 46? The date printed on a birth certificate?

Until the disastrous season of 1991, he felt he was curling better than he ever had in his life. In 1990 his team won curling's richest bonspiel ever, the Moncton 100, and broke its own 1988 money record by finishing the year with more than $140,000. But in 1990-91 they won their first bonspiel, did well in the second and then didn't even qualify in the next seven. However, by the new year when playdowns began, they had started to pull together. In the end they got only as far as the Southern Alberta finals, Ed's worst showing in years.

But if in 1991 his competitive fire seemed to be sputtering a bit, the problem had nothing to do with losing interest in curling. On the contrary, it happened because he was chasing professional status for the sport with so much energy there wasn't much left over for playing.

In 1991 he was preoccupied with organizing a professional circuit for the world's best curlers. Because he was trying to court all the major bonspiels, he played in every one of them, trying in between games to do the necessary schmoozing. But it was too distracting. It wouldn't have been an easy job for anyone, but Eddy is less comfortable than most in that environment. He was quickly exhausted and his game suffered.

Whether he's learned yet that he can't curl competitively and be the sport's major impresario is anybody's guess. Certainly, by the summer of 1991, at least part of the pro tour organizing effort was concentrated in downtown Toronto in the offices of Brian Cooper's Hollis Communications. By then, John Kawaja, another of the world's finest shotmakers, was also involved in the scheme.

Kawaja's involvement may add up to Luke's passing the torch or it may be John's assessment that his business acumen was necessary to the project. He's a clever, organized businessman when he isn't performing his magic with the curling rock. Combining curling and promoting might be easier for him. He's closer to the commercial capital of the country and he plays the less-demanding position of third. The mental effort he has to put into the game is quite different from the intense concentration required of a skip.

As the 1991-92 season got under way, TV Labatt was looking at a proposal drawn up by Hollis Communications, and there was general optimism that the pro circuit would eventually get off the ground.

For Lukowich it would be a landmark accomplishment in a long, successful career. But it's unlikely he would see it as a natural stopping place. He has never in his life taken the long view.

Even now, as he sits sipping coffee in the Winter Club waiting for his squash game and talking about his career, it's the fierce competition with his brother Morris and their upcoming squash game that captivates his interest. Looking ahead, even to the next curling season, is an effort. He's not sure yet what will happen in 1991-92. He'll see.

And even if he hears "time's winged chariot hurrying near," he certainly isn't going to turn and look.

Some say he's the best curler in the world. Never mind that he hasn't won the Brier since 1986. He's consistently at the top of the money charts, and when people are searching for the name of the most complete curler in the world, Edward R. Lukowich tops many a list.

Paul Gowsell, once the most feared man to slip on a slider, says without a second's hesitation that Fast Eddy gets his vote. Gowsell, who wanted to be the first man to earn his living from curling, defers to Lukowich, the first who ever did. Sort of.

The argument, especially west of the Assiniboine River, goes something like this: he may not be the best skip in the world, or the best strategist, but over the long haul, with every angle covered, he's the man. And if ever anyone has had a love affair with the game, it is Ed. Over three decades, he has been the ultimate suitor, the Dante to the game's Beatrice. Fortunately his unabashed devotion has not been unrequited. He's won everything, including the right, in 1988, to represent Canada in the Olympics.

He's also one of curling's most eccentric characters. His team sometimes wonders if he's "in another time zone."

"He has a master plan going in and it's better not to disturb him," says second, Brent Syme. Then after a moment's thought he adds with a raised eyebrow, "At least, we hope he has. Maybe Ferg [third John Ferguson] and I give him too much credit."

In a game that's all angles and carefully plotted linear strategy, Lukowich often seems to be playing by intuition and half-understood hunches. He gambles in situations that leave the two professional number-crunchers on his team aghast.

At 23, Jim Sullivan sometimes seems like a zombie after a big game because of the intense concentration it takes to process every nuance. At 46, Ed Lukowich expends even more effort because of the kind of game he plays. When he's finished a big game, he can be white and exhausted.

So much exertion leaves little energy left over for anything else. His team knows he can't be juggling too many things and play effectively. Fortunately for them his day jobs—there have been more than 30 of them, from teacher to stockbroker—have never commanded his full concentration.

"I'm a rebel," he says. "The rest of the world says you have to give up curling for a job. I've never been willing to do that."

So now at 46 he describes himself as the "most experienced person in the world. I can do anything."

And he just about has. He's written three successful books on curling. He's made a 60-minute instructional video on curling and is currently nurturing a curling mail-order business into existence. For several boom years in Medicine Hat he sold real estate. In Toronto he was a car salesman for 20 minutes, until the guy who was supposed to be teaching him the ropes leapt over him to snatch a customer.

"Not for me," he says now. "I wasn't going to compete with my co-workers for customers."

He was educated to be a teacher and spent six years in university getting ready for the job, but it never worked. "I was lackadaisical with the kids," he has said. But those who know him well talk about his aptitude for dealing with youngsters. "He really knows how to talk to them," says his brother Mike, who also taught school.

But the child-man who's dynamite with kids has a hard time with school administrators. In Medicine Hat, for example, where he moved because he had a teaching job, he lasted only until Christmas—not even one full school term. "They were hassling me about the curling," he says. "They wouldn't give me time off, so when it came time to renew the contract for the second half of the year, I wouldn't sign."

In the 1980s his jobs have been more curling-related. He worked for White Ram Knitting for several years and then opened his own curling shop at the Calgary Curling Club. But even those enterprises did not mesh well with competitive curling. He was busiest with work at the same time that he was most involved in curling.

Now he's starting again, trying to get the mail-order business going—hoping it won't gobble too much of his precious time. He's also working on organizing a pro curlers' circuit. Modelled on the Professional Golfers' Association, the group would organize the existing 15 or so big-ticket cashspiels into a two-tier circuit with about 40 of the best rinks on the tour.

"It takes so much time," Ed laments. With curlers and spiels spread out all over the country, it's a heroic organizational task and much of it hinges on getting TV coverage and finding a big-time sponsor to underwrite the tour.

For Ed, designing the concept and whipping up enthusiasm for the idea is the pleasant part. The hard-headed business aspect does not interest him. His own team complains he does too much "hand-shake business."

"In 1986 after we won the world championship, we talked about getting an agent as Marilyn Darte had done," explains Syme. "We were in touch with some guy in Toronto but we weren't going to let Ed go to that meeting alone. We didn't want it to turn into a lifetime supply of shirts."

They went to Toronto, but after what Syme thought was a good meeting they never heard another word. "It was left that Ed was going to follow up. I don't know if he ever did. Probably it just turned out there was no money for curling."

"He's like me," says Mike Chernoff, a Vancouver oil-patch millionaire who curled with him for six years. "They'd [Lukowich's new team] describe me as a remnant from the past, too. I'd never in a million years dream of an agent in curling."

Chernoff laughs when it's suggested that Ed is a kid who never grew up. "There are lots of us like that," he says. "I'm one of the worst. I'm over fifty—halfway to sixty—and they think around here I'm too old to curl. So I'm playing senior hockey—three times a week. Just like Ed, I still want to play kid's games."

It's obvious Ed would rather play anything than struggle to set up a pro curler's association or a business or grapple with any of the real-life demands of adulthood. But he works away on the pro circuit idea because he feels he owes so much to the game of curling.

As for the built-in problems, such as the opposition of the CCA or at least of some members who fear they could lose control of the game, Ed is vague. He works away sporadically at the organization, dreaming a big company will one day step in, see the brilliance of the concept and take over.

About his own future he's equally vague. His wife, Judy, who has been a competitive curler herself (playing the Scott Tournament of Hearts in 1985 and competing in the junior nationals as a schoolgirl), understands the curling passion. But even she has never seen anything to equal Ed's attachment.

He sounds wistful when he talks about her competitive curling. "It doesn't seem to matter as much to her any more," he says. After a minute's thought about the role curling plays in his family, he adds, "After a while the wives just get sick of it. She'd probably be the happiest woman in the world if I retired."

But to what? And in the unlikely event he were to resign himself to the nine-to-five grind, what would he do with the competitive fires that burn as brightly as ever when he's on the curling rink?

His brother, Mike, refuses to worry about him. Three years older, Mike loved curling as much as Ed, but he didn't have as much of the rebel in him. He was Ed's skip on their junior national championship team—and when they went up to men's, one of the best in Saskatchewan—but he picked life as a schoolteacher over the uncertainties of living by your wits in the curling world. He now lives in Quesnel, B.C., operates a feed store and rarely curls.

He admires Ed's courage. "Millions of people work. Not very many do what he's doing," Mike says.

Chernoff echoes that sentiment. "Ed doesn't need a lot of money. He's not tight, but he doesn't spend a lot. He likes cashspiels, but the game is more important than the money. If you got more money for finishing second, some guys would automatically aim for that. Not Ed, he'd still want to win."

And while so much of modern society focuses on net worth as a way of keeping score in life, Ed happily operates on another plane. He ignores the passage of time and chooses instead to concentrate on perfecting his game. "In sports it's very hard to stand on the peak," he says. "You're either getting better or you're getting worse."

So at 46 Lukowich heads out to the curling sheet or the squash court, not to hold his own, not to revisit past glories, but to keep flying higher, the perpetual Peter Pan.

To understand his grand obsession it's necessary to go back 40 years to Speers, Saskatchewan, and a kindly guy named Button Joe.

Speers had only 150 people when Ed was a youngster there around 1950. His dad was known as "Button Joe" because he ran the little two-sheeter natural curling rink that was the hub of winter sports for Speers. There was no hockey rink, so the little round-faced kid who was dying to play sports made the curling rink his hangout. He'd help Button Joe look after the ice and as a reward was allowed to throw a few rocks. The two-handed delivery punctuated by a belly flop looked funny but it served its purpose. By the time Ed Lukowich was six, he'd won his first bonspiel.

The next year the school unexpectedly barred everyone under grade four from the spiel and little Ed, with tears streaming down his face, was forced onto the sidelines. He still remembers his anger and frustration. The love affair had begun.

"I don't know why, but even then I really loved the game," he remembers. He later found baseball and then hockey. But curling was first and his affection for it runs deepest.

Lukowich is a natural, a guy who was born to be a professional athlete, say both his brother Mike and his long-time third, Mike Chernoff. He could have played any sport. He didn't take up hockey until he was in his twenties but people who saw him then wondered why he hadn't played in the NHL like his brother. His brother Mike insists that he would have been a shoo-in for the NHL if he'd started hockey as a kid. Morris came along 10 years after Ed, just as the town was building its rink. Although he wasn't as big as Ed, he had the same phenomenal drive and will to win. "The only reason Morris played in the NHL (for the Jets, Kings and Bruins) is that he had that extra drive and desire," says Mike Lukowich. "He's only 5′8″ or 5′9″ and he came along at a time when everybody was fighting. But he had so much desire, he didn't lose too many fights. Ed has that too, and with his size and strength he would have been great."

As for baseball, like all Canadian kids, Lukowich didn't have a long enough season to polish his skills. But even out on the prairies, baseball scouts did come sniffing around when he played for the semi-pro Saskatoon Commodores. They only backed off when Ed was already at tryout camp and they found out their quarry was 25 years old!

So curling was the motherlode for the young athlete. It was the outlet that would give him competition, excitement and a chance to excel. Sporadically it would also give him a modest living. He learned to read the ice by working on it with Button Joe. He developed his near-perfect release and delivery by practising longer and harder than anyone else in the game. (Even after he'd won the Brier, people remember how Ed would sometimes get into a frenzy and throw 500 rocks a day.)

His other attributes were natural. He has the athlete's size and strength and he's also ambidextrous, one of the hallmarks of a natural athlete. (Researchers theorize that two-handedness signifies a wider, thicker channel between the two hemispheres of the brain which probably allows information to be transmitted more quickly and improves hand-eye co-ordination.)

By the time Eddie left Speers for Saskatoon, the family of four boys was well known in northwest Saskatchewan and beyond for its athletic feats. In 1962, when Ed was 16, his brother Mike skipped their schoolboys' team to the Canadian championship. At 20, Ed would again play third for Mike as they made it to the Saskatchewan final in men's play. Had they managed to knock off favourite Bob Pickering, they would have been on their way to the Brier.

"Imagine what that would have meant," says Lukowich with a wistful sigh. "Button Joe played lead on that team; for him to play in the Brier would have been just the greatest. That was the last year he ever curled with us."

Both Mike and Ed remember their mother, Ann, now a widow living in Saskatoon, as the perfectionist and the family disciplinarian. It was she who kept their lives orderly and gave the boys their drive. "She wouldn't stand for no guff," Ed remembers fondly.

Button Joe must have given her a tough moment or two. He was a grain farmer and summers were his busy time. Also, in the summer the family had a huge vegetable garden to help them be self-sufficient. But it was often Ed who worked the garden, even though he had bad allergies. Joe had other interests.

When Ed was 10, the summer Morris was born, Joe busied himself making a three-hole golf course on the town's sports field. He made two par threes and a par five for a town where no one played golf. "They were good holes, sand greens but well-designed," says Ed. And then he adds with a laugh, "Nobody played but us, though."

The Lukowiches and their golf course must have been the talk of the town. "My dad was a great sportsman," says Ed. "I learned my love of sports from him, but I think the self-discipline I've shown in sports I learned from my mother."

All through high school, Ed excelled in sports. In 1963, the year after they won the Canadian junior championship, he went to the provincial final as skip. In the summer he went to the provincial track-and-field finals, placing third in the province in the long jump. He liked track but somewhere along the way a doctor diagnosed a heart murmur and Ed backed away a little.

At university, after Mike and Ed almost made it to the Brier in 1966, they went on to have a number of very respectable years on the cashspiel circuit. Mike was developing a name for himself as a big hitter and one of the best skips in the province. But they still needed seasoning, and in Ed's opinion their game was not yet complete enough.

Ed was in no hurry to graduate from university. He wanted time to develop his game and to plug the holes that he saw in a team that concentrated too much on the hitting game. Besides, the workaday world held no allure for him. He was studying physical education with a minor in education, and he knew he was heading for a career as a high-school teacher.

Would that career give him the freedom he needed for curling? Mike had now finished school and was teaching. Ed saw how much his brother had to sacrifice for his job. He had no interest in living like that. "That's one of my only regrets in curling," he says now, looking back on those days. "Mike loved the game just as much I did, but I was more of a rebel. He kind of gave in to the system. There comes a point where you have to decide whether your life is going to be dictated by your job or by curling."

But by then the Lukowich brothers were drifting apart. Mike was still committed to the takeout game, but Ed was more and more drawn to the subtleties of a game of quiet draws. The split came in 1972 when Ed took the surprising step of signing on as third to Rick Folk, the 22-year-old son of a local furrier. Folk was something of a phenomenon around Saskatoon at the time: he was a prodigiously good golfer and was known to have a fine, deft touch on the curling rock as well. But he was younger than Lukowich and still green. If Ed was looking for instruction he seemed to have picked a strange mentor.

There's no doubt Lukowich was quite a catch for Folk. "Ed was a great thrower of the rock," Folk remembers. "One of the best, really."

The Folk-Lukowich combination was an instant success. In their first year together they went to the Saskatchewan northern finals. But the "catalysts were burning all the wrong way," says Ed, whatever that means. He remembers Folk as a very young man who was still maturing as a skip. "The second, Tom Wilson, had a real bad temper. That team wasn't ready yet to win a Brier."

But his exposure to Folk's draw game only whetted his appetite for more. And when Bob Thompson, a friend from university who was playing for Paul Savage, called from Toronto to say there was likely going to be a spot on that team, Luke bought a train ticket. It seems the Savage rink had had a rough Brier in Edmonton in 1973 and Ed Werenich was about to be dumped.

By this time Lukowich had already given up teaching for a career as a stockbroker; Toronto seemed a perfect place to ply that trade. But of course the real magnet was the chance to curl with Paul Savage, one of the game's most famous finesse players.

As he headed east to play the year's final bonspiel with Savage, he couldn't have known that the man he was about to replace was the one who would ultimately be recognized as the genius of the finesse game. Ironically, one of the reasons Werenich was being turfed from the team was that he was too critical of Savage's strategy. They'd finished the Edmonton Brier 6-5 and barely on speaking terms.

But all that was happening in a realm remote from 28-year-old Ed Lukowich and his pure pursuit of curling.

It was late March and the Brier was over. As the finale to the season the Savage rink was playing the Beefeater Bonspiel. Lukowich took over at third, Thompson dropped to second and the team pulled off a respectable second-place finish.

It was the highlight of Lukowich's time in Toronto. He didn't like the cutthroat business practices. Suddenly he wasn't in the stockbrokering business any more. He turned briefly to selling cars. And even in his leisure sports he was unhappy. Baseball was always the highlight of his summer, but in Toronto he couldn't find a team. He saw Savage and the others a bit, but he felt adrift in the huge metropolis.

"I was really like a foreigner. I never felt at ease there," he remembers. At the end of the summer he went back to Folk and Saskatoon. In Toronto, Werenich and Savage patched up their differences and put together another Brier-bound team in 1974.

The next year Ed was back in Toronto, this time determined not to have a summer without a competitive outlet. He enrolled in adult power-skating lessons and found that if he hung around the rink he could find a game of summer shinny most lunch hours.

But neither summer hockey nor the lure of Toronto curling were enough to keep him in a town that made him feel such an outsider. When he got a phone call from Medicine Hat in August offering him a teaching job, he was delighted to accept. Morris, his young brother, was playing in the Western Hockey League there and he knew he would be more at home in Alberta.

He'd played two years with Folk and one bonspiel with Savage and now he was about to launch himself as a skip. He hadn't learned enough yet, he knew, but he figured he was going to have to teach himself. "I guess it happens to a lot of thirds," he says. "The guy who's skipping doesn't quite win it for you and you start to think, 'I can miss just as well as he can.'"

The first year he pulled together a very good team—"one of the best I ever had," he says. Grayson Kracmer played third, Dale Johnston second and Wes Aman lead. The "garbage" game they played took Alberta by storm. In the provincial finals they lost only one game, but it was the crucial one, and they finished second.

Rick Folk remembers the furor over Lukowich's game. "He had a game where there were rocks everywhere, everything was in backwards."

It certainly wasn't what anyone expected from a player with a reputation as a precision shooter. But for Lukowich, with his unflappable confidence that he could make any trick shot no matter how difficult, the garbage game was a natural.

He has fond memories of Medicine Hat. Curling was thrilling again, just as it had been when he was a kid and barrelling towards a Canadian championship. And playing skip suited him down to the ground. "I was able to play exactly the game I wanted to play."

Others have said Lukowich waited too long before he started skipping, that he would have won more Briers if he had started younger. But Lukowich shrugs it off. He started at the moment in his own personal development when he was ready to take the heat and call the shots.

As for his job, it continued to be secondary in his life. The pleasure of that year wasn't at all diminished by the fact that he'd had to quit teaching at Christmas because they wouldn't give him time off for the playdowns.

"That was fine. I sold real estate," he explains. Those were the boom years in Medicine Hat when they were building the oil refineries.

But the real business of life for Lukowich in those years had very little to do with oil booms or real estate deals. The curling rink was the centre of his existence and his powers of analysis were at their height. Morris remembers how he'd even analyse his younger brother's hockey game and point out areas for improvement.

By the 1990s Lukowich had learned to worry about "analysis paralysis," about getting too stiff and self-conscious to perform and about ruining his game by concentrating too much on problems. But in the mid-1970s he was still developing, and the more intense thinking he put into it, he believed, the better his game would be. For several years he knew that people were saying he "gambled way too much." He would never sit on a lead; he'd have the game won and then watch as it slipped away.

But he believes that was another stage on his path of self-development. He had a rough year in 1976 because he broke his ankle playing hockey, and although he wouldn't sit out the season, he couldn't throw the rock with the old precision.

But by the fall of 1977 things had started to click for him. For one thing, Mike Chernoff, who was to become his Svengali, called from Calgary offering to play third. The Southern Alberta Curling Association had just changed the rules. Teammates no longer had to live in the same town.

Still, Medicine Hat is a three-hour drive from Calgary; it seemed a hare-brained scheme. But Lukowich immediately jumped at the chance. He knew Chernoff as a student of the game, someone who liked to analyse as much as he did. And their dedication was obviously similar; neither balked at a six-hour drive for a curling game.

It was an odd collection of players—the Lukowich team of 1978. Chernoff was already in his forties, a wealthy oil man with a passion for cigars. Dale Johnston who played second was a cattle rancher so conservative in his tastes that the day was ruined if it didn't begin with bacon and eggs for breakfast. Ron Schindle, the lead, was a cocky 21-year-old men's clothing salesman in his first season of competitive curling.

Ed had picked him because he was a natural athlete. He also liked the confidence and dedication Schindle showed in practice. Many afternoons the two of them were the only ones practising in the Medicine Hat curling club.

But Schindle was too young and too egotistical for most people in curling. "He not only bothered the other teams, he bothered us," Lukowich remembers with a chuckle. Chernoff can still see him preening and parading before he threw a shot in televised games. His antics slowed down the game and drove Chernoff wild.

Unlikely as this collection of characters seemed, it was about to win the 1978 Brier. There were, of course, a few forbidding potholes in the road, but in the end they put together a winning strategy and steam-rollered to a 9-2 record in the Vancouver Brier. Second was Rick Folk, Lukowich's old skip, with his pal Bob Thompson playing third.

But the strategy that won the Brier that year was not Luke's garbage game but Chernoff's cooler, clearer vision. In November, after a couple of months together, Chernoff and Lukowich were on a terrible losing streak. "We'd lost nine in a row; the worst streak of my career," recalls Lukowich. Their solution was to revamp the roles of third and skip. Ed would continue to throw skip rocks but Chernoff would plot the strategy.

"We were immediately a much stronger team," Lukowich remembers. "I was so offensively minded, I had way too many rocks in play. Mike had more patience. He was a very good skip, but I was better with the broom. Also, he didn't have much in common with the lead and second, but I'd played those positions, so I could communicate with them."

Their renovated team got them the Brier Tankard but, in one of the biggest disappointments in Ed's life, their luck ran out before they wrapped up the world championship in Winnipeg. Lukowich was 32, newly engaged, and just one step from the peak of his heart's desire in curling.

They lost the semi-finals to Norway's Kristian Soerum, who was then eliminated by Bob Nichols of the United States. It was an enormous blow—and it almost wiped out all the pleasure of winning the Brier. Even now he remembers with pain and resentment how much trouble they'd had reading the newly flooded ice. "Part of the process over the week is catching on to the ice," he says. "We thought we had the ice down pat and you step out there and they've flooded it and everything's changed."

Norway won the toss and the Canadians never really got into the game.

"I was really crushed. I felt I'd let myself and the whole country down."

In the summer he married Judy Mayer, a member of a prominent Calgary curling family. Judy, as a successful curler herself, probably understood her new husband's depression. Certainly, the loss haunted him all summer. He began to look at everyone he met suspiciously, wondering what they thought of him, looking for signals of disdain.

It took a trip to Barbados, a new curling season, several wins in European bonspiels and enough solid curling at home to take them once again to the Alberta final, before Ed started to file away that painful loss.

"Ed had the feeling that the Europeans didn't look good, and didn't throw well," remembers Chernoff, "and yet they beat up on us. To him that meant we must have been donkeys."

But life goes on. And even though this was the toughest loss ever, Ed's talent for shaking off defeat finally reasserted itself. In 1979 the team that beat them in the last game of the Alberta final was skipped by Paul Devlin. But it was Devlin's second, Pat Ryan, who was destined to become Lukowich's nemesis in the 1980s.

A new chapter in his curling development was beginning. At last he'd found the mentor he was looking for. To listen to Lukowich tell it, almost everything he knows about the game and about life he learned from Chernoff. "He was one of the nicest friends I ever had," he remembers.

The first lesson was patience. Mike's vision of the game, his predictions about what would happen, were a revelation to Ed. Instead of reinventing the wheel every time out, Chernoff had the probabilities down pat. At first Ed would argue. Chernoff would say something like, "Leave that counter and it will end up costing us."

Ed would disagree, pointing out they already had three in the rings and they should be throwing a guard. But eventually Ed gave it up because Chernoff was right so often.

Chernoff went in with a strategy, a set of options, and he followed it as well as he could. For Lukowich the game suddenly became much simpler—"crystal clear," in fact.

Mike was a perfectionist about style, scrupulous about telling the truth even if it was unpalatable and hopelessly serious about the game. Every one of those qualities appealed to Lukowich. Other curlers—even very good ones—complain that Lukowich doesn't listen. To Chernoff he listened intently and he worked tirelessly to improve his game.

He'd vowed to himself that he would be back to the world championships and he kept his nose to the grindstone, throwing more rocks some days than even the obsessive Pat Ryan, struggling to find that elusive draw weight.

Meanwhile the rest of the team—even Chernoff—was less committed after they'd won the Brier. They were living through the usual post-championship letdown and finding it difficult keeping focused on winning it again.

Their streak gradually petered out. In 1980, the year Paul Gowsell seemed unstoppable, they finished third in the province. In 1981 they didn't make it to the provincials.

By 1982 Johnston and Schindle were off the team and Chernoff was languishing. He'd never been interested in cashspiels, so Lukowich often played with others. On one memorable occasion in Cranbrook, he played with Gowsell. Paul had trouble hitting the rings that day. Eventually it was Lukowich, not Gowsell, who got them thrown out of their hotel and in trouble with the law for refusing to pay their bill. "After that we realized that combination was never going to work," chuckles John Ferguson, who has played third for both.

The next year Lukowich put together a whole new team. It was

1983, and Werenich's Dream Team was hot news in the papers and the talk of the curling elite. Privately, though, Lukowich believed his own dream team, skipped by Frank Morissette with Neil Houston as third, Lukowich at second and Stu Erickson at lead, would give Werenich a solid run for his money. It didn't work.

Although they made it to a few semi-finals on the bonspiel circuit, by the time they reached the Bessborough Classic in Saskatoon they were bounced out immediately. Morissette and Erickson decided Houston had to go and Lukowich went along with the idea.

A week later Lukowich was on the phone apologizing and wondering if he and Houston could put together a team in time for the playdowns. They had to find two more players. Lukowich went back to his mentor. Yes, Chernoff was available. Now, with only one more position to fill, he started striking out. His old lead, Wes Aman, wasn't interested. Neither were a couple of others he asked.

It was not going to be easy. They were very close to the deadline of Sunday December 20, 1982. Every serious competitive curler was already signed onto a team. Then Houston suggested his old high-school friend Brent Syme. Lukowich knew a little about him, but Chernoff had never heard of him. Still, they didn't have time to be choosey. At nine o'clock, three hours before the midnight deadline, Brent finally agreed to go along with his pal for fun to see if "we could beat up on a few people in the playdowns."

At the time curling was a casual recreation for Syme. He played in the Calgary Superleague with three friends, but they weren't even near the top of the charts. True, at one point in his life he had thought about the Brier; he'd played with Houston on a junior team that went to the Canadian nationals. But the Brier dream had disappeared in a flood of real-life demands. Now, with one phone call, the dream was resurrected. Of course, he'd like to play lead for Lukowich, but he was understandably a little nervous. He was very glad Houston would be there to smooth over the rough patches. Win or lose, this would not be an experience to miss.

Nobody dreamed it would be all win. They didn't have time to practise before they started playdowns, but it didn't seem to matter. There was a magic on that team that swept away all comers. By the time they got to the Brier they seemed invincible, racking up a 10-1 record before they lost to what Lukowich now calls "the real Dream Team," Eddie Werenich, Paul Savage, John Kawaja and Neil Harrison.

The pundits describe that Sudbury Brier as the best ever and Lukowich remembers their play as a highlight in his career. Even the loss wasn't devastating. But it did make him hungry. In the new team he hoped he saw his future in curling.

But Chernoff was ready to move on. He'd bought land in Vancouver, where his wife wanted to live, and he was bent on leaving Calgary.

"It didn't matter any more," he remembers. "We had accomplished as much as we were going to. I was getting older and I knew that without Ed there was no way I would be competitive."

Privately he was surprised that Ed's competitiveness showed no signs of wearing thin. In fact, at the Sudbury Brier he'd seen something new in Ed's play, something he'd never seen or dreamed of seeing. Suddenly, inexplicably, Ed had perfect draw weight. Again and again he could draw to the button without a second's hesitation. Chernoff didn't believe his eyes. As perfect and as natural as he'd always believed Luke's delivery to be, he was always slightly suspicious about his draw weight. He noticed that Ed would try anything, a complicated freeze or a trick shot, before he'd go for a wide-open draw. He had a mental block, Chernoff believed. Now suddenly Lukowich could draw like Werenich. All that relentless practice had paid off.

Now he blames himself for not picking up on Ed's new strength in the 1983 Brier. He had never trusted Ed's draw weight in critical situations and he couldn't bring himself to do it now. "I wasn't aggressive enough," he admits. "I just didn't believe he could make every draw shot."

The next year Chernoff's spot on the team was taken by a 26-year-old freckled CA named John Ferguson. Like Houston, Ferguson was a refugee third from Paul Gowsell's rink. First Houston and then Ferguson had played third and functioned as the voice of reason on the rink.

Ferguson came to Lukowich knowing exactly what he wanted, a place to curl competitively without all the emotional wear and tear that went with being on a Paul Gowsell rink. Ed was calmer, more orderly, not abusive and—not coincidentally—poised to win big. It was an exciting possibility for Ferguson, and it worked out just about as well as he could have hoped. In 1984 they sailed through the provincials and went to the Victoria Brier full of hope that this year they would trounce Werenich & Co. They finished with 8-3 in the round robin but lost 6-3 to Werenich in the semi-final. He went on to lose the 1984 final to Mike Riley.

Finishing like this, with their noses jammed against the glass, kept them hungry. In 1985 they lost the provincial final to Pat Ryan who went on in the Brier to rack up that legendary 11-0 round-robin record. It was all for nought though, as he was undone by Hackner's pyrotechnics in the final.

In 1986 the Lukowich-Ferguson-Houston-Syme combination was again a formidable force. At the cashspiels they'd learned how to pace themselves in the early going so they could save their best for the finals. They were rock-steady and confident. The three younger men socialized with each other and watched their skip with a benign eye as he followed his own fitness regimen and became a bit of an eccentric on the curling sheet.

In the 1986 Labatt Brier, Lukowich was easily the most experienced skip on the ice. His team sailed through, demolishing everybody until the 13th draw, when they ran into trouble with Spike Muyres of Humboldt, Saskatchewan.

And Russ Howard, making his second appearance as the skip for Ontario, was not to be trifled with either. Lukowich beat him 7-5 in round-robin play but they both finished with 9-2 records. Lukowich had the bye into the final, but when they finally faced each other on Sunday afternoon in the Kitchener Memorial Auditorium the outcome was by no means certain.

It was a titanic battle that ended only when Howard was forced to take one in the ninth end, allowing Luke a free draw to win. Now Howard was the one who would face a grim summer remembering that one miserable end. He still says that was the toughest loss of his career.

Lukowich had waited and honed his game for eight years, but now he was back and ready to take that long-coveted world championship. The competition was in Toronto in 1986, a city he'd never liked. But neither Toronto, nor the horrible ice at the Coliseum, nor the media trivialization nor any other troubling incident of that week was going to get in his way this time.

His players had always counted on his immense powers of concentration when the game was on the line, but even they were surprised to see the intensity of his focus in Toronto.

They had a rough start. After the first three days their record was 3-3 and they knew they couldn't afford to lose another game. The ice had been so bad they couldn't tell how they were throwing the rock. They needed some good ice to practise on. Each team had been assigned a host club. Fortunately theirs, the Boulevard Club, was close by.

It was just what they needed. A peaceful club, perfect ice and a chance to have lunch alone together and talk. A morning practice at the Boulevard Club became their ritual and it set them up for the win, Houston believes. It was an oasis of calm away from the tense atmosphere at the Coliseum. He could see Ed relaxing and, as the week wore on, his confidence start to soar.

They didn't lose again. There are times when Ed's team knew all they had to do was to stay with it and not mess up—Ed would win it all by himself. This was one of those times.

After the round robin their record was 6-3. Scotland's David Smith was on top with 9-0. But nobody worried; this was their championship to win. First they beat Sweden 6-3 and then Scotland 4-3. Ed was content at last.

The Toronto sports media has earned its reputation as the most ornery in the country, but the curlers were lucky. The scribes and TV pundits were in a benign mood that early April week and it took the heat off the championship.

The city was still basking in the afterglow of the glorious Blue Jay "Drive of '85," and everything the Jays did in spring training was news. And even the Toronto Maple Leafs had dragged themselves into post-season play and were having a final kick at the can by defeating the Chicago Black Hawks in the first round of the playoffs.

So the world curling championship had stiff competition for attention, especially since another curling event went out of its way to upstage them. Marilyn Darte had challenged Ed Werenich to a game that was being billed as the ultimate Battle of the Sexes.

It was tacked onto the Saturday semi-final and got all the attention. "For us that championship was a real pressure-cooker," remembers Ferguson. "It was good that the media wasn't paying too much attention. We were there to win and by the time we did, we'd been through all kinds of stuff. The ice was so terrible it was a great equalizer. Skill didn't mean much."

But the win certainly did. The monkey was finally off Ed Lukowich's back and he could get on with his life. The big surprise was that he didn't quit. His team didn't either—at least not until 1989, when Neil Houston was the first to jump ship.

Since then, for the rest of the team, with their regular nine-to-five jobs, curling has become a part-time job. It's fun—they wouldn't do it otherwise—but there's no escaping that the cashspiel circuit is a wearying 10 weeks of the fall. In January the playdowns take a different kind of toll. The intensity they devote to getting within striking distance of the Alberta provincial championships every year means they have little energy left over for the other commitments in their lives.

"It could have hurt my career," says Brent Syme, "except that my employer has been so understanding. The basic arrangement we have is that anything I go to where I stand to win money, I take as holiday time. If it's the Brier or anything that's just prestige, they give me the time and TSN is good about plugging their commitment during the week.

"My philosophy about curling is that it's a great release, a nice second income and very enjoyable but still something that's secondary in my life."

For John Ferguson, who at 32 is already treasurer of an oil company, Poco Petroleums, curling is an exercise in juggling priorities. So far he's managed to excel at his job and on the curling sheet. But he admits that the marriage that died a couple of years ago was, in some degree at least, a victim of his dual careers.

As for Ed, he remains the most constant devotee. Both Ferguson and Syme know they're lucky to have him. "He lives for curling," says Syme. They marvel at his dedication and intensity. "He's not obsessed," they say, "he can talk about other things, especially sports." But the bottom line is that curling, both promoting it and playing it, is more important than most other things in his life.

On the Brier front, they've had trouble stepping around Pat Ryan to get out of the province since 1986. Just as Ed had in the early 1980s, Ryan spent the mid-1980s practising diligently and concentrating his fierce energy on improving his game. By 1987 he was formidable in the provincial championships. In 1988 he not only won Alberta, he won the Brier. The next year he won Alberta, the Brier and the world championships.

Ryan left Alberta for Kelowna, B.C., in 1989, opening up provincial competition again. But Ryan's dominance had changed the game. Everywhere—even in Alberta—there were rumblings and complaints about the big-hitting style that closed down the opposition and essentially ended the game after the first big play. The Ryan style took the heart out of the game, people said. It made the game boring to watch and demoralizing to lose.

But Lukowich was anything but bored or demoralized, even through the Ryan years. He kept up his vigorous efforts on the cashspiel circuit and in two different years, 1988 and 1990, won more than $100,000 (to be split among the four members of his rink). He also won perhaps the most coveted prize of all: the right to represent Canada in the 1988 Olympics. Although curling was only a demonstration sport in the February shindig in Calgary, there was intense competition for the honour of representing Canada. Not surprisingly, the final game came down to a stand-off between Lukowich and Ryan.

Being the Olympic representative made 1988 a risk-free year for Lukowich. The government and the curling association picked up the tab for the rink's expenses. In theory all he had to do was worry about curling.

But in the end the Olympics turned out to be a profound disappointment for Lukowich and his rink. They knew, going in, that nothing less than a gold medal would do. Curling was Canada's game. Luke and his rink were hometown heroes.

But after the smoke had cleared, they were standing on the bronze medal level, looking up at Eigil Ramsfjell of Norway on the gold and Hanjurg Lips of Switzerland on the silver.

John Ferguson insists they didn't curl badly in the Olympics, but they made one fatal error. They dropped the first game of the tournament to Switzerland. It turned out to be a game they couldn't afford to lose.

"I don't know how to say this kindly," Ferguson explains. "We blew it on strategy, trying to put on too much of a show." He remembers arguing with Ed, trying hard to convince him to take the cautious route, allow a tie the final end of that game and then carry the hammer into the extra end. But it would take a little longer and be a shade less dramatic than executing the tricky come-around double that Ed wanted to play.

Ferguson lost the argument and Lukowich lost the game. They finished the round robin tied with Switzerland but, because of the record, the Canadians were the ones who had to play the hot Norwegians in the semi-final.

But there were other disappointments too. Ed and Judy worked hard that winter promoting curling, hoping to showcase it during the Olympics. Undoubtedly all the work he did had an impact on Ed's game. His team knows he plays best when his life is at its simplest.

But Ed worked on, ignoring the danger signs. His team noticed that on the cross-country tour to showcase the men's and women's Olympic teams, he got overly tired and didn't bounce back. Nevertheless, he and Judy kept working on the curling newspaper. They even organized social events during the Olympics, especially parties for the fans after the draws.

But there were mountains of frustrations. In the end the newspaper didn't survive, the emcees at the curling draws refused to announce the parties and the Lukowich rink finished third.

Ed had nothing to do with the biggest problem for curling at the Olympics, the ticket disaster, but it must have annoyed him as it did everyone else interested in making curling a good show at the Olympics. Every draw was supposedly sold out, and yet for draw after draw the stands were nearly empty. The problem seems to have been with the way the tickets were sold. Organizers apparently were worried that women's curling wouldn't sell, so they packaged the curling in day tickets. Since not even the most avid—or best fortified—fans can sit through 12 hours of curling, they'd leave after watching a draw or two, wasting the rest of their ticket.

Organizers did try to correct the situation by selling a few hundred rush seats, but that only served to underline the irony. Hundreds would line up outside for the few rush seats, while inside three-quarters of the reserved seats went unused.

The curlers were disconcerted, and many believe the quality of competition suffered because they were performing in a near-empty arena in the midst of massive Olympic hype. It was especially awkward because the curling organizations were trying to impress the IOC enough to get medal status. Not surprisingly, the vote was no in 1988, although the IOC denies that the poor attendance influenced their vote. In September of 1991 curling aficionados expect the IOC will announce that they have reconsidered and that curling will be a medal sport in the 1998 games in Nagano, Japan.

But all of the problems of 1988 didn't ruin the experience for the Lukowich rink. "We were disappointed, but not devastated," says Ferguson. The final Saturday night at the Calgary plaza in front of 150,000 people will always be one of the highlights of his life—whatever the colour of his medal. As for Lukowich, who fashions his idea of himself so much on whether he's winning or losing, the Olympics are an experience he doesn't dwell on.

After the Olympics his rink continued to have big years on the cashspiel circuit, but the fraying had started again. Neil Houston quit. The official reason was that he'd hurt his back playing baseball and he was having trouble sweeping. He needed to play a back-end position, but since there was none available on the Lukowich team he bowed out.

"I think it was time," he says now from his new home in Leduc, Alberta. "You recognize the signs, and you know the team needs new blood. But it's never easy; you've been successful together and you don't know if you will be again. But you have to take the risk. Life is full of risks."

Throughout the 1989-90 season the Lukowich rink didn't seem to be badly hurt by losing their world-champion second. Playing with their perennial fifth man, Wayne Hart, they demolished Russ Howard's rink in the final of the Moncton 100 in January 1990. With its prize money of $250,000, the spiel was billed as the richest ever, and to make sure no one missed the point organizers even wheeled the cash out onto the ice accompanied by Brinks security guards. For Lukowich and his team, the win meant a paycheque of more than $15,000 each for the weekend's play. But in the end the cashspiel cost them their chance at the Calgary playdowns and meant they had to win the 160-team Curl Calgary spiel to get a chance at the finals.

They had been playing so well, better than ever before, they all believed, and then Lukowich's old demon, overconfidence, reared its head again. They had won six of the seven necessary games to go on, and the next opponent was Mickey Pendergast, someone they had been regularly beating for years.

"For Ed there wasn't enough fear in the situation," says Brent Syme, but he's quick to add that he's not criticizing his skip. "We've had so much success that whining about something in a particular game or bonspiel doesn't make sense. You have to look at the long range."

Anyhow, it was the end of their season and they were mad. Not at Ed, but at the Southern Alberta Curling Association, which had ignored three different letters requesting that the dates of the playdowns be adjusted so they could take the conventional route to qualify for the provincials.

In that process they could have lost a few more games and

remained alive. As it was, in Curl Calgary they won six and lost one and their back-door route was slammed shut.

By the summer, though, Ed had shaken off that loss and was ready to take the world by storm in 1991. He had good reason to be optimistic. Ryan was gone. They were curling better than they ever had, and even though they still missed Houston, they had replaced him with a strong new second, Rick Valette, from Shellbrook, Saskatchewan.

They were so confident they had struck a winning combination that they didn't worry that they would not be able to practise as a team. Ed's analytic gifts would save them, they figured. He probably understood the components of Valette's delivery better than the man himself, Syme said confidently.

But things went badly wrong and 1991 turned out to be a trough for the Lukowich team. It started well enough. They won the $16,000 first prize in the first bonspiel of the year, the Winnipeg Coca-Cola Classic. Then they headed for the Kelowna Canadian Airlines Double Cashspiel, where they made it to the semi-finals. But after that the record got worse and worse. Ferguson didn't go to many spiels and Lukowich struggled to find replacements almost every weekend.

Usually even the big-money teams don't jet around every weekend to a different bonspiel. It's too time-consuming, too expensive and too exhausting. But as the 1990-91 bonspiel season wore on, Lukowich was dogged. For nine of the ten weeks of the season, he was at spiels. He recognizes now that he was mentally tired and not curling well. But he says he felt obliged to show up at every major spiel because of the pro tour he's trying to organize.

As for the rest of the rink, it was a year of stocktaking. Their bubble had burst. For 18 months they had won every bonspiel in sight. Other teams would automatically lower their goals the minute they heard Lukowich was expected at a bonspiel. And then suddenly Fast Eddy wasn't making his expenses. After the third cashspiel of the year, the team didn't qualify. They weren't working together and it wasn't until the Christmas vacation that they got a chance to work out the problems.

They played better after that and went to the southern finals before they lost to Ed's old lead from the 1978 Brier, Wes Aman. Their playdown success is surprising considering the rough ride they were getting about Rick Valette, their new second. The provincial organization had no residency requirement, but obviously the other curlers did. Is there nobody good enough for Lukowich in Alberta? the press and his fellow curlers wanted to know. It became the issue of the tournament and Lukowich still worries that he lost friends in the controversy.

In 1991 the possibility of a pro curling tour seemed more likely than ever before. With Lukowich as its director, the fledgling organization had nailed down 30 out of 40 cashspiels as potential members of an organization that would accord points to teams for winning spiels. The teams with the highest totals would be invited to a televised Tournament of Champions. Also, as part of the deal there would be six or seven televised cup events featuring the seven best-known teams in the country. Spiel organizers met in Winnipeg at the world championships to discuss the plan, and Hollis Communications is busy looking for a big-time sponsor to make the concept fly.

For Luke it's complicated and often thankless work, but he's done plenty of that for curling over the years. And his team must wonder if this is the end. Will he be able to curl and direct a pro tour? It seems unlikely. They had worried he was spreading himself too thin at the Olympics; this would be much worse.

Meanwhile the tour seems to have taken its toll also on a personal business venture, a mail-order curling supplies business. Lukowich sold a curling supplies shop at the Calgary Curling Club a couple of years ago with a plan to get into a mail-order business because it would be less time-consuming. In September 1990 he expected to have his catalogue available in weeks. By March 1991 he was hoping it would be out in time for the world championships in April, but he sounded far from confident. Business, at least personal business, had again taken a back seat to curling.

And in that spring of 1991, as he waited to meet with the spiel directors at the world championships, Lukowich was vague about his future as a competitive curler. After 25 years of chasing the Brier and curling stardom, he sounded discouraged. "It's just about time for my annual retirement dinner," he joked. He hadn't talked to his team, and the only thing he was certain about for 1992 was that he wouldn't be taking Valette into the Alberta playdowns.

Undeniably he's inching closer to the feeling that every competitive curler seems to be subject to eventually. The challenge gets smothered by one too many defeats. "In 1991 I really learned to dislike the hitting game," he says. "If I had to play poorly and stand there, end after end, watching the other team peel and peel, the game would not be fun for me. I wouldn't do it."

He believes the modified Moncton rule or something like it is needed to rescue curling. He points out that slo-pitch came along as fastball died. The fastball pitchers had become so good the game was nothing more than a duel between pitchers and catchers. The batters, basemen and fielders stood around as props because the ball was never in play.

The same thing has happened to curling. The shooting is now much more precise because of the long slide and better ice. Even the advent of the push broom means there's no corn chaff on the ice to throw an element of unpredictability into the mix. To keep the game fun, Lukowich believes the rules will have to be revised, perhaps with the modified Moncton rule or something similar.

Listen carefully to all this and you hear a man shifting his focus, and sifting through his options. For years the intricacies of the game were enough to compel all of his attention. He was absorbed by analysing the weaknesses of his own or his opponent's game. He threw rocks for hours if he found a kink in his delivery. He experimented to find his ideal playing weight. He worked on his fitness regimen to get the exact kind of slim, strong muscles a curler needs to throw well.

But now those puzzles are solved. Practising won't help him any more he believes. He plays squash, runs and bikes to keep in shape. His weight seems to have slipped into a natural winter/summer rhythm. Now what?

Not surprisingly the scope of his interest seems to be widening. The new picture might include the job as director of the pro tour or it might head him off in any one of a dozen unpredictable new directions.

"With this pro tour Ed is trying to put something back into curling," explains his brother Mike, "and if he ever wants to promote something, he really can." But Mike wonders a bit about the practicality of Ed's idea. Throughout his career, a keen business sense has not been one of Lukowich's assets. He's had trouble following up. Mike Lukowich wonders if the pro tour idea isn't too late, if curling isn't already a dying sport. But even if it doesn't work, Mike knows he'll bounce back with another scheme. "Ed's not like other people. He's not afraid to be out on a limb. He's not afraid to try something different. He'll be OK."

*

You know, Mike is right.

Look at Ed now. Glasses on a face that is pure mildness. His manner now, as always, is slightly vague, as though he's hearing a resonance that you don't hear. And yet he's heading out for that killer squash game with Morris. The kid brother is 10 years younger and naturally more adept at racquet sports than Ed. In fact in all Calgary there is only a handful of people who can beat Morris on the squash court. Ed is desperate to be one of them. And as he heads out for what he describes as "the worst game in town," the "angriest" and most competitive, a game where racquets and hearts (mostly his) get broken with regularity, you can't help but agree with Mike's sanguine assessment. Ed will bounce back. If his fierce desire to win sputters out of his curling game, you know beyond a doubt that it will go underground to bubble up again as the centrepiece for the next stage of his life.

And just as it was with Button Joe and his golf course, whatever Ed does next will be something unique, something well worth watching for.

5

PAUL GOWSELL
The Enfant Terrible *Grows Up*

IN THE SAME Calgary Winter Club where Ed and Morris Lukowich play out their bitter squash rivalry, Paul Gowsell is having a drink on the terrace. He's tanned, short-haired and fit; a far cry from the *"enfant terrible"* pictures flashed across the country a decade ago.

Then, the curling establishment viewed him as their own answer to Alice Cooper. He was walking, talking mayhem. Even on the night he was honoured in Calgary as the Athlete of the Year, he was picked up on an impaired-driving charge and also nailed for possession of marijuana. That kind of thing didn't happen in Calgary in 1977. And it never happened in curling.

But from 1977 to 1980 he was unstoppable—the brightest and most interesting star in the curling firmament. And then, quite abruptly, his luck ran out. It didn't happen overnight, of course, and there is a long collection of reasons why, but the plain fact is the *enfant* became much less *terrible*.

Both Gowsell and Lukowich were junior champions and both had significant success by the time they were in their early twenties. But Gowsell's success was gaudier, more full of promise and much more demanding. At 20, Lukowich, playing third for his brother, was a hair's breadth away from playing in the Brier, but at 22 Gowsell was there, skipping, mixing it up, fighting with his own rink, fighting with the CBC and fighting with anyone else who crossed his path—especially the rival rinks.

"We were easily the best team there," remembers Neil Houston, who played third for Gowsell for seven of his best years. "We should have won."

Trouble was, Gowsell was competitive in everything. He was playing in his home town, the place where his reputation for outrageous partying was most spectacular. He had not only to win the Brier, but also to live up to his press clippings. The competition was stiffer than he expected, than anybody expected. Here was Al Hackner, a quiet-looking guy from Thunder Bay, Ontario, with glasses, short hair and a funny little glint in his eye. Hackner and his rink were eager to challenge for honours in off-ice antics as well as on-ice precision. If he hadn't taken that challenge so seriously, Houston believes Gowsell would have a Labatt Tankard on his mantle now instead of a bitter taste in his mouth.

Hackner erupted on the party scene. But on the ice he was his coolest, most dignified self. Gowsell, the star, spun his wheels and lost 6-5 in the semi-final.

In Hackner, Gowsell faced, probably for the first time, someone whose vein of psychic energy ran just as deep as his own. But Hackner had just started to draw on his, whereas Gowsell at 22 was beginning to get intimations of mortality. "By the end of the week we weren't sharp," admits Houston.

Gowsell's team now wonders at the speed with which he stormed through his glory years. For three seasons on the cashspiel circuit he kept his intensity pitched at maximum. He usually didn't sleep or eat much before a big bonspiel. He was so wound up he'd drink beer and look for ways to still his racing nerves. "When Paul got going, you couldn't stop him until he was done," remembers John Ferguson. But he also remembers the old dilemma: "Drinking was the only way Paul could get through the hours to the next game. He was so hyper."

Even then Houston was astonished by how he kept going on so little food. He'd eat at the Calcutta on Wednesday night and usually not again until the bonspiel was over. He was "too nervous," the explanation went. Sometimes the biggest challenge of the weekend was getting through the periods between games. Gowsell was temperamentally incapable of sitting around watching TV and waiting four hours for his game to begin.

Because their skip was so high-strung, life for all of them was a frantic party. Everything was an adventure, an exploit. And through it all they were conscious they were living a life others their age could only dream of. They were perfectly in step with the dominant temper of the times. And for Paul, at least, that reinforced his rebelliousness. It was an era when "being true to yourself" and "doing your own thing" were unimpeachable statements of purpose.

And so it was that Paul, with his unkempt mane of red hair, his bushy beard and his wardrobe of plaid pants, became a curling star, the hippie kid who had the courage and charisma to take on the best in the world and, in his phrase, "beat them up in six ends."

"I liked what hippies stood for," Paul remembers. "I was too young for the peace garbage, that was the 1960s, but I thought you should be able to be your own person as long as you weren't bothering anyone."

But Gowsell bothered the Canadian Curling Association enormously. He and his rink were world junior champions both in 1976 and in 1978. But their victories seemed to bring more embarrassment than delight to their curling organizations. For Paul, who has a sensitive side under all the chutzpah, their lack of appreciation was like a declaration of war. And war it was.

In Scotland, at the 1976 junior worlds, the big hubbub was about their sweeping. The Scots and the International Curling Federation were up in arms, claiming the Canadian rink's down-on-the-brush sweeping style was illegal.

Gowsell was furious. They'd been sweeping like that since they were 12 years old, he said. He took a scunner at his Scottish hosts and looked for ways to make them uncomfortable. Once he was stopped going into dinner because he didn't have a suit jacket on. He went back to his room, threw on a tie and jacket and pulled off his shoes. He presented himself to the head waiter and was seated before anyone noticed he was barefoot.

The controversy about sweeping confirmed all of his worst suspicions about Canadian curling poobahs and what he considered to be their follow-the-pack mentality. They didn't back him up and he wasn't surprised later on when Canada fell into line about the sweeping rules. Suddenly armies of umpires started swarming over tournaments.

He's far from alone in his opposition to the crackdown on sweeping. Many say anything in sweeping should be fair, short of burning the rock or dumping. "I have a real philosophical problem with people who talk about the 'ethics' of sweeping," says Brent Syme, lead on Ed Lukowich's team. He doesn't think sweeping can manage the rock as much as people believe. Any advantage a sweeper can coax from knowing how and when to brush is part of the skill of curling, he says.

World champions Ed Lukowich and Ron Northcott agree. They

dislike the way strict sweeping rules undermine the give-and-take of a "gentleman's sport" and turn it into a "cutthroat European game."

Eventually the CCA also passed rules to discourage teams from using corn brooms to add a little mulch and unpredictability to the ice when they were losing. Gowsell believes that's another negative, because 85 percent of the icemakers can't make swingy ice, he says. The corn broom is the only way to get some curl into the game of curling.

Belatedly, Warren Hansen seems to have come around to Gowsell's position. He has tried to get the CCA to drop the restrictive sweeping rules claiming they are unenforceable but so far the CCA has resisted.

But in 1976, when Gowsell came home from Scotland with the world junior trophy, he had yet to fight (and temporarily lose) those battles. He was just a 17-year-old kid with a trophy under his arm and a spirit that had now been toughened up by foreign skirmishes.

The Scotland trip had caused so much trouble that the CCA was determined to keep Gowsell on a shorter leash in 1978 in Grindelwald, Switzerland. They had high hopes. The boys were two years older; besides, they were sending a chaperone—er, coach—this time.

They gave them sweeping clinics, extracted promises about following the European sweeping rules and counted heavily on coach Warren Hansen's influence. As a finishing touch to their preparations, they gave them what Gowsell calls a "Dale Carnegie course." The rest of the rink submitted, but Gowsell balked. He got as far as the airport bar on his way to the course and then strategically missed the plane.

However, even without the benefit of instruction on how to win friends and influence people, Gowsell managed to do both. Out on the ice in Switzerland the 19-year-old Canadian was more than ever his own man. He ignored everything but winning.

To the well-heeled, decorous Swiss who follow curling, Gowsell was a revelation. He carried on as he always did on the ice, banging his broom, berating his own team and mocking his opponents. As for sweeping, the Gowsell rink swept as they pleased. Even Warren Hansen was helpless.

But some of the spectators were drawn to the magnetic Canadian. And out of the cloud of controversy he kicked up wherever he went, Gowsell emerged with one more junior world championship for Canada.

It was a perfect touch of irony that at the closing banquet, the Swiss security guard wouldn't let him in. He was skip of the world champions but the guard was adamant. "This is a banquet for curlers, not hippies," he explained in precise German.

Paul Gowsell seems to have been born with his distrust of wealth and privilege. His parents were comfortable enough to have a family membership in the Calgary Winter Club but not wealthy enough for the Glencoe Curling Club. At eight Paul took up ski-racing. It was a good winter outlet for his prodigious energy. He loved it and was considered a comer. But at 13 he dropped out. It was already clear to him that this was a game for rich kids. He didn't like the pressure. He knew his clothes and equipment would never be good enough.

In curling all that mattered was his skill. The year he was 13 he made it to the junior A league as a skip. He was a little kid with a big mouth and a lot of freckles, but he knew how to win. And at the Calgary Winter Club, where Ron Northcott and Hec Gervais often dropped by to play, winning was enough to earn him the respect he craved.

However, he couldn't translate his status around the Winter Club into a berth on his high-school curling team—William Aberhart High School in northwest Calgary, which was a curling power in the mid-1970s. Gowsell was already well known in curling circles as a talented junior skip and as a kid with an attitude.

Presumably it was the attitude the coach had trouble with. "I was a better curler than him," Paul says with a chuckle. In grades 10 and 11 Gowsell didn't make the cut and the Aberhart team got along without his services.

He finally skipped the team in grade 12, after the old coach had moved on to another school. At 16, in their first year together, Gowsell, Neil Houston, Glen Jackson and Kelly Stearne won the Canadian Junior title.

For Gowsell the party had begun. At the celebration at Lorna Doone High School in Edmonton the night after their big victory, Gowsell grabbed the mike and invited the whole dance back to their hotel for an illegal drink. Three hundred kids showed up, Gowsell remembers, and took over the wing of the Van Winkle Hotel where the curlers were staying. It was a night to remember. The police came three times; the hotel threw them out; and the guys had a marvellous time.

For years afterwards, on every trip to Edmonton they had two immediate goals: to register at the Van Winkle and to get thrown out on the first night.

After that explosive beginning, Paul and his rink knocked about in men's for a year, getting badly beaten but learning strategy and style. They practised relentlessly. Paul was out of school and working as a road surveyor, he had plenty of free time in the winter and at the Winter Club there was always a sheet for practice.

Gowsell got an unexpected break in 1977: the rules for junior eligibility were changed, allowing anyone under 19 to compete, whether or not they were on a high-school team. Gowsell was still young enough and certainly game enough to have another run at junior. He and Stearne with a couple of new players, John Ferguson and Doug McFarlane, entered and won again.

Those were heady times. As a double Canadian champ and a hometowner, he was invited to play in the Calgary Bonspiel, his first big-time men's event. The invitation, he knew, was a public relations gesture, nothing more. Everybody knew the gulf between junior and men's could not be stepped over by a red-headed teenaged hippie, no matter how talented.

But then his rink qualified, won money and laughed all the way to the bank. The Calgary invitation led to others, and soon they were regulars on the men's bonspiel circuit and more than holding their own, thank you very much. Their confidence was boundless; if they didn't have any money for the entry fees they'd call ahead and tell the organizers to take the fees out of their winnings.

Early on they went to the Kelowna carspiel, driving over the Roger's Pass in Jackson's old car. Coming home was trickier. It was snowing heavily and they crept along behind a snowplough. But the real problem was that the convoy that came back included three brand-new cars (the fourth was sold back to the dealer) with summer radials and drivers with very little experience. The Gowsell kids had struck paydirt. Lead Kelly Stearne earned enduring style points for flying his brother in from Calgary to drive his car home for him.

Somewhere in this period, the Attitude was born. People who talk about Gowsell's glory years still marvel about the Attitude. Here was a rink of kids with piles to learn about strategy and the finesse game, but they didn't believe they could be beaten and very soon no one else did either.

"It was uncanny," remembers three-time world champion Ron Northcott. "The good things always happened for them. They could look like they were dead and then they'd make a shot you'd only see work one time in 20. Then they'd have the momentum and win. There was never a doubt in their minds that they were going to win."

They were big hitters, curled with high percentages and worked on the assumption that unless their opponents curled 100 percent they were going to win. It was a potent strategy. Especially when Paul took to warning other skips he was going to squash them like bugs. They'd be playing men 20 years older than they were, but as they shook hands before the game they could feel their opponents tremble. "We had them psyched out, and it put us two points up before the game started," says Paul.

Paul played every psychological game in the book. He stood too close to people. He stared. He laughed. He banged his broom and yelled. At a big Winnipeg spiel he even ordered pizza delivered to the sheet. The 1,500 spectators in the stands hooted with laughter as the pizza guy in a crisp white hat made his way down sheet three. Gowsell ceremoniously took the box, tipped the delivery guy and turned to the rival skip.

"You want some?" he asked Larry McGrath. McGrath, his concentration in tatters, lost the game. To this day he claims his last rock caught on an olive.

Occasionally they'd tie Glen Jackson's dog to the scoreboard while they played, and games had to be interrupted for caretaking chores like cleaning up messes.

Needless to say, Gowsell's was always the game to watch. He drew hundreds of new spectators to the curling rink and was touted in *Maclean*'s magazine for his "unexpected star quality." But he was more than the clown prince of curling, he was a winner. His rink won $70,000 in 1978, another $70,000 in 1979 and $40,000 in 1980. It was enough to keep the wolf from the door and enough to keep Paul from the necessity of work.

"I took a lot of pride in not having to go to work," he remembers. "I liked the party life; it was a lot of fun."

The curling, even with the antics, was deadly serious. And so was the partying. Paul, and probably the whole rink, needed an outlet for the intensity. As many competitive curlers will tell you, it's a very emotional game. The party provides the necessary balance for overwrought nerves.

But the Gowsell rink cranked up the intensity meter on parties just as they did in everything else. They developed their own bonspiel style. A stereo was one of life's necessities, so on every plane trip they each took a component, a speaker or a receiver or a tapedeck, as their carry-on luggage. But air travel was only an occasional necessity. Their preferred mode of travel was in the van Gowsell got by trading in the first car he won plus $1,000. The van had a compartment under the false floor where they could hide three cases of beer and any number of other secrets.

On almost every trip that wild hippie van with the music blaring was stopped and searched, but nobody ever found the hiding place. Still, they found enough to ensure that the rink was often in hot water.

"We saw many a jail and even met a few judges," laughs Houston, "but it was all in good fun."

Brandon held a June bonspiel for a couple of years in connection with their June fair. For Gowsell and company it was a perfect opportunity to party; and as so often happened in those years, the hotter the party, the better the curling. They won the $10,000 first prize both years.

They drove to Manitoba in Jackson's BMW with a 10-man tent and all their gear piled on the roof. They found the local campground, got in touch with the Labatt's rep and were soon sitting down to enjoy the tent full of beer he'd provided. Then Kerry Burtnyk's wild young rink from Winnipeg showed up. The event, the Bacchanalian celebration of summer, was on. There was fierce four-on-four football, high hilarity, heavy metal and drunkenness. And in the morning, precision curling.

Well, it was as precise as you could get in a rink where fog obscured most of the ice surface and you had to throw the rock by keeping your head up above the fog and aiming for the only part of the broom you could see, the top of the handle. "The secret was to make sure the handle was straight," Gowsell laughs. It was that little extra turn on the ordinary, requiring flexibility and quick thinking, that Gowsell loved. It upended the conventional skips and gave him one more precious memory from those charmed years.

Inexplicably, after all the raucousness of their week in Brandon, Paul and his rink were presented with huge stuffed teddy bears as going-away presents. He loves to imagine what the other campers must have thought as they watched their noisy neighbours finally leave. The BMW had a monstrous load crammed on the roof and perched right on top four giant, smirking stuffed bears.

*

Through all those high times there were two constants for Gowsell's rink. They always practised, and the skip's metabolism could always bounce him back, not much the worse for wear, no matter how excessive his fun had been. He'd sometimes need a trail of toilet paper or string to help him find his way back to his room, but after a sleep and some coffee he'd be ready for serious, stern practice. If it was a school day, the others might go to class and be home by the time Paul was awake and ready to go to the rink. In those days, besides the practice, they were playing four club games a week and bonspiels every weekend.

But times were changing. The self-involved 1970s gave way to the greedy 1980s and hippies were suddenly out of fashion. Besides, the guys were growing up, passing from teenagers to young adults, and gradually their thirst for the party life was quenched. "You get to a point when you just want out," explains Houston.

Losing the 1980 Brier was an important milestone. It wasn't fun to lose a championship you were supposed to win, especially to lose it in front of your hometown. "Most teams lose a lot before they win," explains Northcott. "It teaches you something. But Gowsell's rink had never really experienced losing."

Northcott believes the slide started when the original team broke up. Jackson left in 1981, Houston in 1982 and Ferguson in 1983. It was time to get on with their lives.

Gowsell was left behind. He had been the centrepiece, but he had also been the one who had given most to curling. The others had kept up, sporadically at least, with their schooling. And when the emotional barometer on their team slipped from manic fun to edgy obsession they had somewhere else to go.

"Paul found out he could lose," is John Ferguson's explanation of what happened. Suddenly the reaming out of his own team, which had been full of wisecracks and fun when they were winning, became nasty and embarrassing to watch. "It got so you couldn't curl well enough for Paul," says Ferguson.

John threw himself into his CA studies, and curling with Ed Lukowich at the Brier. Houston was already playing second on the team. Gowsell went back to his land surveyor's job and tried to find another team that could handle what was now considered his abuse.

And the magic slipped away.

Paul still throws a very nice rock but he doesn't practise any more and he doesn't have a regular team. The old reliable metabolism still works pretty well but it doesn't get tested to the limit as much any more. And he now talks about losing bonspiels because he was loaded.

And every year he wonders about quitting. He's had some decent years in the win column, especially with a team from B.C., but nobody trembles when they shake his hand any more. And to tell the truth, he no longer believes they should. He concedes Lukowich is a better curler, the best in the world. "Of course, he's got my old team," he mutters.

And now, too, there are other things that command his attention. He's married, with children and a mortgage. Looking back he's sometimes a little bitter about how much he gave to the sport and how little he got back. The targets of his bitterness are the rule changes, the curling bureaucracy and his team's desertion.

And all that psychic energy he used to dump into curling has dwindled away. He doesn't keep up. Ask him about the Moncton rule and he needs an explanation. He's not certain who some of the up-and-coming curlers are.

The final embers of his curling fire were doused in 1987 when he wasn't chosen as one of the eight Canadian skips to play off for the right to represent Canada in the Olympics.

"That was a farce—a joke," he says. "They said you had to be in good shape. I went into the weight room for five months and was in the best shape of my life. And who have they got there? Sewage and Stench [Savage and Werenich]? How much did *they* lose? Two pounds?

"I had no chance before I got there. They didn't want anyone who is a rebel to represent the country. Eugene Hritzuk and Kirk Ziola were the last two skips chosen. Give me a break. What have they ever won? I put a lot of time into it and I didn't have a chance."

The pain from that experience still hangs heavy in the air. For Gowsell the only tangible benefit from his Olympic effort was that four years later he still looks strong and fit from the muscle he developed for the Olympics. He works outside, but he insists his only fitness regimen now is to watch football and drink beer.

Will he continue to curl? Perhaps a little, but he's bought a season's pass for skiing for the first time in many years. "I'm just a little fed up. I have more fun skiing than beating my head against the wall in curling. It costs so much to go in bonspiels nowadays. Unless you finish in the top four, it's going to cost you money. It's not worth it.

Not worth the time it takes to be good at it. I'd rather go skiing. There's no pressure."

He smiles at the irony, remembering he left skiing when he was 13 because of the pressure.

"Life's one big learning experience, isn't it?" he says with a grin.

The Brier Tankard—the holy grail of curling.

Canapress Photo Service/Clark

Ed Werenich holds the Tankard during the presentation at the 1983 Brier, as Paul Savage takes a look at his replica and ring. (Paul Gowsell refers to these two as "Stench" and "Sewage", respectively.) Both Werenich and Savage would be participants in the famous "Battle of the Bulge" when they were ordered to slim down for the 1988 Olympic trials.

Hyper, rebellious Paul Gowsell, the *enfant terrible* who seemed unbeatable from 1977 until 1980. The clown prince of curling was well known for his antics on and off the ice. At one Winnipeg spiel, he ordered pizza delivered to his sheet and when it arrived promptly asked the rival skip, "You want some?" Gowsell's was always the game to watch.

Canada Wide

Ed Werenich lines up a shot at the 1984 Brier as Manitoba third, Brian Toews, and skip Mike Riley look over his shoulder. Mike Riley's rink would win that Brier, a disappointment for Werenich's Dream Team who were pursuing what would have been the first back-to-back Briers in 20 years.

Marilyn Bodogh Darte challenged Ed Werenich to a Battle of the Sexes in 1986, pitting the Dream Team against her Scott Tournament of Hearts championship team. Despite their great showmanship, the women lost 10-2.

Ed Lukowich and John Ferguson watch the rock curl down the ice looking as though they hoped their posture might angle the rock in the desired direction. Ferguson joined Lukowich's rink as a third after leaving Gowsell's team.

Reekie/Canada Wide

The Paul Gowsell guide to curling fashion. His trademark finery from his earlier days: unkempt mane of red hair, beard and plaid pants.

Ken Kerr/Canada Wide

"Cool Hand Luke" is considered one of the best all-round players in the game. He is also a tireless promoter of the game off the sheet—he has been instrumental in the efforts over the last few years to create a pro curling circuit modelled on the PGA Tour.

Canapress Photo Service/Jan Vann Horne

Pat Ryan shouts at his teammates to sweep during a match against Saskatchewan at the Brier in Chicoutimi, Quebec, in 1988. Ryan's rink won back-to-back Briers in 1988 and 1989. Well-known for his intensity, competitiveness and precision, Ryan has devoted many hours to perfecting his delivery.

Al Hackner (centre), the "Iceman", and his former third, Rick Lang (right), with a friend. Hackner made the most spectacular shot in recent memory against Pat Ryan at the 1985 Brier. After he made the shot, he apologized to Ryan who had already been signalling victory.

Hackner

Russ Howard (left) and his brother, Glenn, argue over a shot at the 1989 Brier. At one point, Russ remembers someone from the crowd shouting, "Why don't you get your mother to decide?"

Labatt's/Michael Burns Photography

Pat Ryan compares the moment in the hack alone with the rock to the moments right before a pitcher throws the ball: "It doesn't matter about the TV lights or the expectant crowd. It's a moment of meditation, a chance...to be perfect."

Russ Howard wearing the forbidden mike at the 1989 Brier. Howard's roar when he's in full flight has been likened to that of a bull moose. At the 1989 Brier, believing that his teammates relied on his howl to judge the fury of sweeping, he donned this two-way radio when his voice failed him. The CCA was furious and ordered Howard to take it out and when he refused, changed the rules to outlaw radio mikes.

Labatt's/Michael Burns Photography

Kawaja, part of Ed Werenich's Dream Team, in the hack at the 1990 Brier. Werenich's rink won that Brier and went on to win the world championship.

If curling can claim its heartthrobs, John Kawaja is definitely one of them. But those days are over—John married Laura Barker in the summer of 1991.

Jim Sullivan and his rink were known as the "New Kids on the Block" when they made it to the Brier in 1990. Their appearance there was that much sweeter for Sullivan because the team had been overlooked for the Moncton 100 earlier in the year. The only New Brunswick rink to receive an invitation to Moncton was Jack MacDuff. Word was that Sullivan's young rink couldn't compete with the men.

Rick Lang (in the jacket) and Kevin Martin, winner of the 1991 Brier. Martin is using the infamous corn broom that caused many players to criticize him for his win-at-all-costs attitude. Canada Press reported that the broom "literally disintegrated on contact with the ice, leaving chaff and straw strewn around." Martin's strategy will have many curlers "gunning for him" next year.

Kerry Burtnyk, the youngest ever to win the Brier (1981), is now an account executive with Richardson Greenshields, but has not completely left curling. He and former teammate Mark Olson have organized a Manitoba bonspiel circuit for 1991–92.

Michael Burns Photography

Rick Folk (right) with teammates Jim Wilson (left) and Tom Wilson at the 1980 world championship. Folk's rink won the 1980 Brier that everyone had predicted Paul Gowsell would win.

Perroud

A future passion is born. Pat Perroud started out riding the rock instead of sweeping—his father was an ice-maker and used to keep Pat amused by shooting him across the ice on a rock. Talk about being burned by the rock!

Ian Tetley was fired from Hackner's Thunder Bay rink in 1987 because the serious-minded Tetley and the wild Hackner were incompatible.

Canada Wide

Mike Riley, the man that no one seems to know much about, watches the play at the 1984 Brier, which his rink would eventually win. Riley, a health-nut and triathlete, has long been an outsider in the tight-knit world of men's competitive curling—he'd rather be hiking in the Himalayas.

6

AL HACKNER
The Iceman Melts

THERE'S A BITTERNESS in Paul Gowsell's memories. The winning that was supposed to happen never did. And imperceptibly his gaudy, youthful promise slipped away. Al Hackner's memories, on the other hand, are wonderfully sweet. Before he was 30 he'd accomplished his heart's deepest desire. By 31 he'd done it twice.

But in the half-dozen years since then, a certain aimlessness has crept into his life, and sometimes now on cold grey mornings those sweet memories are silent reminders that the present isn't nearly as golden as the past.

Look at him sitting on the edge of a bed in one of the interminable hotel rooms where he spends so much of his curling life. He hasn't slept much. His hair, still wet from the shower, stands up in tufts. There's a pallor to his skin this morning against the brilliant white of the towel around his neck, but he looks good. The dark eyes behind the aviator glasses are clear and wary.

This, you quickly gather, is a typical Hackner Sunday morning on the bonspiel beat. All around him are bits of unfinished business. A friend sits in a corner chair waiting to chat; two women who've played in the charity bonspiel stop by to say thanks; the message light on the phone is blinking and the appointment he was supposed to keep in the downstairs lobby has just barged into the room.

The Iceman doesn't blink. He smiles his slow steady smile and looks over the situation appraisingly. He's handled far worse.

At 37, Al Hackner has won two Labatt Briers and two world championships and he is known for the single most spectacular curling shot in recent memory. Not bad.

But what does he do for an encore? He could gracefully retire, but he watched his long-time third, Rick Lang, try that after they split up in 1989. Rick was back the next year as a skip. He couldn't do it. He didn't like the way his life felt without curling. "If I leave this game behind, I leave so much of me behind too," he explains.

And Hackner knows what was true for Lang would be truer for him. Lang is a social worker and has now started taking promotions and moving up. His job is a big deal in his life. It's a career.

Hackner is a railway switchman. It's a perfect job for curling because there's lots of free time and not too much wearying responsibility. But it's not, as Rick Lang points out, a career. Al used to love the straightforward nature of his job, and the outside work. Now he sometimes wonders if he shouldn't have gone on to university, shouldn't have looked for more challenge in his work.

But it would be wrong to suggest Hackner broods. It's just that the path ahead, which used to be klieg-lit by his desire for curling greatness, is now a bit shadowy. And where his life before was all clarity of purpose, things are cloudier now. Where he always knew exactly what he wanted and how to get it, there are now pockets of uncertainty and craters of unease.

Still, he pushes on, looking for new teammates and new challenges, half-hoping to be ambushed again by that piercing desire to win, a desire that broadsided him unexpectedly when he was a mere teenager and changed completely the course his life would take.

Al Hackner at 14 was a hockey player, a hockey star really, one of the three best players in the little town of Nipigon, 105 kilometres east of Thunder Bay. He was the captain of the team; his father, Tony, was the coach; they'd won championships. Al had been MVP and had had his picture taken with Gordie Howe. Like every other kid with his ability and temperament, visions of professional hockey teams danced in his head.

But Tony Hackner was also a curler, and one day, when his eldest son was 14, he announced it was time for Al to learn to curl. Maybe they could even play together. Al resisted. It wasn't cool. Curling was a game for old guys who couldn't play hockey any more. And he didn't like the idea of being alone out on the sheet learning to throw a rock. He was shy, and the idea of looking awkward in front of his father and his friends horrified him.

Tony paid no attention to his son's evasions. He paid the five dollars extra they charged him to enrol his son and out they went, Al dragging behind and feeling miserable. At that time, he insists, in the whole town of Nipigon there was just one other junior curler.

But after the first session he couldn't have cared less. It was instant fatal attraction. "I was possessed," he remembers.

Right from the moment he first threw a rock he couldn't get enough. His friends didn't understand it. Even his friends' parents didn't understand it. He had been a fixture at the hockey rink, always skating, always available for a game of shinny and always a big scorer on the town's team. His teammates felt deserted—and they were. Now, if you were looking for Al Hackner you'd have to go to the curling rink.

There he'd be, the kid who'd been gregarious, the ultimate team player on the hockey squad, alone in the silent rink, totally absorbed, working on his delivery, inching closer and closer to perfection.

For a year he juggled both sports, but when the inevitable choice had to be made he dropped hockey. It was not a popular move. When he tried to get his friend Ray Dupuis interested in curling, he was met with a blank stare of incomprehension. "No!" Dupuis said emphatically. He didn't bother to elaborate.

Years later Al remembers a high-school buddy dropping by the curling rink to borrow some hockey equipment. He realized with a sudden shock that he didn't have any idea what had happened to his equipment and—more significantly—he didn't care. Hockey was well and truly over.

Curling, or rather his obsession with curling, filled up his life. At 17, he was already skipping and dazzling the hometown curlers with trick shots. When the chips were down he seemed always to be able to pull it out of the hat. "Lucky" they called it.

Lucky and prepared. Nobody talked much about the hundreds of hours of practice, but Hackner knows that his incredible consistency was attributable to those hours alone in the rink. For ten years— maybe more—he practised two or three times a day, always striving for perfection. "I don't have a perfect delivery," he explains now. "But when I was practising that much I was perfectly prepared. I'd set the rock down the same way every time and I knew exactly what it would do, curl a bit on my inturns and float a bit on my outturn. So I knew exactly what ice to take and I'd make every shot."

Whatever the team, and whatever happened in the game, Hackner rarely lost. The winter he was 17, the last year he curled in Nipigon, he lost two club games. He was picked to go to the Ontario Winter Games and his team came second. His fame was spreading in northern Ontario, but he knew if he was going to keep learning about the game he had to move to the city.

He transferred to a Thunder Bay high school for grade 13. He'd been invited by a high-school team that had gone to the provincial finals the year before. With Hackner on board, who knows what glory might be possible. He also signed on to play with a competitive men's team. He was 18 years old, away from home for the first time and full of energy for curling, competing and carousing.

School was the first casualty of his new life. He'd been an A student before sports started dominating his life, but now, no matter how he tallied the score sheet, he couldn't see any point in hitting the books. He didn't want to go to university. He didn't want a fancy desk job. He wanted to curl.

But he was also having trouble committing to his junior team. Their regular third had been bounced to second to make room for him and it hurt team morale. "I felt like I was scabbing in," Hackner remembers. "It didn't feel right. I was just hanging around, trying to get a free trip to the junior nationals."

Besides, he didn't think much of the curling. There was no comparison in the quality of curling between that schoolboy team and the men's team he was skipping at night. By Christmas he'd dropped out of grade 13 and junior curling and was concentrating on the upcoming playdowns.

To support himself he signed on with the railway. He loved it; it was everything he wanted in a job. But even then he would never have guessed he would still be at it two decades later or that Brian Adams, the buddy who signed on with him that day in 1972, would stick it out too and end up curling with him nearly 20 years later.

For all their high hopes and great expectations, Hackner's men's team didn't get out of their club that year. Still, the omens were right. It took the tough-minded, mightily experienced Bill Tetley, a skip who was destined to win the Brier in 1975, two extremely tough games to knock them out.

Al Hackner was 19 and his life pattern was set. He worked shifts on the railway, practised throwing the rock and partied with his friends. There was no master plan to make curling his life. He dreamed of the Brier but the cashspiel circuit was little more than a distant rumour. Thunder Bay was at least a day's travel from any of the major spiels. He could only dream of a time when he might be able to afford the time and money to try his luck in the big time.

He was happy. Locally his team was winning its share, and his own fame was slowly spreading. The future looked bright, too; his game was improving and he had met the woman he would eventually marry.

In May 1976, just before he turned 23, Hackner and Margaret Nicol decided to try the west. They chose Edmonton for three reasons: Al could transfer his seniority with the railway, he had family there and it would give them a chance to see the much-vaunted western curling up close.

Al hated Edmonton. Although he curled that winter, the team was terrible and he had no fun. He felt that nobody in the west had the feeling for curling that is part of the game in the east.

"Everybody could see he was just wasting his talent," Margaret says. People who've watched Hackner curl know he hates to give up on anything. Even when the game seems completely lost he'll struggle on until the 10th end. But in Edmonton in May 1977, after a dismal year, Al gave up on western curling. "I want to go home to curl with my friends," he told Margaret. She started packing their bags. She knew then, as she knows now, that curling is the essential ingredient in Al's life. If the curling wasn't working out, nothing else would either.

Back in Thunder Bay Hackner starting bumping into a wiry little guy with a great smile, an easygoing manner and lips like Mick Jagger's. At parties, Rick Lang was always part of the action, and when the spirit moved him he did a mean chorus or two of "Satisfaction," the old Stones' anthem. This was one neat guy, a perfect match for Al.

On paper Rick Lang had better curling credentials than Hackner. In 1975, at 22, he'd won the Brier playing third for Bill Tetley. It was the first time a Northern Ontario rink had ever won. The very next year Lang again represented Northern Ontario, this time as skip of his own team. Even though his record was only 5-6, he'd done battle with curling legends like Jimmy Ursel and Bernie Sparkes. For a dedicated student of the game and its heroes like Al Hackner, that must have added to Lang's appeal.

But playing together wasn't an automatic outgrowth of their friendship. They talked casually about "someday," but in the here and now each had other loyalties which he took very seriously.

Finally in the fall of 1979 they agreed to try curling together for the 1980 competitive season. Each would pick one other curler for the team.

For Al this was an excruciating task—"the toughest decision of my life"—he says now. The choice was between two friends and teammates, Johnny Salo and Bruce Kennedy. Both as friends and as curlers they were about equal. "It was just like *Sophie's Choice*," Hackner remembers. "It was horrible. It took me a month just to set up the meeting."

Hackner's mother is part Ojibwa, and although he doesn't make much of a deal about it, he carries a treaty card and often attributes his luck to the benevolence of "the Great Manitou." Salo is also a native Canadian and he too came from Nipigon. Those connections bound them a little tighter than ordinary friends, so when Al finally decided that Kennedy would be better on the new team, he was heartsick about telling Johnny.

"I was dying at that meeting. I said, 'Johnny, I picked Bruce,' and he started crying. I almost cried myself."

Johnny left town that year and moved out west, seeking work as an electrician and a new start in curling. Al believes he left because he was wounded and bleeding. Even now, when Hackner talks about that choice you can hear the lump in his throat.

Years later he'd hear that things weren't going well for Johnny and he'd feel the guilt pangs all over again. "About three years ago I remember sitting with him and telling him if he'd move back to Thunder Bay there'd be a place for him on my team."

Johnny took the invitation and played with Hackner in 1989, 1990 and 1991. They weren't banner years though, and when Hackner signed on with a new team for 1992, Salo again wasn't in the picture. But by this time the edge had worn off their intensity and it wasn't nearly such a big deal. "I explained to him. He understood. We're still good friends," says Hackner. "It wasn't anything like the first time."

But the 1979-80 team was charmed right from the beginning. Even as they were putting it together, everybody seemed to feel something special was about to happen.

Still, they were shocked when success came faster than they ever believed possible. Right from the beginning, Bruce Kennedy functioned as both lead and unofficial morale-booster on the team. Every year part of his schtick was to make a preseason prediction.

His first ambitious assessment made everybody laugh. "This year," he told them earnestly, "we will go to the Brier and we will beat Paul Gowsell."

The team response was a collective guffaw. Gowsell was in *Maclean's* magazine, for heaven's sakes. He was winning every big-money spiel in the country. "It was like saying you would beat Hulk Hogan in wrestling," Hackner remembers.

But Kennedy wasn't through predicting. "And we will also," he continued, undismayed by his team's derision, "*outparty* the man."

Right on both counts.

By the time they got to the Brier that year in Calgary, they had tested their party mettle and knew they were ready. "Bruce and I were big-time partyers," remembers Hackner. "Was this guy [Gowsell] made of iron?"

They checked into their Edmonton hotel on the Thursday before the Brier and headed straight to Gowsell's room. They hadn't met, but they were young, wild and ready. They hung around the whole night, until sometime before dawn Paul admitted he was tired and they left.

They'd won round one and everybody knew it.

The pattern was established. Every night they'd pound on Gowsell's door and settle in for a marathon night of drinking and partying. Every night about dawn Gowsell would have to admit he was tired and ask them to leave.

Undoubtedly part of the fun was the way they were unravelling Gowsell's great reputation for stamina. By Tuesday, when the Brier was already three days old, Gowsell wasn't answering the door any more. Victory had been conceded. When the two teams met in the round robin it was no surprise to anyone who knew them that Northern Ontario thrashed the hometown favourites 10-5.

They finished the round robin dead even at 8-3, and Hackner pushed his advantage to win by one point when they met again in the semi-final. Outmanoeuvring Gowsell must have seemed the real goal of that Brier, because they went on to lose in the final 10-6 to Rick Folk's Saskatchewan rink.

They floated away from the Calgary Brier on a cloud. Kennedy had been right, they were world-class curlers—and even more obviously world-champion partyers.

The next year they were back again at the Brier representing

Northern Ontario and ready to cross swords with anyone who got in their way.

Lang remembers believing implicitly in their team. "Hackner had the potential to be the best curler in the world. He could make the big shot under the most difficult circumstances. And I felt confident that playing with him I had the potential to be the best third in the world."

But they were about to be disillusioned. It happened at the Halifax Brier in 1981 and the cause was Kerry Burtnyk, a 22-year-old from Winnipeg whose team would be the youngest ever to win the Brier. Al and company were up 4-2 in the 10th end when something hideous happened. The Iceman, who Lang believed was incapable of missing the big shot, did. He missed a routine draw, allowing Burtnyk to take three. They went down to a dismal, aching defeat.

That moment and that shot still bring tears to the eyes of Mark Olson, who was third on Burtnyk's rink. He remembers how solemn and stony Burtnyk was in the packed arena as he delivered his three-pointer.

"I'm a good loser, the best, I think," Hackner says now, thinking back. "I remember we're sitting in the bar afterward. The world has just crashed around our ears and Rick says: 'What would we be doing if we won?' So we got up and walked into the Patch. A hush fell as we walked in, everybody stopped talking."

All night long as he partied with Burtnyk and his rink, fans kept coming up and saying, "I can't believe you're here." Hackner's stock reply was, "Where would you want me to go?"

Those who cherish the gentlemanly social sport of curling remember the emotional heroics of the Hackner team that night with as much affection as they remember his spectacular 1985 shot against Ryan.

"I think I took it the hardest," smiles Margaret Hackner. "I always say I don't care, but when it comes down to it, I'm the one who gets sick to my stomach. I just know how much he loves it and how much he wants to win."

But the Iceman doesn't let anybody else see that side of him. He says he wasn't too bugged by all the questions that summer about what happened in that 10th end.

But he will admit that by the next year, when the rink again represented Northern Ontario, and—for the third consecutive year—went to the finals, he knew he had to win.

They were expert these four—Bruce Kennedy, Bobby Nicol, Rick Lang and Al Hackner—at handling pressure. They shrugged it off, they danced it off, they drank it off—and they never talked about it. It was the old hear-no-evil schtick. If you don't acknowledge the pressure, it doesn't exist.

So in Brandon, where more than 100,000 people bought Brier tickets, Hackner, the crowd favourite, signed autographs, smiled for the pictures and carefully led his team to an 8-3 record. Good enough for one more semi-final.

The team, expert as they were, handled it. They didn't talk about last year's debacle, about how they were clearly the class of a relatively weak field, about how everyone expected this to be a coronation.

If those thoughts were there at all, they were hidden somewhere behind cheery smiles and an upbeat mood. All Bruce Kennedy said as they waited through the torturous last hour for the semi-final against Manitoba's Mel Logan was, "God, don't let me play this game if we're going to lose the final."

He didn't need to add "again."

But they'd waited their turn. This time the Great Manitou was smiling. They finished off Logan 8-5 and went on to dispose of Brent Giles of British Columbia 7-3 in the final.

They'd consoled themselves after the Burtnyk loss by telling themselves it would be better to win the next year and go to the world championships in Garmisch-Partenkirchen. Going to the German resort in the Bavarian Alps certainly beat the prize for winning in 1981—the right to compete in London, Ontario.

But that was all just theoretical until March 1982, when suddenly they were packing their bags and their lederhosen. Almost 10 years later Margaret Hackner still sighs at the memory of that European trip. "It was spectacular," she says with enthusiasm. "We had this beautiful room with a balcony on the Eibsee and they treated us like kings and queens. The whole trip was thrilling."

Nobody could ever accuse Hackner of letting the good times pass him by. For him too, Garmisch was a revelation. "There's no sense being here if we're not having a good time," was his watchword for his team. They enjoyed themselves and tried to keep the competition in perspective.

Leave it to others to talk about the pressure. Let Russ Howard or Ed Lukowich fret about the consequences of losing. Hackner's rink was so confident, they scarcely considered the possibility. They were 27 years old. They knew this was as good as life got and they weren't about to miss it.

While the other teams concentrated on their training regimens, the Canadians concentrated on staying loose. They took the funicular up the Zugspitze, had drinks on the balcony overlooking the crystal waters of the Eibsee and drank in the restorative air—and beer—of the Bavarian mountains.

And still they won. They finished the round robin first with a 7-2 record, while five of the other nine teams finished second with 5-4 records. The turning point of the tournament came in the semi-final, when Canada wiped out Soren Grahn of Sweden. After that tough psychological battle, the final against the Swiss defending champions was almost a walk in the park.

Swiss skip Jurg Tanner, whose father scooted around in a Maserati and who epitomized the privileged young European curler, went down 9-7 and managed to be gracious in defeat.

But the best was yet to come. Back home, Thunder Bay turned itself inside out. It's not often the small northern Ontario city of 125,000 gets a chance to celebrate a world championship. This would definitely be a party to remember.

Al remembers the hoopla with a chuckle. After all, great things had been expected of him since he was 19. Now he'd fulfilled the promise and he set out to enjoy the prize.

He wasn't the only one. For Rick Lang, too, this was a charmed moment in his life. Ten years later he would look back on the Hackner years darkly and say: "We only had one thing in common, curling." Ultimately that would be true. But in that glorious summer of 1982, no dark clouds were on the horizon. There was no time or energy for deep truths. Besides, as Lang admits, "Curling was 80 percent of our lives in those years and we both had exactly the same goal."

Both Lang and Hackner use the image of a marriage to describe their years together. Al jokes about "250 nights in the same hotel room." Rick talks about the "emotional ups and downs" of the partnership and uses his social-worker language to talk about the adaptations one partner must make for the other.

They both acknowledge the inevitability of the breakup, explaining it in virtually the same metaphors. Their partnership had all the stresses and strains of a marriage, but it had none of the bonds of children and shared property that sometimes hold marriages together against all odds.

But in those honeymoon years of 1982 and 1983, Hackner and Lang were an enviable dyad. Hackner was magic and Lang never thought to doubt him. He watched him carefully, savoured his cool, and tried to learn to relax. Lang was the facilitator who made life easy for them all and held things together.

Benignly he watched over Hackner, sometimes gently extracting him when the party got too wild and the stakes the next day were too high. "A moderating influence" is how he saw his role. And there were times when nobody could handle Al, except Rick. The mutual respect went very deep.

Rick Lang had learned early how to work around obstacles. He was the youngest and smallest of a large family that played every sport: football, volleyball, baseball, hockey. "In grade nine I was four-foot-six and weighed only 67 pounds." He remembers the frustration of trying to compete with his family. In some sports the size and age difference combined kept him off the field completely.

TV is a natural solace for a young teenager having trouble fitting in. And as he watched curling he realized with a jolt that he'd found a sport where his size wouldn't be a handicap. He knew no one who curled, but the family lived close to the rink and there was a high-school team he could try out for.

Like the rest of his family he had natural co-ordination and aptitude for sports. And his desire was immense. He won the first 20 curling games he played. By then he was hooked and like Hackner, 100 kilometres away in Nipigon, he concentrated furiously on the sport. Three years later he lost the Canadian junior final, and three years after that he was a late recruit to play third on the team that won the Brier. After seven more years and a fruitful partnership with Hackner, he would add another Brier win and a world championship to his string of successes.

The kind of drive and desire that nurtured both Lang's and Hackner's curling careers doesn't evaporate after one championship season. The summer was full of elaborate celebrating, but by the fall of 1982 they were eager to get on with their championship year. On their dance card they had nine bonspiels, a couple of trips to Europe and of course the playdowns and a chance to repeat their glory.

But very early that season they realized the keenness had gone out of the team's desire. For lead Bruce Kennedy and second Bobby

Nicol, once was enough. "Nothing was further from their minds than repeating," remembers Margaret Hackner.

Ten years later, Al still remembers the frustration. "They dropped down a notch in their play," he explains. "Now I have too, and I'd be able to play with them, but then. . . ."

It took two years of trying, two years of not getting to the provincials, two years of burnout, before Rick and Al accepted that they would have to change their team to get back to their old fiery intensity. "We started looking around for two young guys for the front end. We wanted a unit," remembers Al.

They were doing play-by-play TV commentary on the local zone playdowns when they first noticed Pat Perroud and Ian Tetley playing on Bill Tetley's team. They saw a pair of young men who communicated flawlessly and had an intense desire to win. Perfect. What the pair lacked in finesse and polish could be taught.

Rick made the advances and Ian and Pat jumped at the chance. "It was like being invited to play with curling gods," remembers Perroud.

Ian remembers his father giving his blessing. "If you're ever going to get to the Brier or do anything with curling, it will be with those two," he said.

Bill Tetley, of course, knew exactly what he was recommending. Although now past his prime, he still threw rocks every day, and since his Brier win in 1975 he had presided, in his gruff way, over the rapid development of the Thunder Bay curling scene. He saw Hackner and Lang as protégés. And his son Ian believes unequivocally that the pair would never have developed into world-class curlers without his father's example.

But this was another era. Perroud and Tetley remember their jitters. They were two unknown university students suddenly thrust into the limelight. They had all the terrors that rookies always feel the first time they see themselves written about in the sports pages, the first time they realize they have no control of the shadow of themselves that is their public image.

Perroud, the quiet easygoing son of the local icemaker, kept his head down and swept. Tetley, who likes to control his world in much the same way Hackner does, had a tougher time containing himself.

Looking back, people who know them both say it was clear Hackner and Tetley would be oil and water on the same team. On the curling sheet they respected each other's ability, but something in their personal style was at odds. The problems were there from the beginning, but through that 1984- 85 season Perroud and Tetley were on such a steep learning curve the problems stayed below the surface.

At first Perroud and Tetley couldn't believe the subtleties that were unfolding for them. They'd never guessed there was so much to this game they'd played and watched all of their lives. When the ice was straight, Al would bring out the corn brooms and that too added a completely different dimension to the way they played the game.

This was the major leagues: they were learning how to feed the rock, to think two shots ahead and always to keep the professional, the intimidating edge. "There were lots of eyes on us."

There was a new lifestyle too. Suddenly they found themselves jetting around to bonspiels from Montreal to Winnipeg, throwing themselves into a life they had scarcely dreamed existed.

Hackner and Lang had not expected instant success. This was to be a building year. But somehow the edifice they were creating got taller and stronger than any of the others around.

It was a come-from-behind season that put them all on an emotional roller coaster. In every bonspiel they lost early and played out the rest of the spiel with their backs to the wall. And when they showed up at the Brier representing Northern Ontario, they were well aware they had lost the maximum number of games they could lose and still be there.

In the Brier they did not shine. Their record was an unspectacular 7-4, good enough to finish second in the round robin, but no one, not even Tetley and Perroud, believed it was good enough to win.

Pat Ryan was the invincible force of that 1985 Moncton Brier. Everyone stood aside as he and his Edmonton rink swept away all opposition and rolled up an 11-0 record in the round robin. Not since 1969, when Ron Northcott went 10-0 on his way to his third Brier, had anyone approached such perfection.

But Northcott had not been required to play a final game. In those days, when television took little notice of curling, it was enough to win the round robin. Northcott had not had to go the extra mile and play the last winner-take-all game.

But even though it was technically possible, nobody believed Ryan's momentum could be stopped. When Hackner's rink went out in the semi-final against Saskatchewan's Eugene Hritzuk, many believed it was immaterial who won. In the end the 1985 Brier would simply go to reward Ryan's impeccable hitting skill.

The Hritzuk game went as many others had that year for Hackner. Hritzuk had only to make his guard to win and sink their hopes. But he didn't, and the Hackner rink went on to a 7-4 victory.

The stage was set for one of the most dramatic curling games of all time—Hackner facing Ryan. A "magic skip" facing unrelenting preparation and seamless skill. But Hackner knew a thing or two about preparation himself. He studied the statistics. He knew if there was any chink in Ryan's armour it was on the inturn draw in a pressure situation. His percentage in that situation was a mere 82 percent.

The Moncton Coliseum was packed on that Sunday, March 10, 1985. Feelings ran high. Would Ryan make the perfect 12-0 score or would the scrappy and popular Iceman and his pocket "Manitou" pull off the impossible?

In the tenth end it was all over. Ryan was up 5-3 and even though Hackner had made a perfect split and put two of his stones in the house, Ryan had followed with a good hit and roll that gave Hackner virtually no shot with his last rock. As the rock finished, Ryan's arm went up in victory.

In the stands Margaret Hackner sighed in resignation as she watched her husband move toward the hack. She knew it was too soon for Ryan to celebrate. Her husband would always throw his last stone, try the impossible, test his luck. "He didn't have a chance," she says, "but he's like that, he will never give up no matter what."

The noisy enthusiastic crowd of more than 5,000 fell silent as Hackner stepped into the hack. Thirty seconds later the Coliseum erupted in deafening applause. The Iceman's miracle double takeout had worked. Stonily as ever, Hackner turned to Ryan and breathed the word "Sorry."

They headed into the extra end but the momentum had shifted. Ryan's third, Gord Trenchie, missed a couple of key shots. Hackner threw up two perfect guards which forced Ryan finally to make the inturn draw on his last shot. It was a Hollywood script. Ryan's shot looked perfect as it entered the house, but it wouldn't curl and in the end slid an inch too far and wide of the target.

Tetley exploded in a leap of delight. Suddenly he felt himself in the vicelike grip of his skip. "Stay out of the house," Hackner hissed in fury. Tetley remembers the hurt. Hackner's outburst had pricked the bubble of delight for the only member of the team who seemed to feel any. As newspaper reporters later commented, they were the grimmest-looking winners anybody had seen for a long, long time.

The air of gloom over the Hackner rink receded a bit as the night and the party wore on, but it didn't completely evaporate. "We just won the Brier. Why do I feel so bad?" Rick Lang asked after the awards ceremony.

Much later that evening Hackner mulled it over with Tom Slater of the *Toronto Star*. "A thing like what happened today has destroyed curlers in the past," he said glumly. "Just knowing how I felt in 1981 (when he allowed Burtnyk to steal three points and win the Brier), I know how Pat Ryan must feel. It's important he put this behind him. That's what we had to do and we came back to win the Brier in 1982."

But the win was never really satisfying. They were all infected with the feeling of being undeserving. "It wasn't nearly as exciting as 1982," Margaret Hackner remembers. "Curling is a lot of luck. Al happened to make the shot."

Three weeks later, still in this odd state of numbness, they headed off to Glasgow, Scotland, for the worlds. For Tetley this was a perfect setting for a curling world tournament. He felt the hair on the back of his neck prickle with pride as the bagpipes played in the opening ceremonies. Scotland was a "sister" country and the karma was perfect. Perroud remembers it being a zillion times better than his next world championship—1990 in Västerås, Sweden.

But the veterans felt differently. Al and Rick couldn't help comparing it to Garmisch, and finding Glasgow wanting. Beside the sparkling sunshine and picturesque lakes of the Alps, they had to place the damp, cold, bleak iron-and-steel town on the dark River Clyde. The difference in personal comfort was equally striking. The 1982 world champions couldn't help but grumble a bit about how difficult it was to get a meal. Breakfast and lunch were served early and at very strict hours; only the most punctual guests ever got any.

Altogether the experience was flatter. The people were very kind and friendly, but there was none of the expansive pleasure they had glimpsed in Garmisch. And the pampering that had made them feel like royalty was completely missing from the Scots' style.

But none of those little personal letdowns showed on the curling ice. They led through most of the tournament. At the end they lost a key game putting themselves in a three-way tie for first place and in the best possible spot for playoff action. They played the less power-ful American team and watched the Danes and Swedes battle it out.

Al was his usual controlled, calm self throughout, but Lang was far more intense, far more fretful than his team had ever seen him before. "Nobody could have been more uptight about winning than Rick," remembers Perroud. "He kept telling us how it would taint the Brier win if we lost."

Somewhere in all of them, Lang's nervousness struck a chord. They knew they had stolen the Brier; they didn't want to let Canada down and lose the world championship. The memory of Pat Ryan's skill was still fresh.

The magician in Hackner came to life at the end of the long week. In the semi-final and final he curled lights out and showed why he had, with one incredible shot, won the Brier. The final against the dreaded Swedish rink of Stefan Hasselborg and his corn brooms was vintage Hackner. He didn't fuss about the debris on the ice, as Werenich would have. His concentration was perfect as his team used the wide-angled brushes he and John Bubbs's rink had dreamed up in a hot tub in Saskatoon a couple of years before. For a year he hadn't lost a game against corn brooms, using the wide brush.

He calmly waited for his chance. It came in the third end when he scored three. After that the result was never in doubt.

Afterwards Lang explained that the 1985 win was sweeter because they had struggled so much. But the 1982 was "much more of an accomplishment," he explained to freelance curling journalist Gerry Campbell. "I think back to '82 where we started out by saying we wanted to win the Silver Broom and we stayed on top of our game the whole year."

Tetley and Perroud remember the wild party the night they won in Scotland. It lasted all night and in the morning they headed straight to the airport, where they were seated in the nose of the plane and given the royal treatment. The media met them in Toronto, and at home in Thunder Bay there was a huge parade with 10,000 people and Hackner waving from an open car, like the conquering hero he was, to his hometown fans.

The obvious cracks in the team were papered over by their unex-pected success. It's amusing to read Hackner's cautionary words about how they were going to husband their powers the next year and not burn themselves out by going to too many bonspiels, as they had in 1982.

Heart and head have trouble sometimes getting in sync and that's
what happened the next year with the Hackner team. In the end they
lost out in the district playdowns and everybody felt a sense of relief
as they disbanded the team.

But in between that triumphant moment, when they sat as celebri-
ties in the nose of the plane, winging their way home to the adoring
fans and the media in Canada, and the dismal, quiet break-up a year
later, there was a very rough patch of road to navigate for the new
world champions.

Now, when the urgency of their goal was gone and the Great
Manitou had retreated a bit from watching over them, the personal
differences came to the fore. Already at the playdowns in 1985 Tetley
had taken on his hero, but "only in jest," he explains. He and
Perroud were trying to sleep in the room adjoining Hackner and
Lang's Party Central. Hackner's ubiquitous ghetto blaster raged
beside them. Tetley remembers it was four in the morning when he
finally banged on the wall and shouted, "Give it a rest, Hack. Go to
bed."

Ten months, a Brier and a world championship later, he would be
less diplomatic. There are various versions of what happened at the
Bessborough Classic in 1986, but the way Tetley remembers it, he
finally lost patience with his skip. "Even Rick was sick of going to
bonspiels, getting piss-drunk and losing. Saskatoon was a triple
knockout and Al was hammered. We were out after four games. I
didn't think it was fair. I was giving up my time, my year at school."
(Both Tetley and Perroud had reduced their course load at Lakehead
University so they would be freer to go to bonspiels or pursue any
business opportunities their agent turned up.)

Tetley's angry rebuke of Hackner went something like: "It's all
right, Al; at least I'm doing something with my life." Hackner's
withering reply is unknown, but it was obvious that from that
moment the team was over.

Tetley was also champing at the bit, not only to reform the skip,
but also to run the team's business. "I thought maybe I could do a
better job," he explains.

Hackner, on the other hand, wanted Tetley to back off in every
area. He didn't appreciate his unsolicited suggestions on which shot
to play; he didn't want the 22-year-old business student's advice on
how to handle their business; and he most particularly didn't want
any advice on how to live his life.

"As soon as we started to dictate," Tet remembers, "he'd rebel and go the other way."

Hackner remembers a year of bickering and interfering that finally got him so angry he told Lang he was through. "I'm not curling with that guy [Tetley] again. Nobody will ever make me that mad on the curling sheet again," he vowed. "That's not the way curling is supposed to be."

Lang's advice was to give his head a shake and get on with the game. But he must have known that despite the group's talent and potential to win big again and again, that chapter was ending.

Lang was the agent who gave Tetley his walking papers. But they hadn't anticipated that Perroud, who was very quiet and "knew his place," would go with his long-time friend.

"I was disappointed when he said he was sticking with Ian," says Al. "It's too bad we split up. When you look back we had a good team: even when we were grouching at each other we were winning spiels."

Perroud remembers feeling burned out. Because they were champions, everybody they faced played a little above themselves. There was never an easy game. There were spiels, parties, social obligations and, under the surface, constant tension on the team. Perroud kept dropping courses at university, trying to manage all the demands. "I'd never trade the experience," he says now, "but it did wear a little thin." When Ian was cut, Pat knew it was time for him to go too.

After their big win in Glasgow, Al had found them an agent, Frank Caputo, a Sault Ste. Marie lawyer. Caputo remembers how, when he first talked to them, the sky had seemed the limit. Al was 30 and he'd already won two world championships. He'd played in four of the last six Brier finals and won two of them. Surely there would be enough income in endorsements and other business to secure Al's future. But the rosy future depended on one thing—they had to keep winning.

Curling, Caputo quickly found out, is a difficult sell. But if an athlete is so clearly the top of the field, so absolutely outstanding, he or she steps onto another plateau of marketability—no matter what the sport. This is the scenario Caputo expected. He didn't know curling, but looking at Al's record, it seemed plausible to expect continued greatness.

Through the 1985-86 season he watched in dismay as the team

slowly came apart and they lost when they should have won. He remembers his surprise at the atmosphere at curling bonspiels. "I was used to professional hockey," he says. "You know how competitive that can be. They like to drink and party too, but they pick their moments. Never in the Stanley Cup finals."

Curling, where the partying continues, however high the stakes, baffled him, but he didn't blame the partying for the team's lack of success. "Al won two world championships living that lifestyle," he points out. Still, after he'd negotiated a few endorsement deals with curling suppliers, there was little for an agent to do unless the team suddenly took off into the history and record books. And by the 1986-87 season he saw clearly that was not going to happen.

Al Hackner had stepped off the glory train. Although there would be other teams and two other Brier appearances he would never again—at least in the 1980s—make it back to the finals.

Part of the reason was loss of desire. When he signed on, Caputo believed they were gung-ho to roll up the kind of records curling had never seen before. And maybe they thought so too. But the daily dedication and commitment it required was beyond them. Maybe if the prize had been bigger or the rewards automatic, as they are in golf or tennis or any of the pro sports, it might have been easier. But in curling, where you win a cup and a crest for being the best in the country and a silver tray for being the best in the world, it's hard to stay motivated.

Hackner, who used to be legendary for his ability to concentrate, began to find his attention wandering on the curling sheet. Lang, too, who had been consumed by a desire to win since he was 14, began to find other things that mattered a great deal.

In January 1986 both Al and Rick became fathers for the first time. Since then both families have had a second child. The universe changed forever for both of them. The purity of their drive was diluted.

And as their intensity dissipated a little, it became increasingly hard to find a good front end that would trust Al implicitly and keep its distance. Even Rick, who had always handled Al and his tendency to excess with aplomb, began to be a little critical. He noticed that Hack's recuperative powers weren't what they had been, and he was a little impatient that Al chose not to notice.

Rick had always been the moderating influence, the one guy who could tell Al it was time to leave. Now, with a wife and family responsibilities, he performed the role with less enthusiasm, less patience and ultimately less skill.

"He was getting hyper too, just like Ian had been," remembers Margaret Hackner. Lang had always been positive and upbeat on the sheet, but as the losses piled up after 1986, his comments were more critical, more negative. Al couldn't understand why his long-time friend had stopped trusting him after they had won two world championships together. He was alternately angry and hurt. Inevitably he began to lose confidence, to start second-guessing himself in a destructive way.

Margaret remembers the Chicoutimi Brier as the personal nadir in Al's seven Brier experiences. Before they began play, Rick and Jim Adams chartered a plane to Fredericton, New Brunswick, where their wives were playing in the final of the Scott Tournament of Hearts.

After witnessing that comfortable 11-4 rout, they came back to their own dismal reality.

Again there was dissension on the team. Hackner seemed vague. His laserlike concentration was on holiday. Rick was always prodding him to "get in the game." Doug Smith, their new lead, was always marching down the ice to give unsolicited advice about everything. Al's usual cool had deserted him along with his concentration. He was having trouble containing his fury at their votes of non-confidence. "You could see it in his face," says Margaret. "He sure wasn't the Iceman then."

After each game, instead of having a team meeting and trying to work out their problems, Al would either blow up or more often bottle up his anger and frustration and head off to party. Margaret knows that's his usual reaction to emotional roadblocks and she also knows it only makes matters worse, but there was little she could do. The next day Hackner's team would be more angry and more critical, and the skip would have more trouble concentrating.

In the end they finished the Brier in fifth place. It was the first time Hackner had made it to the Brier and not played in the final. With a bleak 5-6 record, the team split forever.

"Al and I will never curl again together," says Lang now. "Anything less than a double world championship would be a failure."

"Failure" isn't such a big word in Hackner's lexicon. "We might curl together again," he says. "It won't be for a few years though." He could be thinking of a seniors' competition tour which, according to the CCA, may be on the edge of an explosion similar to Masters' golf.

Although Hackner and Lang are still casual friends, the downside of their mutual dependence has weakened their friendship. And the split, however desirable and amicable, seems to have had devastating effects on their curling lives. Rick didn't curl competitively in 1989; he looked after the family while his wife Lorraine went on the championship trail as third on Heather Houston's Team Canada rink.

Hackner continued to curl but gave up his daily practising. "Miraculously," he says, he was back in the Brier in 1989 with a new third (his second's twin brother, Bill Adams) and a new lead, Johnny Salo, whom he'd cut from the 1980 team 10 years before. But the 1989 season was very patchy, just like Hackner's play. "I began to believe I'd lost it," he remembers. He'd have one good day mixed in with half a dozen bad ones. For example, on the first day of the playdowns he was curling 50 percent, but by the end of the week he was good enough to win the right to represent Northern Ontario again.

He showed up at the 1989 Brier in Saskatoon half-convinced he shouldn't be there. Nothing in the week that followed changed his mind. "After the first few games I said to my team, 'We aren't going to win anything here. We may as well have a good time.' I was awful, awful, awful."

He flinches when he remembers the embarrassment. For the first time in his life, he'd let the rock go and have no idea where it was going. There was no way out. "In a bonspiel when you're playing bad, they let you go home after three losses. Here they keep dragging you back again," he told the reporters who swarmed over his misery. He remembers it as "torture." Even in the last game, he was counting the ends before he could shake hands and head to the Patch.

He couldn't even take the heat off by turning the skipping duties over to his third, Billy Adams, the wild man with the shoulder-length hair. Hackner, in his sixth appearance as skip, had to win only four games to become the winningest skip in Brier history. Turning over the skipping duties would have been an insult to the fans who were waiting to see Ernie Richardson's 1964 record broken.

While other skips might have done that, for Hackner it would have been unthinkable. In the end he tied Richardson's record of 45 wins. But finishing in second-last spot with a miserable 3-8 record made the accomplishment bittersweet.

Besides, the journalists and just about everybody else were quick to criticize his sub-par performance and dismiss it as the after-effects of too much partying.

But if Hackner's curling career had proved anything, it was that he is a game competitor and an amateur in the truest sense of the word. After the Brier he played two local spiels and suddenly his touch came back. Now he believes the shoes his sponsor had given him with the anti-slip bars on the bottom might have caused the problem. As soon as he slipped on his old shoes everything seemed to click back into place.

And it appeared that his touch was back. Occasionally—even without practice and dedication—he could plug into the old magic. He was beaten out early in the playdowns in 1990, but he had his best money year ever, winning a comfortable $55,000. His seesaw fortunes took another dive in 1991 when he had what he describes as a "wishy-washy year." Again he dissolved his team. There was no moderation on the team. "Billy Adams was worse than me," he laughs. "I'm not used to telling my team we have to go. I didn't have the nerve and we ended up partying way too much."

In 1991 it was Rick Lang who roared back with the old competitive fires blazing. This time he was skipping. He doesn't like either the pressure or the attention that goes with skipping, but he "needed a challenge," so he put together a team that he believed could be "the best in Thunder Bay."

He no longer thinks in the grandiose world-beater terms he did when he was 25, but the results were just about as good. The team which included an old rival, Scott Henderson, at third and Ian Tetley's older brother Ross at second made it to the tie breakers of the Brier with a 7-4 record. But he knows he has leapt back on the treadmill. "Next year, for this team to be successful, we have to make it to the finals," he says with a grimace.

Neither Lang nor Hackner mentions personal rivalry as a motivator, but clearly part of their image of success is besting their old partner.

Al is wrestling with his own demons. The team he put together for 1991-92 includes, at third, a 49-year-old perennial contender from Thunder Bay named Larry Pineau. "I respect him as a curler and as a man," says Hack. "He likes a good time, but he's not the type to be out boozing all night and I won't jeopardize his year by doing that either."

He knows that to win he has to rein in the party animal in his soul and practise more. Both are difficult to manage. "I don't have the energy to practise any more, but I know I have to. Sometimes, even when I go down to the curling club to practise, I end up having a couple of beers with my friends and going home without throwing a single rock. I have to realize if I'm not willing to work at it I can't win.

"I always think about the day when I lose it. I know I won't go around chasing bonspiels when I'm not qualifying. Even now, sometimes, my friends and I go into little out-of-town bonspiels and play for a TV set or something. I won't take my regular team, that wouldn't be fair, but we can have a little fun doing that."

It's not yet clear whether the Iceman will stand by benignly and watch himself gradually melt into mediocrity in curling. Certainly there are curlers who have refused to bend, who keep at the game they love with discipline and enthusiasm. "I find what Werenich and Lukowich are doing inspirational. I don't know if I could do that or not. I'd like to go to the Brier and curl competitively, but that burning desire to win the world championship is not there any more."

But he knows one thing: he isn't about to give up either curling or the party life. "I can't see me quitting curling ever. But I couldn't stand going out, losing and not partying. At least if you have a good time, you've got something from the experience.

"I like to be sociable and I like to win. There's a fine line there."

And it's that fine line that the Iceman now has to find.

7

RUSS HOWARD
The Bull Moose Roars

FOR AL HACKNER the social side of curling is as seductive as a siren's song. And while Hackner, like Ulysses, figures out ingenious ways to restrain himself from yielding to the seduction while still relishing the sweetness of the song, another Ontario world curling champion watches in disbelief.

Russ Howard is 35, a couple of years younger than Hackner. He's the conventional hometown hero. Handsome and athletically gifted, he has perfect teeth, a great smile and a calm and happy marriage to his high-school sweetheart. But for all his natural assets he has a way of making his competitors grit their teeth.

Why this is so is one of those funny questions that can't be satisfactorily answered. It would be simple to label the feeling "jealousy," except that those whom Howard annoys would deny it vehemently.

The truth is he doesn't quite fit in. He's too guarded, too sensitive, too self-absorbed to be one of the good old boys. And although he senses some resentment from the other curlers, he's not interested enough in their attitudes to brood about it or go out of his way to court favour. He gets from them a grudging respect and that's about all he wants.

The emotional centre of his life is elsewhere—with his wife, Wendy, and two children, Steven and Ashley. And then there's the Howard clan. Russ's younger brother, Glenn, is his third, and his curling alter ego. And his parents, Barbara and Bill, are still a very big part of his life. When Bill Howard was the icemaker at the Midland Curling Club, his sons were the star attractions. But Bill had an argument with the club management, and before they knew it they'd lost not only their icemaker but their star team as well. When the chips are down, the Howards know exactly where their loyalties lie.

Glenn Howard, six years younger than Russ, is one of the smoothest thirds on the globe. He's even more handsome, more full-toothed, and more unassailable than his brother. And out there in the elite circles of Canadian curling, he's regarded with even more suspicion.

For the Howards the social side of curling is irrelevant. Competitive curling is about winning, not about socializing. "It just isn't me," says Russ finally when pushed to explain. "One guy I really like in curling is Rick Lang. I'd love to sit down and have a drink with him. But," he adds, "I don't go looking for the guy."

The unwritten code that rules the lives of curlers like Hackner and Werenich simply doesn't matter to Howard. It's an uncomfortable straitjacket he refuses to don.

At the 1991 Ontario Tankard in Owen Sound Howard and Werenich faced each other in the final game of the round robin. At stake was first place and a bye to the final game on Sunday. It was the normal nail-biter. By the 10th end it looked as if Eddie was a shoo-in. He was up 4-3 with last rock. With his final stone he faced two unprotected Howard rocks in the house. A routine hit and stick close to the button would win the game. For many that would be a pressure shot, but it's the kind of move Werenich has built his reputation on.

Then Luck intervened. The rock was scarcely out of the Wrench's hand when it picked something and slid unceremoniously into the boards. Both Howards immediately raised their arms in triumph as Eddie's misfortune gave them the game.

Later a dispirited Werenich went on to lose the semi-final to Kirk Ziola, and the defending world champion abruptly found himself making plans to go to the Brier as a spectator. Howard continued his streak and was soon on his way to the Labatt Brier for the fifth time in 12 years.

But whatever his success, that little mis-step in the Ontario Tankard, that jubilation at another's misfortune, contravened the code and had to be paid for. The competitive curlers were harsh in their judgments. Werenich complained out loud, calling Howard and his team a "classless bunch of guys" at a press conference in the week leading up to the Brier. He went on to say that if anyone on his team breached etiquette so blatantly he would be looking for a new team next year.

Werenich, of course, was the most outspoken, but other curlers agreed, quietly shaking their heads and marvelling at how little the Penetang rink seemed to know about how to act.

The year before, in the 1990 Ontario zone playdowns, Wayne Middaugh, Howard's young second, contravened the code in another way. He smashed a chair in fury in the locker room after his team was eliminated. His outburst earned him a stern warning from John McCrae of the Ontario Curling Association, and from the rest of the more sedate curling fraternity more headshaking.

But Russ Howard sees no advantage in a lemminglike run off a cliff simply because the code decrees that's what one does. For him the rules are one of the conditions of the game. If you can use them in your favour, that's another way to shave down your opposition. Let less competitive souls rely heavily on the spirit rather than the letter of the law, Russ and Glenn take their luck where they find it.

But if this occasionally irritates the competition, it has no impact on the "Russomaniacs," as the press has dubbed the Howard fans. If Werenich with his acid tongue and bitter grudges wears the black hat of Ontario curling, Howard is resolutely cast in the white headgear. Some fans love his cleancut image, his technically perfect delivery, and his ferocious competitiveness expressed by a roar in the rink that outdoes the bull moose on the prowl.

That roar, which he doesn't know he's emitting, is Russ Howard at his most abandoned. Even then he's usually coiffed and perfect, but nothing like the casual perfectionist you see if you catch him at Brooklea Country Club in Midland, Ontario. It's the hottest day of the summer and the two staples in the club house are hot tempers and cold beer. Russ indulges in neither. He's busy but unflappable. Watch him selling in the pro shop (which he owns) or fielding queries from a Big Brothers' luncheon. What you see is red-headed, open-faced affability at work. There's plenty of charm here, but it's parcelled out carefully, on his terms. And if at Avonlea you hear softness and affection in the voices of the people who want Eddie Werenich's attention, here you hear respect and deference as people approach Howard.

He looks every inch a golfer with his three-button, pastel golf shirt and pleated slacks. It's the way he's looked and probably acted from the time he was a preteen starting to work seriously on his golf game. It all happened right here at Brooklea, where his father now manages the golf operation and Russ is head pro. The job's been his since he was 23 in 1979, but it was only after he won the world curling championship in 1987 that he became such a hot ticket in southern Ontario golf. Brooklea's business went up almost 50 percent, and although there may have been other factors involved, having a world champion curler as head pro was certainly a key element.

"That Brier and world championship changed my life completely," he says now, still a little incredulously. Winning had meant everything to him before, but he hadn't thought much about the rewards. In the purest sense he had wanted to win for the sake of winning. That it would mean money in his pocket, overseas travel and immense, if brief, celebrity was surprising and a little unnerving. Everything, including Russ Howard, changed, and his desire to win would never be as uncluttered again. "I'm more sentimental about the money now," he says, as he tries to identify and explain the ways he has changed.

The changes wouldn't be terrifically obvious to people who had known him in high school. He looks older but otherwise very much the same as he did then. He was never gangly, awkward or pimply. He never owned a pair of jeans, never grew his hair long. He never played pinball or pool or hung out at the plaza.

It's a different world if you grow up at a golf course," he explains. "I've looked like a golfer all my life." But he knows that doesn't really explain a thing, and when he thinks about it he wonders too why the tyranny of the group never got to him.

He was always close to his parents, but they didn't demand conformity; he was free to choose. But as he looked around, he found their life, which focused on the curling club in winter and the golf course in summer, far more appealing than the other options available. When it came time to spread his wings a little, he wasn't interested in going too far from home. He picked his own route, and if the wildness and excess of youth were missing, that was his choice.

He played hockey and was a perennial all-star, but even then he wasn't in the mainstream. And at 16, when he chose curling over hockey, the rest of the team probably didn't go into a tailspin as it did when Al Hackner quit. Howard was good, competitive and a fine natural athlete, but he wasn't the soul of the team. In fact, expressions like "soul of the team" mystify him a little. He's not really sure a team has a soul.

One of the most curious chapters of his young life was his flirtation with golf. He was good. Damn good. The best in Simcoe

County for sure, maybe the best in southern Ontario. But astonishingly, he has no idea how much farther he would have had to go before he met his match; he never went looking. He never entered a national tournament. He didn't need to know if he was the best in the country in his age group.

"When I got out of school I was absolutely the best golfer in Midland, so I guess I was content," he says now. But he wonders himself what held him back from testing himself against other fine golfers. "Maybe it was the fear of failing. Maybe deep down I didn't think I was good enough. I don't know."

But even though Russ says he's a little embarrassed by his lackadaisical approach to golf as a kid, he's still the same. He regularly shoots under 70 but he doesn't go looking for a CPGA card, an item that would give him more clout as a golf pro. His reluctance surprises even his brother Glenn, who is similar in temperament. "I guess maybe he was a tad insecure when he was a kid, but I ask myself now why he doesn't go after it."

Russ talks about realistic expectations. "Sometimes I'm almost too realistic. I don't kid myself: 68 on my own course is not 68 on Augusta Downs. I might shoot 77 at the Masters and it might make me a hell of a golfer but it won't make me any money."

So now, although he has no idea how far he might have gone, he lives with the poignancy of knowing that at 17 he was one stroke shy of the world record for 18 holes. He shot 61 at a time when the Guinness Book of World Records pegged the record at 60.

"You have to remember it was my own course, which is 400 yards shorter than the regulation 5,000 yards," he says firmly. After a few seconds' silence he continues in a softer voice, "But still, 400 yards over 18 holes isn't much..."

At the time, recruiters with golf scholarships to big American universities stuffed in their pockets were hovering around. But Howard chose instead to study journalism at Georgian College in Barrie, just down the road from his hometown. "I didn't want to go too far from home, from my Mom's cooking," he explains with a dismissive chuckle.

So the idea of life in the fast lane of the PGA tour remains just a pleasant daydream, one that still crops up now and then when he's doing his inventory of might-have-beens. "I sometimes think of the seniors tour," he says. "I could get a bit more serious about golf. By the time I'm 50, Jack Nicklaus will be over 65 and I'll beat him.

After all, I never thought I'd be a world champion in curling either."

Back in high school his loves were curling and golf, but he worked harder and was probably slightly better at golf. Even then he had the mechanically perfect rock delivery that the Japanese are now so anxious to learn from him. It was the legacy of his father Bill's careful, precise teaching. The family loves sports—a great aunt, Jean Thompson, even competed in the 1928 Olympics. Bill Howard managed a grocery store for years, but when he took early retirement his real avocation showed. Now 68, he's been an icemaker, owned a driving range and managed both curling and golf clubs.

The heritage showed early. Russ was a phenom in high-school curling. In grade nine he made it as second on the school curling team. His teammates were 18-year-olds in grade 13. In the car on the way to the provincial final the coach decided that Russ at 13 was their best bet and should take over as skip. It was his initiation into the wonders of skipping and he lost all three games.

But the next year he was back again skipping a new team. They finished second in the Ontario juniors. The year was 1972, his opponent, Dave Merklinger. For both boys it was an auspicious beginning to a lifelong rivalry.

That second-place finish and a championship later in an Ontario high-school tournament were the highlights of Howard's high-school curling career. When he moved on to community college he played everything, including badminton and football, but it was his prowess in curling and golf that earned him a school letter and the distinction of being Athlete of the Year. He remembers with a laugh how the 6′8″ basketball players, the football players and the other "real" athletes in the school used to razz him for his old men's sports. It didn't matter a whit. He'd taken that heat since he was 13. Besides, he'd never minded the outsider's role, and if the truth were known these games of control, touch and finesse were infinitely more satisfying than the rough and tumble of more physical sports.

But school continued to be a burden. Glenn had adapted, treating school as one more arena in which to compete, but Russ balked at what he considered the pointlessness of the endeavour. He saw no practical reason to know history or many of the other subjects, and even in journalism school he struggled—especially when he saw so many of his classmates take jobs at small newspapers or radio stations that offered barely a living wage.

He remembers dropping in at Brooklea on his way home from Georgian College after graduation. He came away happy. He'd accepted a job for the season as a greenskeeper. "I think I probably needed some quick cash," he remembers. But of course a golf-course job is also a natural to combine with the life of a competitive curler. After all, there are very few jobs in journalism that give you the winters off.

He was working on the golf course for a living but curling was already centre-stage in his competitive life. Just before graduating as a 21-year-old college student he'd been the youngest skip in the Ontario Tankard. And although he didn't know it yet, he'd already taken the first few steps on the road to the world championship 10 years later.

His lead on that team was Kent Carstairs, an accountant who had taken up curling the year before to get a little exercise. Carstairs was a natural—both smart and athletic—and the two became fast friends even though Carstairs was a few years older. When Russ and Wendy were married four years later, Carstairs was best man.

The 1977 Tankard showed Russ and Kent how much they had to learn. They were completely unseasoned and slightly in awe when they faced Howard's curling hero, Paul Savage. So far they had coasted on shotmaking ability, but now they found their strategy woefully lacking. "They were throwing up rocks in front and I thought they were just lousy curlers," laughs Howard. "Our strategy just killed us."

But this was their chance to learn "big time" and they took it. By the time they got back to the provincials again, in 1980, they were the powerhouse and others had to stand aside.

They went on to the infamous Calgary Brier as unconsidered upstarts. Nothing they did that week changed opinions very much. As it turned out, the real action was taking place outside of Howard's realm of experience anyway. He was only 24, but he had no role to play in the young men's drinking and partying sweepstakes that Paul Gowsell, Al Hackner and others were conducting off ice. Nor did he have their precision and magic on ice either.

While Gowsell and Hackner finished tied for second in the round robin with 8-3 records, Howard finished fifth and out of the playoffs with 5-6. But Howard was learning every time out, playing catch-up because he'd never had the level of competition the others had grown up with. While Hackner had left Nipigon to find the competition he needed to polish his game, Howard had stuck close to home. Now he had to turn up the jets on his game in the midst of a national championship and the adjustment was a little more than he could manage—at least in 1980.

But if he was disappointed when he measured himself against Hackner and Gowsell, he wasn't discouraged. And in the long run Howard's approach showed some clear advantages. While Gowsell's shooting star was brighter and much flashier than Howard's little candle, it was also much briefer. In 1980 Hackner was a colourful aurora borealis that put on an astounding show through the first half of the decade. But in the second half the lights faded to a twinkle, while the small candle of Howard's skill in 1980 grew and grew until by 1987 it was a conflagration capable of winning the world. Then Howard stood at the pinnacle in a spotlight far brighter than either of his contemporaries.

The most important twist on Howard's upward spiral was the addition of his brother Glenn at third. By the time Russ made his second Brier appearance in 1986, Glenn Howard, his adoring younger brother, was at his side. The two are near clones. Glenn is two inches taller, 20 pounds heavier and six years younger, but in appearance and character they are uncannily similar.

In most things Glenn follows the path struck by his elder brother. He too is a fine golfer. He too ignored the lure of the United States and stayed close to home for his post-secondary education. He was a more serious and committed student than his brother but he didn't like it much. "The first few months of university were pretty rough," he admits. "Partly it was homesickness."

In curling his career has paralleled his elder brother's too. As a teenager, he skipped a junior team that came second in the province just as Russ had six years earlier. In university other curlers were in awe of his skill. He was pegged as a definite comer on the national curling scene.

Of the two it was very clear the elder brother would be the leader. "My dream was always to play third for Russ," explains Glenn. "In every sport he had a six-year jump on me." But even now, when his curling ability has caught up with his elder brother's, he still—in most cases—defers to his experience. "In the '88-'89 season we were struggling and Russ felt he was losing some control. He even asked me if I wanted to skip. But I want no part of that," Glenn says emphatically.

There are subtle differences between the two men. "I'm competitive when I have to be," explains Glenn. "Russ wants to win at everything he does."

Russ is more controlled and less likely to blow up when something bothers him. When Ed Werenich, deeply into his mind games, "bodychecked" Glenn at a provincial championship in 1988 because he was in the way when Werenich was trying to sweep after a shot had crossed the T-line, The Wrench picked his quarry wisely.

"He wanted to upset him, throw him off his game," says Russ grimly. "And to tell you the truth it worked. But I take it as a compliment. There aren't many teams Ed Werenich has to use those tactics with to win a game."

But when 21-year-old Glenn first started playing on his brother's team, there was still a big gap between their levels of skill, and neither knew if Glenn would ever be the world-class curler Russ had developed into. In those days, too, the six-year age difference meant a correspondingly large social gap as well.

So they were on a mission of discovery in 1983 when they started together. For Glenn, who was still in university, it meant putting aside the books for the weekend and travelling to meet the team at the bonspiel. Practice was out of the question. The time commitment was already extravagant for a university student.

Their bonspiel record was undistinguished, but in both 1983 and 1984 they seemed to jell in time for the playdowns. Both years they made it to the provincials, lost out in the tie-breakers and watched Ed Werenich waltz away with all the marbles.

And after he had finished off all comers in Ontario, Werenich didn't stop. He went on to win the Brier and the Silver Broom in 1983 and nearly took the Brier again in 1984. The Howards watched in amazement. They had played the Dream Team; they knew that these legendary heroes of the Toronto media had not only chinks in their armour but also, occasionally, feet of clay. Werenich's success taught them they were simmering close to the top of the world of curling.

Glenn longed for the end of his schooling so that he would have the time he needed to devote to practice. In 1985, with Glenn very busy in fourth year and a new team member, Tim Belcourt, they came within a game of making it to the provincials. If they were looking for signs in the tea leaves they were all there.

As soon as Glenn finished university he headed home to live with his folks and devote himself more fully to curling. He had no specific career path in mind, although he was toying with the idea of teaching. He'd been accepted at teacher's college and the job appealed to him, but there were significant drawbacks for his curling career. It would mean another year of schooling and a lifetime of awkward moments when he needed time off for bonspiels or playdowns. He had teacher friends who had either been fired or demoted for calling in sick when they had to go off for curling. Putting himself into that kind of jeopardy was not an appealing thought. And the only absolute about his future plans was that he wanted to curl.

Enter Brewer's Retail. He was offered a job in their management-training program. At first he saw it as a stopgap measure, something that would allow him to "keep all the doors open." But he liked it. The money was good and so were the opportunities. It wasn't long before the idea of teaching had faded to the status of one more road not taken. The beauty of working in a beer store in Ontario's cottage country is that the summers are hectic but the winters are relatively slow. Although not quite as seasonal as being a golf pro, the beer store certainly had advantages for a competitive curler. Glenn insists he has never regretted not using his environmental studies degree.

And so they began the 1986 season with very high hopes. Glenn was practising as fervently as Russ. Their new second, Tim Belcourt, 24, came complete with an upbeat personality and tremendous confidence in Russ. At the end of the 1985 season he'd played a bonspiel with them in Parry Sound and they'd won handily. They felt he was the shot in the arm they all needed to spark them to the next plateau. This time they wouldn't be turned back at the provincials. This time they would beat Werenich and his—by now slightly tattered—Dream Team.

But once again as November unfolded they found themselves very slow off the mark. As usual the ice in their curling rink in Penetanguishene, a small tourist centre on Georgian Bay 185 kilometres north of Toronto, went in a month later than it did in the bigger centres. And as usual the various work schedules of their team meant they couldn't make more than half of the 9 or 10 bonspiels before Christmas that the competition usually played.

By the time they got to the playdowns they felt they were starting to cook, but they knew they needed to turn up the heat a bit. Russ and Glenn practised together twice a week now, using a rule Russ invented that has since been called the "Moncton Rule" because it was first used in competition in the Moncton 100 bonspiel in 1990.

The rule prohibits leads from peeling, and Russ devised it so he and Glenn would have to play more finesse shots. They knew Werenich with his exceptional touch on the rock was their chief opposition.

But their dreams of world domination were immediately dashed. They were beaten in Simcoe County. Unless they could make it in through the much more difficult Challenge Round, they were finished. But just when hope had faded they seemed to catch fire.

Glenn now confides that as he watched their play go from good to extraordinary, he felt they were destined to win. Even in the tie-breaker against Larry Snow, when lead Kent Carstairs bumped an opposing rock, they were allowed to keep their win. The officials ruled the accidental hit didn't significantly alter anything, basing their ruling on the fact that Glenn thought it was good because he raised his arm before the guard was burned. This controversial ruling had people shaking their heads long after the Howards had gone on to much greater things.

After that, they harnessed their momentum to down Wayne Tallon in the final and roar into the Brier. "In that final, I think I curled the best game of my life to that point, 94 percent," remembers Glenn.

Many young teams are outfoxed by the veterans when they get to the Brier, but the Howards were different. First they were picked by TSN commentator Ray Turnbull as a dark horse in the tournament. For Glenn it was pretty heady stuff. He was only 24 and now he was returning to Kitchener-Waterloo, where he had graduated from university only a few months before, as part of a team to watch in the national championship. It went beyond his wildest dreams. But he stayed inside the very comfortable cocoon of his brother's team and concentrated on his game.

And as the games rolled by they suddenly found themselves 9-2 and tied with Ed Lukowich for first place. "We were bouncing off the walls," Glenn remembers. "There haven't been too many first-time winners. Everybody is so in awe of the Brier."

In the final against Cool Hand Luke, Russ looked every inch a champion until the ninth end, when he took a little too much ice and missed a hit and stick. There was no time left to recoup the error, and Luke won it all with a wide-open draw to the four-foot in his final shot of the tenth end.

As they trooped off the ice, downcast but far from demoralized, Carstairs quipped: "Well there goes $100,000." It was intended as a bit of outlandish overstatement at the time, but now Russ believes the accountant on the team underestimated by 50 percent. A Brier win is worth about $200,000 to the winning team, Howard believes.

But that knowledge would have to wait—until the next year.

By the time the 1986-87 season opened, the Howards and their front end had got used to their elevated status as Brier finalists. They were serious contenders. They might be from a small town; they might be ignored by self-absorbed Toronto; but they would be there when the final reckoning was made, they felt certain.

"It was no fluke we were in the final," Glenn says. "Lukowich beat us because he curled 1 percent better on the statistics."

For Russ the goal was now crystal clear. He'd always been able to channel great energy into specific, clear goals, and now winning the Brier obsessed him. They all upped the intensity of their practice, but none as much as Russ.

Nobody had quite as much cause as he, either. The loss in the 1986 final hadn't seemed gargantuan at the time. But gradually as he endured a summer of constant questioning about what happened in the ninth end, he began to see it as a devastating failure. After he'd told and retold the story hundreds of times, he realized he never wanted to come so close again without winning. For your own mental health it's far better to lose in your club than to miss the championship by one spectacularly ordinary shot.

He tried to keep above it, but the critical edge to the questions, the implication that he had "choked" under pressure, kept him slightly unhinged. He couldn't wait for the competitive season to put it all behind him.

In 1987 they were a team on a mission. This time they didn't just suspect, this time they knew they could win. This time they would do whatever it took, and the edge in percentages would be in their favour.

Russ practised incessantly. Glenn was a close second and the others did what they could. But despite all their practice, all their good intentions, they got off to their traditional slow start. Again they lost in Simcoe County.

Would they call it quits for this year and try to correct things for next? Was it time for analysis and introspection?

Russ Howard is a stickler for perfection. He rarely goes into a slump, but when he does he lies awake nights going over and over his delivery until he finds the flaw. He's so careful about every nuance of his game that he still asks his brother after every single shot if he's on the broom. But for all his belief in analysis Russ did not think it would help them now. They needed to play. They'd gone so far the year before, he argued, they should explore every avenue to get back and do it again.

Once again they went into the Challenge Round as the court of last resort. And once again they battled through unscathed and wound up winning the province.

In some ways the Brier in Edmonton was a curler's delight—a sold-out Northlands AgriCom, and enough heroes and heroics for everyone's taste. But Russ Howard's was the team of destiny. Everything went their way and they finished the round robin at 9-2 with a bye to the final. The two coasts battled it out in the semi-final but Bernie Sparkes of British Columbia, using straw brooms, finally bushwhacked Mark Noseworthy and his Cinderella team from Newfoundland 8-6.

In the final for the first few ends Howard's team was forced to watch the unfamiliar sight of their skip struggling. They were curling well and keeping him in the game but they were having trouble with Sparkes's straw. "We weren't used to it and we started to forget what it does," remembers Glenn.

But somewhere in the middle of the game Russ seemed to come to life with a jolt and realize that his most cherished dream was on the line. By the seventh end they were tied four apiece and Russ and Bernie were playing tug-of-war with the debris from the straw. It was helping the rocks curl, but Sparkes was trying to throw his rocks and clear the path in such a way that the Ontarians couldn't use it. Russ, with a face as dark as a thundercloud, took his push broom and shoved it back on. They went up two in the eighth and Sparkes came back with three in the ninth. But the Howard rink was here for the kill and when the chaff settled after the tenth end, they had themselves a five-ender. Final score 11-7. Television ratings showed 4.5 million watched the showdown.

It was a controversial win, but that didn't matter an iota to the brothers from Midland. Pictures show Glenn leaping almost four feet into the air in absolute, unfettered happiness. The dream of a lifetime had come true and it was all they had hoped and more.

Now all they had to do was beg, borrow or buy a little more time off their jobs and dig up enough money to fly their wives to

Vancouver, and the opportunity to defend Canada in the world championships would be theirs.

It wasn't easy, but three weeks later there they were in Sparkes's home province at BC Place with the red maple leaf on their backs, defending the world championship Ed Lukowich had won for Canada in 1986. Maybe it was the irony of the location, maybe it was the first turn on the world stage, or maybe it was simply the horrid conditions, but the rink from the Penetang Curling Club did not—at first at least—look as if they belonged in the championship. They lost their first game to France. "The first time Canada has lost to France in the history of curling," says Glenn ruefully.

But after the first loss they pulled together and zeroed in, as they had so many times that season. They went on to finish the round robin second to veteran Norwegian and world champ Eigil Ramsfjell. But in 1987 Ramsfjell was vulnerable. He allowed himself to be knocked out in the semis by Rodger Schmidt, a Canadian playing in West Germany. Schmidt's win set up a seesaw final that rocked and rolled until the ninth end, when Schmidt took one and handed Howard the hammer coming home. It was a fatal error. Russ pulled off another spectacular five-ender finish. The rink that had been knocked out earlier in the season in regular play in their own country now stood astride the entire curling world.

The changes in their lives were quick and dramatic. First there were the automatic trips abroad. The team from small-town Ontario had never even been west to play in bonspiels before. Now they were on tap for an exhibition tour to Japan. They were being lined up for bonspiels in Switzerland, Germany and Scotland. Russ was suddenly sought after as an after-dinner speaker and the fees being discussed ranged as high as $700 for a few of his words of wisdom. Curling-supplies companies, even car dealerships, were coming up with sponsorship packages. It was a heady time, especially as the summer wore on and Russ began to see the advantages of being a celebrity. Receipts at the golf course skyrocketed as curling fans from far and wide came to play at Brooklea and shake the hand of the world champion. And there were no more questions about what happened in the ninth end in 1986.

For a team that had thought only of the prestige and satisfaction of winning the Labatt Brier, a team that was used to going all out in a bonspiel whether they were playing for a suit of clothes or a toaster, this was a revelation. And inevitably their dreams, some of them at least, began to take on a distinctly more golden hue.

In 1987 one more tier was added to the curling championships. The CCA held a playdown to determine who would represent Canada in the 1988 Olympics. The competition, held a few weeks after the world championship, was the finale of the rancorous $600,000 process of picking a team. The Howards were almost relieved when the torch was handed to Ed Lukowich. But they weren't the only ones who found it peculiar, if not absurd, to have one Canadian team win the world championship and another team—one that hadn't even made it out of their province to the Canadian championships—represent the country in the Olympics.

By this time they were all done in. In fact Glenn, who was also going through some personal problems at the time, wound up in hospital suffering from exhaustion. "We were mentally tired out," he explains. "Competing at that level is exhausting and then we had to go right back to work when we finished."

Fine, but as this amateur game gets more professional, more competitive and more demanding, the toll on the players gets higher. "Except for Pat Ryan, not one of the big names of the '80s has had a career," points out Rick Lang.

In Howard's case the toll was more on the team than on the skip. "Work almost gets in the way when you're competing like that," says Glenn. "I'd love to take two or three days off after a bonspiel or competition to settle down, but I can't."

Kent Carstairs had a responsible job as chief of the accounting department at a local seat-belt manufacturer. Tim Belcourt was working in a sports store and later opened his own. Whenever he needed time off, someone else had to be brought in to work his hours. For the others there were no replacements, and when they got back they were expected to buckle down and catch up without so much as a breather.

Only Russ could go home and have the luxury of time off to get geared up for the next competition. In the summer at the golf course he works long hours, but that makes up for a winter of free time.

It was clear from the beginning there would be stresses and strains in their world championship year. In November they headed off to Scotland, where they won the bonspiel and $11,000. Their all-expense-paid junket next whisked them to the Continent, where they toured Germany and Switzerland for a few days before they settled into more bonspiels.

Back home there were invitations for expense-paid jaunts to big-time western spiels that they had never been able to enter before. But eager as Russ was, they couldn't really cash in. Glenn had used up his two weeks' vacation time. Kent was already working on vacation weeks from several years down the road, and on the whole there was great pressure to stay home and keep their lives together. In January they even had to pass up the glories of Grindelwald.

In their championship year, a time when many teams dream of cashing in big, the Howard rink finished ninth on the Canadian Curling News' Gold Trail with $13,125. Even added on to the money they won in Europe it only totalled a little more than $20,000 in a year when Ed Lukowich won $101,250. Russ, who could have gone to every spiel, was beginning to champ at the bit a little.

But they were still focused on the playdowns, hoping to make their third Labatt Brier in as many years. As champions they had a bye to the provincial level but they were nervous. They didn't have a mea-suring stick to gauge how they were playing, and in the very first game of the round robin they had to face none other than their old nemesis, Ed Werenich, this year playing third on Paul Savage's rink.

Emotion ran high in that first game, especially after Eddie and Glenn got into their famous pushing match over sweeping after the T-line. When they met again in the final, the stage was set for a very tough grudge match.

Glenn blames himself for the loss.

The Howard rink had just come off a five-game winning streak and for the first seven ends managed to dominate the wily Savage. But Glenn inexplicably missed both of his shots in the seventh end and handed Savage a three-ender. They struggled back, but finally Savage, curling better than he had for years, drew to the four-foot in the 11th end to win.

It was the first February finish the Howard team had faced for years and it felt strange—especially because their expectations had been altered by their Brier and world championship wins.

By the next fall Russ's frustration from the year before had begun to bubble over. He knew the team had jobs and other commitments but he couldn't shake the feeling that he alone seemed completely dedicated to their success. And another problem had begun to crop up as well.

From the beginning he'd been the undisputed leader of the team. He often discussed a shot with Glenn before making the call, but that was usually just for confirmation. Now, however, things had shifted a little. The respect seemed to have dwindled as the team's stature on the world stage increased. They now questioned his judgment and he began to have attacks of self-doubt, wondering if they had lost faith in him.

Al Hackner has had the same problem with his teams. It's a debilitating feeling. Russ reacted by asking Glenn if he wanted to skip. The pressure, the responsibility, and the criticism were getting a little too much. Glenn was technically as good as he was and he seemed to be full of ideas. Why didn't he try skipping for a while?

Glenn dismissed the suggestion out of hand. He was not even slightly interested in taking over the control. And privately he marvelled that his brother would ever suggest such a thing. Russ was not one to talk much about his feelings but Glenn dismissed the whole conversation as "just talk."

But nothing improved, and Russ's talk now turned to taking a breather from curling. By the provincials, relations were a little strained on the team. Russ had been in favour of more commitment, more bonspiels and more practice. The others were pulling back a little. Privately Russ gave them a very slim chance of doing well in the playdowns. He believed they'd gone stale like so many other championship teams before them.

Russ admits he was a little surprised when this team, which he thought was stagnating before his eyes, made it through the conventional route and wound up at the provincials. He was even more surprised when they finished the round robin at 7-2 in a three-way tie for first place.

But the team that had seemed lucky so many times before now looked as if it was in for a spate of very bad luck. For the tie-breaker Glenn was in very rough shape. He believed he had food poisoning, but it turned out to be just a rather virulent case of flu. He played in the tie-breaker, but "I was dying ," he said. "I didn't play very well."

It wasn't until the very last moment that he decided to try to play. His decision postponed the heroism of their 50-year-old fifth man Larry Merkley for the next day.

Glenn's illness seemed to ignite Russ's competitive fires. Even though Glenn was out there going through the motions, Russ knew he was playing for both of them. He made some of the best shots he's ever made in competition, says Glenn. In the tenth end they were up one with their old rival Dave Merklinger sitting with a couple in the house. Russ was already into the swing for his last rock when, master of the touch game that he is, he felt something was on the 44-pound rock. It was too late to abort, but as he released it he jiggled it a bit and put a spin on it. The rock cruised down the ice excruciatingly slowly, spinning 10 or 15 times as it went. And it ended up shot rock and almost completely buried. Only outrageous skill and blind luck had kept them in the game. Now Merklinger had only one very tough chance to come back.

But Merk's luck was uniformly bad. As his rock passed the hogline it picked a hair and did a right turn into the boards. Game over.

Afterwards, in the dressing room they shared, Glenn overheard the Merklinger rink's dispirited conversation. He was still feeling miserable despite the win and was annoyed by their talk. He thought they were dismissing Russ's great shot as pure dumb luck and he took exception. Suddenly the two stars of "the roaring game" were living up to the sport's nickname with some very ungentlemanly shouting.

For the Howard rink there was one more tough game on the horizon. They still had to meet Werenich, Kawaja, Tetley and Perroud in the final. By this time Carstairs was also sick—in fact shaky, cold and weak enough to be admitted to hospital. Merkley was pressed into action to play in the final. The only rocks he'd thrown in more than a week were a perfunctory few at team practice sessions. Nobody had any idea how he would curl.

But they were on a surprising streak and nothing fazed them. At the end of a hard-fought game, Russ rose to the occasion and beat Eddie Werenich by stealing three. It was a sweet victory and Howard shed his earlier misgivings about his team. Now, in their third Brier in four years, they would show the world curling finesse at its best.

And so they did at the beginning of the week. It was an exceptional Brier in 1989. Five of the twelve contenders were Brier or world champions or both. Saskatoon was breaking records for the most spectators in history to attend a curling match. And Russ could feel his blood rising to the challenge.

But unfortunately his voice was another story. Howard's howl when he's in full flight, deeply intent on winning, has often been likened to the roar of a bull moose. The bellow that Howard insists he does not realize he's emitting is as close to abandon as the man gets.

Without it his game suffers. With the crowd going wild, Saskatoon was a perfect setting for his ear-splitting performance. But after Tuesday all that was coming out was a lame croak—a sound so puny that his front end couldn't hear him. They were used to the excessive lung-power he used in smaller, less noisy venues. How could they adjust to sweeping in a vacuum? Besides, Russ believed Kent relied on the intensity of the howl to judge the fury of the sweeping. Glenn even burned a rock looking up for directions because he couldn't hear.

They were driving back to the hotel after their Tuesday morning game, discussing the problem, when somebody remembered seeing a Radio Shack two-way radio that could be worn unobtrusively in the ear and used the bones of the head to vibrate the sound waves. The driver was commanded to do a U-turn and off they went to Radio Shack.

The device worked perfectly, and by evening Russ could croak his instructions so that Belcourt at the other end of the sheet with the receiver in his ear knew exactly what he wanted them to do. The problem was solved. Russ curled 95 percent in that Tuesday evening win over Saskatchewan.

But when the CCA got wind of what Russ was doing they were furious. After three ends they dragged Belcourt aside and told him to take the receiver out because it was jamming Warren Hansen's signal. Russ ignored the warning, but as soon as the game was over, they were all escorted to a meeting with the CCA brass, a meeting that quickly degenerated into a shouting-croaking match. Basically the argument boiled down to the CCA's insistence that no electronic devices be used and Howard's canny "where's your rule?" defence.

Howard kept repeating, as each round got nastier, that he was trying to win the Brier. And although that might have been a compelling argument in sports where the athletes have more clout, here it didn't work. Inevitably the CCA played their trump card; they made up a new rule in the middle of the Brier. Howard was forced to comply, but the episode still leaves a very bitter taste in his mouth.

"Basically I ignored those guys in 1980 and 1986, but now it's getting harder," he says. It infuriated him that in the middle of trying to win a Brier they would subject him to such rough and thoughtless treatment. They'd stalk him, escort him off the ice and set up late-night shouting matches. One official even threatened to have a rock pulled if he didn't knuckle under.

Of course the controversy became a media circus. Howard remembers he "felt like JFK." Every time he came off the ice he was surrounded by dozens of reporters looking for a story not about curling but about electronic devices. All of his free time was eaten up by media and meetings with the CCA. And if he did get back to his room for some peace, he would get calls from reporters around the country or fans offering support.

The whole controversy was distracting and exhausting. By Friday Howard was drained and dizzy. "All I wanted to do all day was drink Pepsi," he remembers. He spent a lot of the day talking to Wendy. Curling was a great pleasure in his life. The Brier was supposed to be the pinnacle, and here he was exhausted and miserable. His attitude was abundantly clear in his final round-robin game when he lost to former world champion Ragnar Kamp of Nova Scotia in a terribly curled 8-1 fiasco.

On balance it was incredible that he finished with an 8-3 record—good enough for a three-way tie for first. "I was bitchy, upset and tired," he remembers. And the way the team was playing behind him wasn't helping things. The tendency to challenge his decisions, which had bothered him earlier in the year, was now rampant. The whole team, including his brother Glenn, seemed to have lost confidence in him and everybody had to voice an opinion on every shot. At one low point Russ remembers someone from the crowd shouting "Why don't you get your mother to decide?"

It was an ignominious moment in what had been a proud Brier record, and Russ silently vowed he would never put himself in that position again. Not surprisingly, they lost in the semi-finals to Rick Folk 6-4 and were mercifully allowed to go home.

Russ's idea of quitting the team had already been conceived before the Brier. In fact, he'd mentioned it several times to his brother as the year went along. But the experience in Saskatoon brought the matter to a head.

"I thought, 'I don't need this. There is no goddamned way I'm going back on the ice in that situation.' But I guess I knew in the back of my mind that if I did curl at any level my brother would be with me. We'll curl together forever—or until he gets sick of me. There's no question there's a special kind of bond . . . We're brothers."

But Russ was not an impetuous guy and Glenn imagined that

after the turmoil had subsided a little he'd have a change of heart. He couldn't imagine Russ giving up curling or "freelancing" or whatever else he was talking about.

"I always knew deep down I wanted to curl," Glenn remembers, "and I didn't want to break up the team. But if it came down to it I wanted to curl with Russ. He's my brother and I believe the best skip in the world."

Still he was horrified when about three weeks after the Brier Tim called to tell him that Russ had called Kent and quit the team. "I didn't know a thing about it, but I told Tim I'd find out."

Russ had told Kent he wanted to freelance as Rick Lang had done in 1988. It was a total shock to Kent. Things hadn't gone well over the year but Russ had said absolutely nothing about what was bothering him. Russ had never been much of a communicator, especially when the subject was awkward feelings, but it had never mattered as it did this time.

Kent was angry and hurt. It was a betrayal, he felt, of their close friendship over the dozen or so years they had played together. It didn't help any that a month later Russ and Glenn played in the Jamaica bonspiel in North Bay with Peter Corner and Wayne Middaugh, a pair of young curlers just out of junior.

Both Kent and Tim suspected Russ had quit the team to play with them and had made up his mind about it before the Brier. They didn't like the way it had been handled. They also didn't like the chatter they were starting to read in the paper about the problems with their team—especially when they had never discussed it themselves.

"Tim and Kent had trouble swallowing that explanation," admits Glenn, "and to tell the truth things aren't really right to this day."

"It was really sad, I hated what happened," says Russ, "but I don't think it would have worked." He talks about the difference in their commitment to practising and travelling. "After the world championship I really had my eyes opened. Everybody's going around the world and we're going to Barrie, Ontario" (about 80 kilometres from home).

The *Midland Free Press* ran a written statement from Carstairs explaining his version of the break-up, and Russ, who had felt badly about it before, felt even worse. "Everything he said in there was factually true," says Russ with a heavy sigh. "I phoned him and explained everything. It's what I should have done in the first place."

Although there's still a decided coolness between Russ and Kent, the team got together in January 1990 for the Moncton 100 and made it to the finals. They won $51,000 for their trouble and "got along pretty well," says Glenn. Still, that chapter in curling history is very definitely closed.

Through the hot spring of 1989 Russ toyed with the idea of playing with Middaugh and Corner. They were certainly eager. As soon as they heard of the Howard team's break-up they had been on the phone. They were good, too; they had been skip and third on the runner-up team in the Canadian juniors in 1987, the year Jim Sullivan won. They also seemed to be on the Howards' wavelength; they were interested in keeping fit and they loved golf. Middaugh in fact was an assistant teaching pro at St. George's Golf and Country Club outside Toronto.

In the early summer the foursome played a few rounds of golf and they enjoyed each other's company. Undoubtedly there was a quickening of interest because they were young (21 and 22 respectively), enthusiastic and, perhaps the quality Russ liked best, unrelentingly positive. They gave the same impression of having unshakeable confidence in him that Belcourt had in 1985 when he joined the team.

For Russ, who knew he had been losing control of his 1989 team and who suspected his game had been affected, this was the ticket he needed. It wasn't long before the foursome was making plans to play as a team in the 1990 season and beyond.

Their play reflects the new feeling on the team. It's more direct, simpler and puts "a little less strain on the brain," says Glenn. "We win but we seem to win easier than we did before." says Glenn.

It was a luscious year on the cashspiel front for the Howards. In three weeks they won $74,000, more than they had ever pocketed before. Ironically, most of the loot came from the Moncton 100, which they played with Kent and Tim because the invitation was for their former world championship team. In the semi-final they eliminated Werenich's 1983 Dream Team before being buffaloed by Lukowich in the final so completely that Russ ended up waving a white towel in the eighth end with Luke lying five and the score already a lopsided 11-3.

They won $51,000 for their trouble and Russ was roundly congratulated for dreaming up the rule that had made the curling so entertaining.

The Howards enjoyed the Moncton 100, but the real business had been conducted a couple of weeks earlier when they had played much better with their new front end and won a $23,000 prize at a Calgary bonspiel. This was the future. Still their elaborate success in Moncton was not lost on Wayne Middaugh and Peter Corner. They were thrilled to be so close to the big show and continued to throw the big takeouts as if they were born to them.

The new team was flying as it headed into the playdowns. But once again somebody in Simcoe County pricked their balloon and they fell to earth with a thud. The shock prompted Middaugh to take his disappointment out on the chair in the dressing room, but soon they were back on a track that had become very familiar to Russ and Glenn—the Challenge Round. And as usual they triumphed and went on to the provincials.

At first everything went according to the script. "We dominated the provincials in a way we had never done before," explains Glenn. "With the old team we had to work at it a little harder."

But the domination gave out suddenly in the semi-final when they faced a very hot Bob Fedosa. Fedosa went on to almost upset Werenich in the final.

The Howards were far from disappointed in their showing. Their pockets were bulging with cash and they'd finished third in the province behind the team that would ultimately win the Brier and the world championship.

But the biggest payoff was that the game was more fun again and all the near horizons seemed conquerable. The only flaw in their satisfaction that summer was the still sandpapery relationship with Kent and Tim.

It didn't improve in the fall of 1990 as they began their second season with their new team. Still Russ and Glenn were far from apologetic about the change. More than ever they were convinced that their choice at front end was inspired.

In December they won $15,000 in the Skins Game, missing the $38,000 winner's share by a mere two centimetres. At the end of 10 ends there was no clear winner and Russ and his perennial rival Ed Werenich were forced to draw to the button for the big prize. The pressure was felt even by Warhorse Werenich, who tried to get his lead, Pat Perroud, to throw for him.

In the end he was a shade closer than Russ and, as usual, took home the lion's share of the cash.

But the new thing was that the Howards were serious contenders for cash. They won $30,300 and were fourth in the country in a year when there wasn't too much money floating around. Before the new team was formed the best they had ever done was ninth in the country. The way the new team played the game made it a little easier, and they were all more relaxed. As the 1991 playdowns began they could, they believed, win it all—Werenich willing.

"Let's face it," quips Russ, "if there had only been one of us in the province over the last 10 years he would have been a lot more famous." (And a lot richer.)

The playdowns handed the Howards their usual dose of good fortune which, combined with their upbeat mood, made them heavy favourites as they headed into the Hamilton Brier. Nobody was sick. There were no simmering team problems. The CCA was not hovering. And the field looked eminently beatable. Nobody of the stature of Pat Ryan or Bernie Sparkes, whom the Howards had conquered in 1987, bore down on them, at least on the rink.

But there was one old foe—and a formidable one—lying in ambush. At least that's how the Howards read what happened next. It happened on the Tuesday, three days before they were to leave for the Brier, a time when Brier contenders, whatever else they may be doing, are into the Deep Think of preparation.

Glenn was working and trying to keep his mind as uncluttered as possible. Russ was practising and working on his positive attitude. Neither had any inkling they were heading into the trenches for a bout of psychological warfare.

"Wrench fires out at Howard rink" read the headline in the *Toronto Sun*, and the story by the *Sun*'s curling writer, Perry Lefko, did not mince words. "They're a classless bunch of guys," was Eddie's inimitable quote. It seems he was still fuming over their gesture of triumph at the Ontario Tankard when his last rock picked a hair in the final of the round robin.

At that bleak moment he was infuriated that the Howards would raise their brooms in glee at his misfortune. Such behaviour is not in the curling code and Eddie does not ignore contraventions of the code. Sixteen days later he was still incubating his anger. And when he let fly, the Howards were caught off-guard.

Long after the 1991 Brier was history, Glenn could still quote verbatim Werenich's tirade. "I don't know how he has the nerve," Glenn says, still fuming. "I didn't think it [the triumphant gesture] was that big a deal. I apologized to every one of them as we shook hands. But if he had a problem he should have phoned us. I couldn't believe he'd bring it up like that when he knew it would be a big deal at the Brier. That's all anyone wanted to talk about.

"It's his intimidation factor. Not many people stand up to him. But if he's going to play head games he should do it on the ice. Not after the game's over. Not right before the Brier."

And so the stage was set. The last time he appeared at the Brier, Russ had faced batteries of microphones and media. Everybody wanted to know about his remote radio fight with the CCA. This time he was bracing for a tougher, meaner scrum with more personal questions.

But it wasn't—except to the Howard rink—the big deal they imagined. Oh, there were questions all right, but the issue died as the Brier got underway. The wounds were secret and personal.

The Howard team went in as heavy favourites but after the first three games the big guns on the team started firing duds. They finished 6-5, and out of the action. It wasn't an inexperienced rookie front end that brought them down, either. Russ and Glenn both struggled.

So why did it happen? Nobody's sure. But there are of course theories. For one thing Russ deliberately tried to restrain his roaring to avoid unnerving Corner and Middaugh. But in the end he had trouble keeping himself in the game.

Spectators commented that you could almost see the desire fade. By the end of the week Russ seemed tired. He told reporters he had to fight to concentrate.

Also, the team didn't bounce back well from the fiasco Wednesday evening, when careless TV crews left the huge double doors open on a rainy night. Ice conditions inside went from fine to frosty in an hour and only the most robust and determined of the competitors mastered the tricky changing ice. At that point Russ Howard was neither robust nor determined.

Observers watching as the Brier slipped away wondered if a decade of chasing the Brier was enough. Was Howard burnt out? Although he didn't admit he was playing badly, he did talk about fading motivation. By Friday, even though they still had a mathematical chance, he was announcing they were finished.

And after the Albertan young bloods had ploughed their way to victory, Glenn and Russ quietly folded their tent and headed the 240 kilometres down the road home.

Throughout the week Werenich lolled in the stands with his feet draped over the seats in front, watching his old rival self-destruct. Watching him, you couldn't help but wonder what was behind those hooded eyes. Did he know he'd drawn blood? Did he care?

"I think Werenich's comments hurt us in a small way," says Glenn attempting a post-mortem. "Usually we can crank it up a notch for a big tournament. But we couldn't this time. I don't know how we're going to prevent it from happening again. We're talking about seeing a sports psychologist and we probably will. That might help."

As for Werenich and how to cope with the wild cards he deals, Glenn is very unsure. "I don't understand it," he says with a slight quaver in his voice. "All we've ever done is compliment their team."

... And been luckier and more narcissistic than most. And had straighter teeth and flatter stomachs than curlers are meant to have. And, not by coincidence, made one thousand fewer trips to the bar.

So the rift that's all style and no substance continues. It's the showdown of two lifestyles, two mindsets and two eras.

And the smart money says it's beyond fixing.

8

PAT RYAN
The Express Steams West

RUSS HOWARD NEVER wants to be too far from cover. There are always guys around with slingshots and he knows he's got soft spots. But while he frets about Werenich's not-so-off-hand remarks and wonders why the game is so rough, another world champion, Pat Ryan, born a year earlier, in thrall to the same mistress of curling, bedevilled by the same competitive spirit, dances on the edge of the precipice—and enjoys the view.

Like Howard, Ryan stands a little apart from the curling world. He's the only skip of the big teams of the eighties who really has had a career, and although the good old boys may not be lining up for his autograph, he commands respect for his tough-mindedness.

"He has no vulnerability. It's like he has a shield around him," says Randy Ferbey, third on the Ryan team that won back-to-back Briers in 1988 and 1989 and tacked on a world championship the second year. For the most part Ryan's shield goes down over his team as well. In Edmonton, if there were hostile crowds, catcalls and a critical press, the team calmly circled their wagons and "talked out our worries." Nothing went beyond the foursome, no hint of trouble or pain, not even to their wives—that was part of the schtick.

It didn't always work perfectly. In his first year of skipping Pat describes his team as "four racehorses pulling in different directions," but for most of the 1980s the power of his drive and the purity of his desire to win usually overpowered everything in his way. His teams, often chosen because they were malleable and committed, played it his way—at least at first.

After the world championship in 1989, the team was coming apart. The schisms were there for everyone to see, but it clearly didn't matter to Ryan any more. He'd removed his shield from the team and shunted his show to the next stop.

Confidence is the key to the Ryan style. Watch him at the opening banquet of the Brier in 1990. His navy blazer is conservatively cut, so is his hair. His movements are precise and purposeful; his gaze extremely direct. On the other side of the room Eddie Werenich is impersonating a gangster, wandering around in double-breasted splendour, a fedora teetering on the back of his head. Ryan could be impersonating a West Point grad.

But that's only half of the story. As the night wears on, fans start coming to his table to request an Elvis tune. Elvis? Pat Ryan does Elvis? This certified management accountant who is precision incorporated? This person, who exudes logic and practicality, impersonates a twitching, gyrating, out-of-control Elvis Presley? Impossible.

Fortunately, on this night, he's reluctant. But it soon becomes clear that his reluctance has nothing to do with the obvious problem that, even if he can sing, he's at least one hemisphere of the brain away from being able to really do Elvis.

But that's not it. He's reluctant, it turns out, because his performance usually goes over too well. Afterwards, his life's not his own. People are always bugging him to do it again. It's a fatal mistake, he tells you, to perform on the first Saturday with eight more nights to go. In Edmonton, after he lost at his hometown Brier, he sang, and he ended up hiding under the table because there were too many fans, too many groupies and they were too persistent.

"I felt like a piece of meat," he says with a shudder.

But that memory has had a few years to fade now and, besides, this is a crowd of sedate eastern Canadians. So up he goes with his military bearing and short hair, the most unlikely Elvis ever.

In the spotlight everything changes—except the length of his hair. He puts the collar up on his jacket, loosens his tie and caresses the microphone with far more authority than the hired talent had been able to muster. The voice—a big husky baritone—fills the cavernous hall with the mournful opening of "Heartbreak Hotel." The body moves, twists and syncopates. The left hip swivels against nature's intention, just as Elvis's did. He ends the song down on his left knee to thunderous applause. By now the accountant who used to be sitting beside you is only a dim memory.

Now Elvis is into it. His next song is a romantic ballad—groupies be damned. But when that's over, despite the roars for more, he jumps off the stage and heads back to his table—with barely a hint of a swagger.

What would his father think? Pat has to chuckle a little at the thought. Twenty years ago Glen Ryan was worried about his eldest son. Too intense, too competitive, too solitary, he needed social connections, a team of his own, something to draw him out a little. Curling seemed ideal: it was a sport he could play for life. It imposed a team on the individual and the ambience was resolutely relaxed and friendly. The intensity he was displaying at home would get swallowed up in the sociability.

Pat soon found curling was everything his father had said and more. The "more" was the individual part that his father, who used up his competitiveness playing semi-pro baseball, hadn't really noticed.

"When you sit in the hack, you're your own man," Pat explains. "The team doesn't count. It's all you and your level of concentration. You can get really close to perfection. At the end there's a degree of unpredictability. You put the rock as close as you can but you don't know if it will continue to slide. If it stops, you can be perfect."

For an intense, driven teenager this was perfect. "I was obsessed," Pat remembers of his earliest experiences curling. Every day he was at the rink, Assiniboine Memorial in Winnipeg, practising. There were other kids with what some call "the sickness" there too. Mark Olson, a couple of years younger than Ryan, was, if anything, more committed. In 1973 Olson was eight years from winning the Brier. Pat would have to wait 14 years before he held up the gold tankard in victory. Others, like Kerry Burtnyk, who skipped Olson to the Brier win in 1981, were also hanging around, devoting themselves to developing the perfect delivery.

When he wasn't at the rink Pat and his younger brother, Jeff, would play "shuf" in the basement. On their hands and knees they'd slide 16 hockey pucks out onto rings they'd painted on the basement floor. The cement was slightly irregular and the pucks, which they waxed with shuffleboard wax, curled a little. At lunch-hour and after supper, for hours on end, they'd be down there quietly absorbed in mastering the game Pat had created.

Pat made up other games too—some much less subtle, like "Frisby Kill" or "Badminton Kill"—in which he and Jeff, four years his junior, could test each other. In the frisby game they would stand six metres apart, wind up and fire the frisby at each other as hard as they could. It was a variation of the old game of chicken. The first one to drop the frisby 10 times lost the intimidation sweepstakes and the game.

There were other games too in those long summer days at Victoria Beach on Lake Winnipeg. All of them were Pat's creations or at least his refinements on already existing games.

"Whenever I started to beat him at these things he'd change the rules," chuckles Jeff. "But we didn't argue much. I remember it all as fun."

Pat's competitive spirit was also very evident at the curling rink. By 1973, when he was in grade 12 and playing schoolboys' for the last year, he won the province playing third on a rink skipped by Dave Iverson. There was a certain inevitability about that win. Burtnyk, who was three years younger and also playing third, remembers feeling like David going up against Goliath when he faced Pat Ryan.

But Goliath was pretty small stuff outside his own province. "That was my first taste of the rewards that curling could bring," Pat remembers. "At that time I'd never taken an airplane anywhere. It was great."

They flew to the Maritimes and placed third in the national championships. It was, as Pat says, "an eye-opener." In Manitoba it was taken for granted that they would win. That third-place finish was the first inkling Pat had that Manitoba curling pride can be a millstone around a competitive curler's neck.

Glen Ryan was still hovering. Now he was worrying about Pat's obsession with curling. There were far too many men around Winnipeg who had wasted their lives on curling. You could see them every day at the rink, behind the glass, having a beer with their cronies and reliving old triumphs.

Some of the "curling bums" were young men who had been exceptional at the junior level and plunged into men's curling with little thought for their education. They hung around the edges of curling greatness without realizing that the men they were trying to impress were likely finished as competitive curlers. Even if the youngsters ended up playing for their heroes, it was unlikely the team would win: the heroes had stepped past their moment of greatness. The kids were sacrificing their education for nothing.

Glen Ryan saw this great pool of unfulfilled promise and he didn't
want his son to slip into it. So Pat enrolled in general arts at university. A year later he transferred to Red River Community College
and started taking business courses. He curled for the college team
and two years in a row won the western Canada college championship. He even entered one men's cashspiel with his college team and
walked away triumphant. But he stayed clear of the enticements of
the Brier.

"Curling," he now says, "is a rose on the side of my life." In those
years between 1973 and 1977, when he concentrated on school and
avoided men's playdowns, the description may have been accurate.
But by 1978, when he was playing third for Paul Devlin in Edmonton
and sniffing the possibility of a Brier berth, there was nothing deco-
rative or extra about curling in Ryan's life.

But by then his career was nicely launched. Oil was a boom
industry and he'd moved to Edmonton after college to work for
Imperial Oil. Three years later he moved on to corporate financial
planning for Strathcona County, a municipality that adjoins
Edmonton. He was a natural for the job—strategic planning had
been the M.O. of his life so far.

But he'd also managed to manoeuvre himself to the top of the
heap in Edmonton curling, a feat Al Hackner had essayed briefly in
1977 but quickly abandoned. Curling in Edmonton was too bleak
and hostile an environment for him. But the fierceness of the
Edmonton scene didn't faze Ryan in the slightest. In his first-ever
entry into the playdowns in 1978, as second on the Devlin rink, he
and his team made it to the provincial final before losing to Ed
Lukowich, who then went on to win the Brier.

It was an exhilarating loss. In 1979 it buoyed them again to the
top, where they beat Luke in the final and went on to the Brier. Ryan
now says the years he stood back from the playdowns allowed him to
develop and mature in a more rounded fashion. It gave him a context
for curling. But in that early Brier, where they hung in the middle of
the pack while Barry Fry's Manitoba rink rolled up a huge margin to
win, the context blurred a little.

A Brier victory seemed much more possible at home in Alberta
than it did out there in Ottawa under the TV lights with the likes of
Fry and Rick Folk.

The next year another Calgary powerhouse faced them in the
Alberta finals. Paul Gowsell seemed destined to win everything in

1980 as he downed the Devlin rink and waltzed onto the Brier stage in his hometown.

By now, still sticking with his strategic plan, Pat was immersed in studying for his CMA (Certified Management Accountant) designation. The young men his age who were making big names for themselves in curling had chosen to ignore school. A less confident person than Pat Ryan might have worried that he'd made a mistake. "Curling will always be there," is the way he put it to himself. At that time "school will always be there" might have seemed a more relevant assessment of the situation.

However, in 1980 Gowsell didn't win and businessman Rick Folk did. But the next year Ryan's theory was tested even more severely. Devlin tried replacing his third and the move turned out to be a mistake. They were out early, so Pat had plenty of time to watch the Burtnyk-Hackner Brier showdown on TV and to ruminate on life's uncertainties.

As for his own prospects, Ryan was unsure. His team seemed to be falling apart. He'd watched Devlin's confidence take a severe battering without his habitual third, John Hunter. They'd probably missed their chance at the brass ring; it was time to move on. As he looked over his options, he decided he would have his best shot at success skipping his own team.

"When Kerry and his team won," remembers Pat, "it was enough of a kick in the backside to go out and skip my own team. He opened my eyes—it could be done. We were all very good curlers. He didn't have any help, no Orest Meleschuk or big name from the past. He opened a window. These were my friends."

"I don't think anyone in the world is as competitive as Pat Ryan," says Randy Ferbey. Ferbey has trouble imagining Ryan in any role but skip. "He's too competitive not to play skip. Too good a curler."

But in the tightly knit factions that made up Edmonton curling in the early eighties nobody knew that. Ryan was unproven and there was no line-up of topflight curlers waiting to play with him. Finally he did pull a team together, the "four racehorses pulling in opposite directions," but it was a nightmarish year for him. A year, he says, that could have made him quit curling. "Some interesting experiences," he sums up with a rueful laugh and no elaboration. His wife, Penny, remembers 1983 as the only year he ever needed bolstering at home.

However, there were a few small successes. For one thing they beat

Pat's old skip, Paul Devlin, in the zone playdowns. And overall they played well enough for Pat to attract the attention of a perennial contender on the Edmonton scene, Gord Trenchie.

Trenchie was already into his forties when he noticed the style and competitiveness of 27-year-old Pat Ryan. "My objective was to get to the Brier and to win money on the bonspiel circuit," Trenchie recalls. "I thought his attitude was conducive to winning big."

In fact, in putting that 1983 team together, attitude seems to have been more important than anything else. Pat appreciated the vote of confidence Trenchie had placed in him. They'd played against each other five times in 1982 and Trenchie, skipping his own team, had beaten him every time. But for the new team he agreed to step down and play third. He was a "pillar of strength" in the first two years, explains Pat. He knew the game; he knew the Edmonton players; and Pat relied on him.

For the front end they recruited two players who shared their approach to winning: Dave Hay and Don Bartlett were relative newcomers but they had a ferocious will to win. The rest could be taught.

Pat and Gord left no rock unturned in their attempt to build a winning team. The two of them practised every lunch hour. The whole team practised at five o'clock. On Saturday mornings they'd spend an hour and half in a team meeting talking out everything. There were rules about drinking (no hard liquor), rules about how to stand on the sheet (as if you own it), on how to look at the opposition (through their heads as if they weren't there) and many, many more.

Many of the things about attitude on the ice were borrowed from Paul Gowsell. And they got help on the mental preparation from Duane McPhail, who had played and coached on Father Bauer's Team Canada hockey team. McPhail was a friend of Pat's from work and he enjoyed helping the team control their destiny.

"Curling is so competitive," explains Pat. "If you're going to win you need to find a little extra edge somewhere. McPhail was part of their edge; so was making a corporate plan. After all, few believed in the corporate plan with more tenacity than Pat Ryan, whose work life was dedicated to making corporate plans for the county.

Trenchie was more than ready to buy into the plan. For a dozen years he'd been looking to shave every corner to win. At last he'd found someone whose commitment matched his own. McPhail had a great settling effect on the front end. With all this energy and spirit and with clear, shared goals the team was soon doing better than they had dared hope. They qualified in every bonspiel they entered and in 1983 nearly snatched the provincial title from Ed Lukowich.

They beat him in the first game. He nailed them in the second and then, in the third, they were leading until Ed made one of his patented circus shots in the eighth end and their hopes died.

Trenchie took the loss extremely hard. It was perhaps a precursor of what was to come. "I was very disappointed, very discouraged after everything we'd done," he says with a tremor in his voice even now. "I'd been trying for so long to get there, I thought we'd never get another chance."

But his spirits picked up dramatically when the next year they almost beat Ed Werenich and his Dream Team to claim the big $60,000 booty at a world tournament organized by the Calgary Stampede Association. They finished second with $30,000. Now they knew they belonged in the big time. They finished the cashspiel season with $48,000 but there wasn't much time for smugness. They were abruptly into the playdowns and heading for another acute disappointment.

"We let things outside curling control us," explains Trenchie. He remembers arriving late at the airport for the flight to Grande Prairie for the provincials. The scene that greeted him in the departure lounge was a hollering match between Pat and Norm Cowley, the curling writer for the *Edmonton Journal*. Cowley had turned his set-up article for the provincial championships into an attack on the hometown Ryan rink.

Pat was not amused. "He doesn't back down," says his brother Jeff. "He's pretty small and when we were kids he'd get into fights but he'd never back away. He's still like that. He'll always get into something if he thinks he's right; he's always very outspoken."

Trenchie hadn't seen the article Pat was waving at Cowley but he gathered the gist. "He said we were frequently breaking the sweeping rules, in effect that we cheat."

Pat was incensed, not because he couldn't take criticism—he was used to it. Besides, there may have been some truth to Cowley's accusations. No, what infuriated Ryan was the timing. On the eve of the provincials the article ensured that every official would be gunning for them.

There had been laxity in enforcing the new sweeping rules, but now Cowley had made sure that wouldn't happen in this tournament. In the end Pat threw the newspaper in Cowley's face and they boarded the plane.

But that wasn't the end of the trouble. The plane was overbooked, and since Trenchie and Hay had been last to arrive, they were asked to deplane and wait for the next flight several hours later. Trenchie refused, adding that it would take physical force to get him off the plane. A few minutes later the airline hostess returned, knelt down beside his seat and assured him that if he didn't go voluntarily they would indeed physically remove him. Despite the fact that many of their group were non-curlers flying to Grande Prairie as spectators, nobody offered to give up his or her seat. In the end, Trenchie and Hay trooped off, missed the opening banquet and arrived, very upset, just before they were scheduled to curl. (Lukowich had arrived a couple of days early to get the feel of the ice and the competition venue.) But even with these setbacks, the Ryan rink finished third in the province—again a disappointment but not a devastation.

"A lesson-learned kind of year" is Pat's summary of 1984. This time they had learned—or at least they thought they had—not to let problems outside curling into their thoughts in competition. "That experience was a good teacher. We learned you have to control your emotions. You have to isolate yourself from everything except curling," says Trenchie.

But the next year, his third with Pat, he would be sorely tested on that maxim. His marriage had failed and by the 1984-85 season he was going through the painful court process of dividing up assets and responsibilities. "I was trying to control it, but it was very hard," he explains. "I couldn't rest my mind."

The relationship with Pat had been one of the most solid things in his life in the previous two years, but just before the provincial championships in 1985 he heard rumours that Pat had been trying to replace him before the December 15 deadline. At first, he says, he didn't believe it. There were always vicious rumours aimed at teamwrecking. And Pat, confident, successful, and very good at getting what he wanted, was always a prime target. But then for some reason the sources got better and Trenchie began to believe it was true.

Instead of confronting Pat, as their team philosophy dictated, Trenchie absorbed what to him was a devastating betrayal and kept playing.

There was another weird twist to this provincial championship. After they'd won the northerns their second, Dave Hay, announced he was leaving the team. He was an actor and he'd been given a part in a CBC production that was just too good to turn down. In one of the moves that drove Pat's opponents to catcalls and fury, he somehow had the rules changed or bent so that he could replace Hay with Don McKenzie, who had just been knocked out in the northerns. Such a substitution wasn't supposed to be possible and nobody was quite sure how he did it. "It was in our favour and I didn't ask questions," says Trenchie.

Pat chuckles now when he hears how mystified everyone was about that coup. The Alberta Curling Association had made an exception the year before for some lesser-known curlers, he explains. All Ryan had to do was argue the precedent. Game, set and match.

But even with a solid replacement at second the feeling was different on the team. "In the provincials on the ice we were a team, but inside I didn't feel we were any more," says Trenchie. Ironically, this was the year they finally beat Lukowich.

They went to the Moncton Brier in an odd frame of mind. McPhail went along to make sure their group goal-setting and so on was tuned up. Pat had managed finally to mitigate his intensity and was a little more relaxed. He says he saw no signs of any hairline cracks in his team. But for Trenchie the suspicion that Pat had tried to replace him was a festering wound that he was having more and more trouble concealing.

On the ice the performance looked seamless as they finished the round robin with an impeccable 11-0 record. But under the surface there were enormous tensions. Trenchie remembers what he describes as one "touchy incident" on the Wednesday.

They'd beaten their biggest rival, Al Hackner, in the afternoon 5-3. Trenchie thought it was the best game he'd played so far. But when he was looking over the stats afterward, Rick Lang pointed out that he had been scored wrongly on the first end. Pat walked by and they showed him the error. As Gord remembers, Pat's offhand remark was, "The way you were throwing out there, you're lucky to get that."

"Then he walked out of the room. I didn't know if he'd been kidding or what," says Trenchie. But by the evening game that remark had stirred up all the other pain he was harbouring. He came to the rink fuming, marched up to his skip in the practice session and hissed out the words: "Pat, never make a remark like that again or I'll drop you."

They beat Quebec that game 6-5 in an extra end. It was Wednesday night; their record was 8-0—and there was definitely trouble in the camp.

The pressure was unrelenting, and for Trenchie particularly it had been a very long year. By the tenth end on Sunday afternoon, when Al Hackner made his historic double take-out to tie the game and they headed into the 11th end, the tension both on the ice and in their hearts was palpable. Trenchie missed both his shots in the 11th end, and Pat's final draw to the four-foot circle slid an inch too far.

The commentators said the Ryan rink was demoralized by Hackner's shot. They lost momentum, the conventional wisdom insists, and flushed the Brier, the year, the team and their grand dreams down the drain.

Six years later Trenchie is still emotional on the subject. He blames himself for the loss. His knee had been giving him trouble and was ready for arthroscopic surgery. He'd taken very good care of it during the Brier, carefully wrapping it for each game, and it hadn't bothered him. But in the 11th end, with the crowd of 6,000 in the Moncton Arena holding its breath and millions more watching on TV, he turned suddenly with his foot in the hack and twisted it. It locked for a minute.

Instead of waiting for the knee to come back, instead of walking down the ice and telling Pat that he was in pain, he succumbed to the pressure of time and got ready to throw. As he hit the ice with his slide, the pain surged through him and he let the rock go too early.

"I told somebody about my knee and they said I was making excuses, so I don't like to bring it up," he says now. "It's true I wouldn't have mentioned it if the shot had been good."

Still, he takes responsibility for poor judgment in not delaying longer and hoping the pain would subside, or in not taking himself out of the game.

Pat takes responsibility in a similar way. He thinks they were too overwrought by the 11th end. He should have tried to pull everybody back into focus by speaking to each one and making sure they were OK. "Just talking to them would have made the difference," he says.

Afterwards Trenchie remembers that the glum little foursome went out for drinks but no one said anything. Did they know the team was finished?

"Virtually we never talked after that," says Ryan. "But I still have nothing but respect for Gord Trenchie. He took a chance on me. I have his picture up in my house. He's one of my guys."

Trenchie remembers he was waiting for things to heal a bit after the Brier. He fully expected a long two- or three-hour state of the union discussion with Ryan. Instead he got a phone call on a Saturday morning a month after the Brier. It was an announcement, not a discussion: Pat was going to play third for Randy Ferbey in 1986. The knife twisted sharply. Ferbey was the name Gord had heard in the replacement rumours in late December.

Since then Trenchie hasn't curled competitively. "I'm down to about 35 games a year," he explains now. The first year (1986) he couldn't have curled anyhow. The arthroscopic surgery wasn't successful and he had to have it again the following summer. Since then he's had offers to curl on good teams but "it's never been quite right," he says. However, for the 1992 competitive season there is finally an offer that interests him.

On the subject of Ryan, he's more sad than bitter. "I still think he's great, but there've been very few words between us. We're both stubborn, I guess. It was not the way I wanted it to end. I still have very strong feelings about the team."

He still has trouble mastering his intensity, still hates to lose and even in club play gets very uptight when he does. He watched the Ryan rink go on to win two Briers and one world championship without him and he felt "a little bad that I wasn't involved. Even as a fifth man I would have been happy."

But one of the axioms of curling is that marriages like the Trenchie-Ryan affair break up. Especially when there are significant differences in age and lifestyle. Three or four years is about the lifespan of a men's team. The individuals seem to wear out each other's intensity. To get a new shot of incentive it's usually necessary to get new blood.

But to hear Randy Ferbey tell it there was no reason, in 1985, to believe his blood was rich or royal enough for the Ryan team. "There's no doubt he was the king of the castle around here. He was the best we'd had for a long time. My team was going nowhere. I hadn't accomplished anything," says Ferbey.

He modestly forgets to mention that he had faced down and

beaten Ryan in the final of a one-on-one tournament at the end of the 1985 season. After that evening he and Ryan talked for five minutes about playing together. Ryan said he wanted to play third. "He thought it would be easier to leave his team that way," remembers Ferbey.

The whole idea of skipping Pat Ryan made Ferbey, a Northern Alberta Institute of Technology (NAIT) printer, profoundly uncomfortable. He insisted he had no credentials to skip Pat Ryan. And before he knew it, Don Walchuk, an all-star second from Pat's Brier team, was also on his rink. "Here I am skipping these guys?" Ferbey's voice still registers wonder six years later.

But it was only a month and two bonspiels before Ferbey was allowed to step down and Ryan took over. "It was an honour, but Pat's too competitive not to skip."

Pat says he'd learned his lesson in the 1985 experience. He was now looking for solid compatibility on his team. It was easier to find recruits now that he'd come so close to winning the Brier. In Ferbey he thought he saw a younger version of himself. Ferbey was an incredibly good hitter and almost as stubborn and competitive as he was.

But Ferbey was about to get lessons in the meaning of the word "competitive." In the summer before they started to play together the team that included Don Walchuk and Roy Hebert took a golf trip and a camping trip. Both trips turned into near-parodies on the competitive nature of the male of the species. They bet on everything.

The game Ferbey remembers best was a competition to see who could throw or roll a yellow tennis ball closest to a tent pole stuck in gravel. The uneven and unpredictable angles in the gravel meant that skill played almost no role in the game. It was all luck. Still they played for hours—until Pat won.

The same with golf. They had trouble keeping the legitimate score because they were betting 25 cents on ten different things every hole—the longest drive, the best putt, and so forth.

It would always start in fun and end in argument because everybody was obsessed with winning. Competitiveness was, after all, the main credential for being there. They had to be willing to do whatever it took to win. But in the end it was almost always Pat who would go that extra step—whatever it was—to win.

He loved this milieu. It reminded him of the marathon games with

Jeff at home in Manitoba and, besides, he knew this was good for his team. He was going to make sure there were no soft spots. Mental toughness was an essential part of the team ethos.

But togetherness in the Ryan team meant a lot more than just living in each other's pockets for a few days a year. Excursions into each other's psyches were also part of their new team's conditioning. "When we played together I was closer to him than I was to my own brother," says Ferbey.

Pat believed they hadn't understood each other as well as they should have on his last team. Now he attacked that issue with his usual ferocity. They read books like *The Inner Game of Tennis*; they studied the Russians' ideas of biofeedback and they kept a squeaky-clean emotional slate with each other.

But in 1986 Lukowich again proved indomitable. He won in a walk, and the Ryan rink was left wondering what else they could do.

One thing was to quit playing mixed. With their wives Ferbey and Ryan had represented Alberta at the mixed national championships in 1986. They lost the men's final in the afternoon and had to be on the ice that evening in another city for the opening game of the mixed national competition.

All year the curling brass had tried to get them to drop one of their events, but Pat steadfastly refused. His argument was that if they weren't allowed to play in more than one event, they were being penalized for being successful. The association reluctantly bought his argument, but after 1986 Ryan and Ferbey decided the mixed event probably was diluting their intensity for the men's competition.

Once again, though, when he played in the 1986 mixed, Ryan was seen to get his way with the curling poobahs. Many ordinary curlers were miffed and mystified by his power.

But that was fine with Pat—a little mystique added to the potency of the team. Nobody beyond the four of them needed to know what they were doing, how they were training, what they were reading. It was team business and it shouldn't go beyond the closed door of their meeting room.

Ryan had seen Gowsell in action. He admired and tried to learn from his tactics. He remembers how, when he was an unheralded second on Devlin's rink, Gowsell knew all about him when they met for the first time. The wild redhead called him by name and seemed to know how he threw the rock. That knowledge gave Gowsell power.

He could also spook the opposition just by looking at them deeply as if they were transparent, Pat remembers. And it wasn't long before the Ryan rink was striding out to take their places with a similar attitude.

At the end of the 1986 season lead Roy Hebert was transferred to Calgary. They replaced him with Don McKenzie who had filled in in 1985. The substitution made the team a little bit stronger.

In the summer they repeated the camping and golf trips, the barbeques and the long team meetings from the year before. As the days got shorter and colder, the dividends started to roll in. They could feel themselves starting to jell. And finally, when the provincials rolled around, they found themselves edging out Lukowich, the defending world and Brier champion, with a perfect draw to the four-foot by Ryan.

It was almost beyond imagining that they were to represent Alberta in their hometown Brier. They imagined themselves feeding off the crowd and pushing, as Pat always hoped to do, beyond their known limits.

Pat had every reason to believe this was a better team than the one he'd taken to the Brier in 1985. There were certainly none of the fissures that turned into gaping chasms on that team. "But it turned into a disaster," remembers Ferbey. Instead of 11-0, they finished the round robin with an undistinguished 6-5 record.

"I expected too much," confesses Randy. "I expected there would be a great wave of feeling, of fan support, and it turned out to be almost the total opposite. They were pulling for everybody to beat us. You'd hear catcalls from the stands and afterwards you'd hear who it was and you couldn't believe it. It would be a friend."

Even the invulnerable Pat Ryan was affected by the harshness of the crowd. "I don't know how you could feel good about yourself with guys screaming really personal insults from the crowd. If there were rifles up there we would have been pieces of Swiss cheese.

"It was tough. It was Randy's first Brier—something he'd worked for and dreamed all his life of playing in. You have to really wonder if it's worth it."

The fan reaction put them off balance, but it didn't matter much because Russ Howard looked like the rink of destiny at this Brier, whatever happened. The crowd heckled him too but he didn't seem to hear.

The Brier experience gave Pat a new perspective on himself and his team. Tough-mindedness has to go deeper than just looking invincible on the ice.

They had one more chance at competition that year as the Olympic trials to pick the Canadian team for the 1988 Olympics were held in Calgary after the world championships. But this was to be another disappointment. Ferbey for one had mentally packed away his broom for summer by the time the eight-team triple knockout rolled around a few weeks after the world championships.

Randy had been ordered to lose weight along with Werenich and Savage but, unlike the Ontario curlers, he'd immediately complied. The only thing that bothered him about the dictate was that it was mentioned in the papers. The intrusion into his life was not an issue—he was used to it.

Ferbey says he saw the Olympic tryout camp as one more glamorous bonspiel. For some reason he didn't connect it with the Olympic hype that was already beginning to build in Calgary. And although Ryan says he was more plugged in, he'd never been to an Olympics and it was hard to gauge how grand the event would be. They still wonder a bit at their naiveté, especially since they've been able to watch first-hand how many invitations and perks have come to Pat's wife, Penny, who was on Linda Moore's gold-medal women's Olympic team.

Their Olympic camp was far from a disaster. Once again they came close, losing another final to Ed Lukowich. If you ask Pat about his unending struggle with Luke, he insists he's lucky to have had such a benchmark to measure himself against and to play up to.

At the time they remember not feeling terribly sorry they'd lost. It meant Lukowich would be out of their hair for much of the 1987-88 season. Or so they hoped.

The real issue for them that summer was bouncing back from a very tough Brier. They needed time together, Pat felt, to deal with their loss as a team—the lessons of 1985. But in the juggling act that he has performed so superbly in his curling career, there were a couple of new items to work in. His wife, Penny, was going to be on the road a lot with the women's Olympic team. Pat, even if he did some curling, could not travel too far or too often because of the couple's two very young children.

Besides, he'd been promoted in the summer to director of finance for Strathcona County. Work was consuming more and more of his time.

He remembers that fall telling his team he was "95 percent certain" he would not be able to enter the playdowns because they were taking place during his fiscal year-end at work and he couldn't spare the time.

Their bonspiel season was a disappointment. They won money in Europe, but in Canada they had to watch their big rival Ed Lukowich crisscross the country, all expenses paid, as Canada's Olympic representative. He played in everything and won big. He finished on top of the Gold Trail with $101,250, breaking all records for curling winnings. Meanwhile, the Ryan Express finished up the track at 61st. Canadian winnings: $4,200. The year before the team had finished second on the Trail with more than 10 times that amount.

But they had won a spot in the playdowns, a wild-card spot that went with winning a small local bonspiel. Things had often gone against them in the past, but this time destiny seemed to be pushing them towards the Brier.

If they hadn't won a wild-card spot, Pat wouldn't have been able to play. He was too busy at work to take nearly a week off. But the wild-card sewed up a spot in the northerns which luckily were close to Edmonton in 1988. They won the northerns without Pat having to miss more than a couple of days from work. The next round, the provincials, were played right in their home club.

A guy with two kids at home and a career who is still trying to curl at the elite level needs breaks like these. It was just possible—if he worked in the morning and curled in the afternoon. The Fates now were not just smiling on them but positively beaming. "The years I don't really invest myself, we seem to win," says Pat, still puzzled by the perversity of curling fate.

Luke missed the provincials completely in 1988, losing out in the city bonspiel. He had been wearing himself out ringing up the cash register all over the country. It was high time, the Ryan rink must have felt, to even the score a little.

Ryan and company were peaking at the right time. Even so, they lost two games very early in the triple-knockout tournament. It didn't matter too much. After those first two losses they won 28 straight games.

Ryan had been criticized in 1985 for choking at the big moment after seeming invincible. And although he didn't accept the analysis, he hated the way people patronized him after the loss. There would be no repeat of that performance.

Nor would the 1987 debacle be repeated. He was ready to screen out the fans. He was focused. This was his third Brier in four years and he was ready to win. The signs were all there. Off they headed to Chicoutimi to face one of the strongest Brier fields in recent years: three former champions and a couple of the country's biggest cash-spiel winners.

The crowd was quieter than in Edmonton—especially after Pat persuaded the officials to announce the new rule about abusive fans being removed from the arena. And the intensity in the rink from Alberta was building.

It didn't matter that this was the lowest total gate for more than a decade, but it did matter that Hackner, who had plucked away the 1985 Brier, was one of the contenders. For added drama, Ryan's old clubmate, Kerry Burtnyk, was there too, representing Manitoba for the first time since his Brier win in 1981.

They rolled into the Brier on a winning streak and abruptly rekindled their 1985 momentum. Once again, Ryan stormed through the round robin undefeated. But in the final against Saskatchewan's Eugene Hritzuk, it looked as if victory might slip through his fingers again. Only one end was blanked. The others were bitterly fought seesaw battles. The Ryan rink straggled into the 10th end holding the hammer but on the wrong side of a 7-5 score. But this time it was Hritzuk who cracked under the pressure. Facing three Alberta counters with his last rock, he hogged the shot. Ryan finally won his Brier, finally got his perfect score—and he didn't even have to throw his last rock.

Pat believes 90 percent of curling is "upstairs." By 1988 he'd learned a lot about mental control. "Sometimes I don't know what my mind's thinking out there. I wonder if I'm buckling under the pressure. Then I stop and I tell myself, 'You're spinning out here, your heart's racing.' Then I sit in the hack and I turn off my mind. You can't think yourself through a shot. You have to believe in your practice and let your body do it."

One of the things Ryan loved about curling right from the beginning is that moment in the hack. It doesn't matter about the TV lights or the expectant crowd. It's a moment of meditation, a chance, just like the chance a baseball pitcher has, to be perfect.

So the Ryan rink that mopped up in Chicoutimi in mid-March

1988 had reason to be confident about the upcoming world championship in Lausanne, Switzerland. To keep tuned up they played a bonspiel in Cranbrook, B.C., and again went undefeated—except for the niggling fact that they lost the final.

Unfortunately, it was an indication of what was to come. Among themselves they expected Lausanne to be a pleasant trip and an easy competition. Indomitable at home, they expected to be twice as powerful abroad, where curling is still in its developing stages. The world championships began just as everyone expected, with the Ryan Express roaring down on the opposition, defeating everything in its path. Eigil Ramsfjell's Olympic champions were squashed 10-2 in five ends.

But the Norwegians had a nasty surprise up their sleeve. Eigil as usual had kept his counsel and watched Ryan carefully. In the final he came out ready to play a completely different game. "He pulled one on us," says Ferbey. "He probably didn't try to lose, but he didn't prepare at all for the first game. We came away thinking he wasn't that good."

After the first end of the final they knew they were in for a fight. And finally it was a fight that was too much for them. They lost 5-4 giving the Lausanne spectators all they could hope for in a curling match.

"At first the loss didn't bother us," remembers Ferbey. "Everybody kept saying the Brier was the thing. But that's total garbage. As the summer wore on, we began to feel among ourselves that we didn't really accomplish anything. So we were second in the world—big deal."

Pat, now 32, felt as if his goal had been snatched away again. He had the Tankard on his mantel but in his heart there was a heaviness that went more with failure than success. It was as if, when he finally ended the race, someone moved the finish line. For a decade he'd chased the Brier with all his confidence, dedication and energy, but now he saw that the Brier without the world championship beside it was incomplete.

He talks about "sampling the salad bar" of a curling life. He will tell you that you can't excel at anything unless you're well-rounded. But he sometimes forgets his own advice. This time he suffered from a bad case of tunnel vision by focusing only on the Brier and not really considering the importance of the world championship. Now he would pay.

"You think losing the worlds is going to haunt you your whole life," explains Ryan about the way he felt after the 1988 world championships. "You say to yourself you were beaten by some guy from Norway—and you begin to think somebody upstairs wants to toy with you. I never thought I'd ever get back."

But unlike most Brier winners, the Ryan rink, unchanged and undiminished—or so it seemed—steamed back to do it again in 1989. From the outside there was none of the usual loss of energy or flagging of spirits. It was almost as if they needed to win again, needed to right the wrong of the world championships.

That was what the world saw. In reality they had a lot of trouble getting themselves going, says Ryan. They'd always had emotional ups and downs as a team. He remembers the big fight they had at the Vernon carspiel in 1986 after they lost their first two games to teams they'd never heard of.

"The next day everybody was afraid to open their mouths," says Pat. "But we won seven in a row and won the cars. I learned something there. Sometimes a consoling chat works, but sometimes a good fight is a better motivator. A skip is like a symphony conductor; you have to keep changing the instrumentation and sometimes you don't know what will work."

But this time it wasn't a cathartic fight they needed. Splitting up was very much in their minds. Ryan was tired, tired of never having holidays or free time and tired of working long hours at the office. He was ready for change. He wanted to take the next step in his career and that, he knew, would mean leaving Edmonton.

Even before he told his team about his plans, some of them were thinking it was time to split, to look for new partners and new intensity. And so, with very low expectations, they eased into the 1988-89 season.

Their bonspiel season was better than the year before, but the end-of-an-era feeling hung over everything they did. By November Pat had landed a job in Kelowna and was getting ready to move in the new year. But they didn't fall apart as other teams have done. Just as in 1985, when the Trenchie split was coming, they rallied when it counted.

Because he was changing jobs Pat had a little more time flexibility for the city playdowns, and they won. By the time the provincials rolled around, Pat had already moved to Kelowna and a big new job as director of finance at the 750-bed Kelowna General Hospital. He flew in for the provincials and they won. The next time they met it was at the Saskatoon Brier.

Ferbey admits he was worried. They had talked almost every day on the phone, but nothing Pat had said was particularly reassuring. He was talking about how he had someone new holding the broom in practice and how he'd pinpointed a problem with the delivery of a certain shot. Ferbey listened and felt his heart sinking.

Pat was always interested in anything new. Now Ferbey was afraid he wouldn't recognize his old skip.

When they got to the Brier, although they were defending champs, they were not the favourites. That honour went to a rapidly tiring Russ Howard, who was using an electronic device to communicate with his team. The fickle curling world had already passed on to something new. Ryan's rink had lost the worlds and they were splitting. They were already old news. It irked them to be ignored, but it probably eased the pressure too.

"It was our quietest Brier and probably our easiest win," says Ferbey. This time they were far from invincible. At one point they were 6-3 and hoping for a playoff berth. But at the end the right teams won and lost, and they wound up in a three-way tie for first place with an 8-3 record. They had a bye to the final because they'd beaten the teams they'd tied with, Russ Howard and Rick Folk.

By this time Howard was caving in under the pressure and confrontation with the curling powers. He lost the semi-final 7-4 to Folk.

Pat was getting a bit of a rough ride in the media, too, over refusing to wear a mike so TV viewers could hear what he was saying to his team. He was called the "money-conscious Pat Ryan" because he complained the CBC was making money from the curlers and putting nothing back into the sport. (Although they are paid expense money to play in the Brier, there is no compensation for the time off work.)

"Curlers are left behind [other sports]," he told Perry Lefko of the *Toronto Sun*. "They are like an abused herd of cattle. They [the TV networks] herd you over there and say, 'Entertain us. It's too bad you lost a week's pay.'"

Rick Folk, a few years older and mellower than Ryan, was a hometown hero in Saskatoon because he'd grown up there and won the Brier for Saskatchewan in 1980. But now he'd opened a store in

Kelowna and was also a big deal at the Kelowna Curling Club, where Pat and Penny joined when they moved.

For Pat there was plenty of drama in meeting him in the final. Leading up to the 1989 Brier the two former champions were staunch regulars at practice time.

There was not a lot of common ground between these two teams. Their styles were very different. Ryan's team oozed confidence and set out to "own the ice." Folk favoured the quiet fade-to-black style, so you never quite knew who he was or what to expect next.

"You would never have said we were friends," says Ferbey thinking back to the 1989 final. Pat stepped onto the ice that March 12 Sunday afternoon knowing he and Folk were going to lock horns the next year at the curling club. When an elderly spectator called out: "This is for the bragging rights around the club," Pat knew the comment wasn't far off the mark.

"I had the experience of losing to Hackner in 1985 and being on the receiving end of condolences for a year. I didn't want to go through that again," he remembers with a chuckle. "I couldn't take another year of people saying how sorry they felt for me."

The game was an unmemorable peeling contest with Ryan coming out on top 3-2. The turning point came in the sixth end, when Randy made a perfect freeze and Folk couldn't make his straight-back raise takeout.

It wasn't exactly exciting, but it was good enough to win, and with a team on the rocks that was plenty good enough. Milwaukee, where the world championships were held, was another disappointment. In Europe they'd been treated like Wayne Gretzky, Ferbey says. In Milwaukee nobody seemed to know there was a world championship going on. They drew fewer than 1,000 a night and most of those were Canadians who had travelled south for the curling. The final drew only 2,500 to the 11,000-seat Mecca Arena.

The poor crowds and lack of excitement added to their own feelings of malaise. The team was splitting anyway. What did it matter what happened in this little, second-rate, nearly empty arena?

After four games they were 1-3, not communicating well and not trying particularly hard. Pat was chippy. Members of the French team, skipped by Dominique Dupont-Roc, were swinging their brooms over their heads in excitement and Ryan complained he almost got "bopped" a couple of times. When the third on the team got in his way as he was watching his rock, the Frenchman ended up on the ice. Others, like the Swedes, complained that Pat was miserable and didn't enjoy the game.

Then they started to win. They won five in a row, then the semifinal, and then suddenly they found themselves coasting to a world championship.

Something had sparked them awake and there they were on the edge of winning the world. The game with Switzerland's Patrick Hürlimann ended 5-4. Finally, after five long years, they had done it. They could, at last, rest content.

But the tensions on the team didn't disappear. The 1989-90 season was their second year of "farewell tours." They were bored with each other but the European bonspiels were too great to turn down. So off they trundled, amid exaggerated rumours of discord.

Their team had run its course anyway, Ferbey believes. They'd won two Briers and one world championship. What else can you expect of life's chance acquaintances? After all, they weren't brothers. They weren't the Richardsons or the Howards or even the Sullivans.

And like the partner in many a tired, stressed marriage, they were guilty of "taking advantage of each other," says Ferbey. The rest of the Alberta curling world was talking about the trouble on the star team. They'd always been a team that presented an absolutely united face to the rest of the curling world. Now there were those who delighted in the fact they were openly feuding.

Ryan, whom people had ridiculed a little because he insisted on kneading the team into a unit with identical goals, a guy who had struggled to refine every nuance of their team relationship so they would never surprise each other with their reactions, was now being accused of going his own way too much. "He isn't much of a team player," people would say knowingly.

"That year we were four individuals rather than me being the leader [of a team]," Pat says, shrugging. "I didn't try to get everybody together. I had moved; everybody was growing and changing."

As the calendar flipped to 1990 they were in Moncton for the fabled $250,000 bonspiel, celebrating Moncton's centennial. It was to be their last hurrah as a team, and on the surface it seemed an odd choice. The spiel was designed to sidestep their big-hitting style with Russ Howard's rule that leads could not peel.

Ryan, who was supposed to be the popularizer of the peeling game that was taking over curling, was not expected to do much in that bonspiel. But he had never accepted the rap that he couldn't play the aggressive game. Nobody ever got ahead by peeling, he points out. "We were the best at keeping it clean after we got ahead, but that doesn't mean we can't play the other style," he insists.

Still, there were and are many doubters in the curling world, and nothing the Ryan rink did at the Moncton 100 altered that. "I didn't go there to prove anything," Pat says. "I thought we could make a lot of money. It was a game we could certainly play."

But the team had come apart, and the group that assembled on the ice for their first draw were four very different individuals. "There were personality changes on the team," says Ryan. "It's amazing what a world championship will do to a personality."

So the Moncton 100 turned into a social affair with too many late nights to produce winning mornings.

When the teams voted on how they liked the new rule that leads can't peel, Rick Folk's and Linda Moore's team both rejected it and Pat offered alternative suggestions.

Ferbey says when they started with their peeling game it was something new. They never guessed it would end up subverting curling to low-scoring games full of blank ends. "There isn't a curling team in the world that doesn't peel if they get the chance," he says. But when Ryan first started doing it, no team ever believed it would work on them. The opposition always started into the game convinced their chance would come and they could capitalize and win.

Ferbey now looks back at the 3-2 world championship win and wonders about the changes in curling. He says he would be a "little embarrassed" about winning with the big-hitting game now. He's looking forward to rule changes that will prevent the peeling style from taking over curling. "Nobody wants to watch a 3-2 game. It's boring," he concedes.

Pat too accepts that the game needs some fine-tuning. He's made a proposal about a ninth rock that would be placed somewhere outside the rings as a guard before play on each end begins. Instead of eliminating the lead from the action, this would make his job more important, says Ryan. So far he's had no response from the curling authorities.

When the 1990 playdowns rolled around, Ryan passed. In 1989

curling had at long last begun to feel like a second job. Besides, Penny and Pat needed to settle into their new life in Kelowna, a pretty town in the interior of B.C. The location is as close to perfect as they could find. In the mountains, three hours from Vancouver, it's a small (but rapidly growing) community-minded city where Pat can indulge in his newest passion—windsurfing. On weekends, if the weather is remotely warm enough, he's out on Lake Okanagan or driving south to the magnificent gorge on the Hood River in Oregon.

He's interested in singing, says he'd have a band if he didn't curl; he loves to take photos and even made a team video once to the Bette Midler tune "Wind Beneath My Wings"; but it's windsurfing that has really captured his imagination.

"You wouldn't believe the power and control you feel," he says with a hint of rapture in his voice.

But Kelowna, it should not be overlooked, is also a curling town. And the big new house the Ryans bought in a leafy subdivision is two minutes from the curling rink.

"I like to be good at a lot of things, but I'm best at curling," Pat says. Ferbey insists that when they curled together curling was not relegated to some little off-beat corner of their lives. It was the main priority, before family and career.

Since he stopped curling with Ryan, Randy says his marriage has improved, his status at work is better because he's not always asking for time off and he's "totally happier."

But then ask if he'd do it again—and he takes the bait whole. "In an instant," he says.

It's like a drug addiction, he explains. It affects everything in your life 24 hours a day but you don't care. You don't like asking for time off. You don't like telling your wife there will be no paycheque this week because you're going curling. But you do it—over and over and over again.

"The weird thing is I don't think you can be a success at the game if you don't do it that way, and yet when it's over, what have you really got? Nothing."

Ferbey's bleak view is not shared by Penny Ryan. "Our lives are absolutely better because of curling," she says.

But Penny too, according to her husband, has trouble compartmentalizing the game. "She lives it, she gets very wrapped up in it. She thinks about it all the time. If I'm not doing it, it's the last thing on my mind."

It's easy for him to say that now when the pressure to win is off—for a few years anyhow. In fact, in the 1991 competitive season he was relaxed enough about curling to play third for an old adversary, Rick Folk, on what was billed as the "Super Team." Bert Gretzinger, another national name with impressive cashspiel winnings, played second. At lead they had Gerry Richards, who had played at the national level as a junior and skipped a team to the national firefighters' championship where Eddie Werenich earned his skip's stripes.

But these heavy hitters fanned in their first year. They didn't make the Gold Trail at all. They played in four bonspiels, always qualifying but not making anything beyond their expenses. According to Gretzinger there's nothing to worry about. The games were close and they were each responsible for one of the losses.

In the playdowns they won the title for the interior of B.C. but lost three of their first four games in the provincials and were abruptly sidelined.

"We would have liked to make some more cash," explained Gretzinger, "but we got along well and Pat loved playing third." Whenever Folk couldn't make a game in their Superleague play, Gretzinger skipped.

Long ago Lukowich played third for Folk on his way to learning the intricacies of the finesse game, but Pat Ryan denies he's serving the same kind of apprenticeship. He knows the aggressive game, he insists. He's playing third so he can take more chances, because the skip is always there to clean up after. He points out that with his championship team the style was always to press to the edge of the envelope, trying to increase the difficulty of each shot and heighten the pressure until the opposition cracked. Ferbey's constant refrain when asked whether to play it safe or dangerous was "Live by the sword, die by the sword."

"We would always go the full-limit gamble," says Ryan, "to force ourselves to make difficult shots and force the other team out of their comfort zone. We won the world championship on the edge of a razor blade. We knew Hürlimann's percentages were a little lower on the angle hit, so we put him in the position where the pressure was as high as it could possibly be. You have to wait, stay on the guy's heels and go all the way to the last rock and hope that's his breaking point."

Whatever edges of envelopes are reached, Pat Ryan will not be playing third in Kelowna for Rick Folk forever. "You only go through life once," he says trying to explain his restlessness. So, as the powers in curling struggle with rule changes and style changes, one thing you can certainly bet: Pat Ryan won't be left behind playing in some outmoded style.

In the whole galaxy of curling stars there are few as capable of renovating themselves as Pat Ryan. It's one of the specialities of the self-made man. When the new "Super Team" was getting organized, Ryan brought up some of the rules that he felt had made his old team successful. One was, "No hard liquor." "Well, that's my first call," said Folk, pulling rank as skip for the first time. "I might have the odd drop of rye."

Ryan, who's known in curling circles as a dogged negotiator, immediately dropped the issue.

As for group camping trips and other summer excursions to foster togetherness and mental toughness, he never even suggested them. Gretzinger, a guy in his forties who's paid his dues, grins. "It's too late to go camping," he says.

But while Ryan may have reined himself in and decided to accommodate the personalities on his new team, the probation period will not last forever. Already in the spring of 1991 after the Super Team had posted one mediocre season, rumours were flying that Ryan would be moving on again, this time to play with Brent Giles.

Ryan denies it. In the Olympic year the Folk team will be back together, he insists.

But everyone knows if not this year, then next. In his game plan there is absolutely no room for failure. No possible chance Pat Ryan would stick with a losing team.

9

KERRY BURTNYK
Bubba Becomes a Broker

PAT RYAN REACHES into his life and tries to shape everything he confronts. If the team isn't right, or the job or the playdown structure doesn't suit him, he makes changes. At 36 he's lived in three provinces, played three positions, and kept the door revolving on his team. He's also had a number of side passions like photography, music and windsurfing. Even the changes in the Canadian curling style in the eighties have the Ryan stamp on them.

Kerry Burtnyk, Manitoba's curling hero, is the exact opposite. He and Ryan grew up in the same club, Assiniboine Memorial in Winnipeg. But where Ryan recoiled in horror at the sight of "curling bums" who hung around the rinks and put curling ahead of everything else in their lives, Burtnyk, or "Bubba" as his buddies call him, embraced that life.

For 13 of the last 15 years, curling has been the whole story on Kerry Burtnyk. To be sure, the story has had plot, character, drama and tension, but only one theme. Kerry hung around his club. He won a Brier. He lost a world championship. He bonspieled enthusiastically. And over the last six years, although he only made it to the Brier once, he brought home more than $100,000, making him one of the most consistent money winners on the circuit.

He rarely made changes to his team. Occasionally there would be woman problems on a team of young bachelors, and there have been impulsive resignations. But mostly they've hung together, a little knot of Assinboine Memorial kids who realized their dream and grew up to be elite curlers.

Ron Kammerlock, for example, has played with Kerry for all but a couple of the last dozen years. When Jim Spencer quit in 1990 he'd been a regular on the team most of his curling life.

And just as Kerry didn't try to change things too much on his team, he didn't worry much about taking charge of his life either. He made no attempt to stash curling in one corner. It ruled, and he went with the flow. He won early and he won big, defying Ryan's rule on the prospects of curling bums. But after that early win, when he was 22 and his team broke records as the youngest ever to win the Brier, the losses started to mount. After the 1981 world championship when they lost the final to Switzerland, they never again scaled those heights.

Finally in 1988, after seven years in a wilderness of losing in the provincials year after year, they finally won Manitoba again and went back to the Brier. To Kerry the loss in Chicoutimi wasn't as important as being there. The spell was broken. They had proven 1981 wasn't a fluke. They'd shown everyone again that they could be a force. And now, finally, he could pursue the business life that he had tentatively begun.

Today if you're looking for Kerry Burtnyk, skip the curling rink. You have to go to the glitziest green-glass office tower in downtown Winnipeg. There, in the plush offices of Richardson Greenshields, a receptionist will summon "Mr. Burtnyk."

Curling fans who think of Burtnyk as a young, slightly wild lion in a windbreaker and ball cap with a can of beer in his hand wouldn't recognize the bespectacled young man in the Brooks Brothers suit, snowy shirt and conservative tie who appears and ushers his visitor into the company boardroom. This is the new world of Kerry Burtnyk, stockbroker or, as he prefers, "account executive."

Nor would they recognize the curling bum in the eager professional who talks about loving his work and finding his niche, about buying things like a house and a new car and even about getting married.

"I'm really happy about it," says long-time curling mate Kammerlock about the impending marriage to competitive curler Patti Tressor. "I didn't think he'd ever settle down."

But eons ago, when 13-year-old Kerry Burtnyk, small for his age and very quiet, pushed his way through the door of the Assiniboine Memorial Curling Club for the first time, the script for his future was already written. It's not the foray into business but the long dalliance with curling that is the surprise.

At 13, in grade eight, he was already something of a math whiz. He was serious, painfully shy and liked to play chess. He loved sports, but the next year in high school he was one of the smallest kids in the school. He didn't have much of a chance in hockey or other sports where strength and size are key ingredients. Luckily he was already, with only one year's experience, a good curler.

Good enough to win a spot as third on the school team for the schoolboys' championship and almost good enough to beat Pat Ryan, who was opposite him on Dave Iverson's rink. The Iverson-Ryan combination eventually went on to win the provincial championships and come third in the country. Burtnyk would accomplish the same feat a couple of years later.

In his high-school yearbook, Burtnyk was summed up this way: "Born with a Silver Broom in one hand and an Aero bar in the other."

The Silver Broom reference showed he'd already made his mark as a curler. The chocolate bar was a tip of the hat to his math prowess. The math teacher had a habit of getting tangled in problems at the blackboard. He'd offer an Aero bar to anyone who could extricate him. Kerry collected more than his share of the rewards.

But the centre of his life those days was Assiniboine Memorial. Olson remembers how competitive they all were. The curlers hung together all summer playing everything: soccer, baseball, football and road hockey, competing furiously through the long summer days. There were always fights when their fierce competitiveness boiled over. And when they rested, the talk always turned to curling and how they'd win the next year.

"We grew up where they idolized curlers," explains Olson. "I remember I couldn't have been more than nine when I was asking guys who had played in the Brier for their brooms. We lived and breathed curling. The Brier becomes your sole goal."

Burtnyk was shy, Olson gregarious. It was a comfortable arrangement. Kerry soon found himself spending all of his spare time at the rink. And their devotion paid off. Two years in a row they won the huge Winnipeg schoolboys' Christmas bonspiel that attracted 300 teams. As they got older their fun got a little more adventurous. They organized all-night junior bonspiels at the curling club. They'd start at midnight and go to 7 A.M.—first prize $100.

Mark was a year older, and already out of junior in 1978 when
Kerry and the team finally won the right to represent Manitoba at the
national junior championships. Olson went as coach. Burtnyk kept
track of his curling games that year. In six months he played 185
games, at least one a day. "And that's not counting throwing rocks,"
he laughs.

They didn't know what to expect, heading into the junior nationals. They were prepared for the strong teams and, in fact, beat every
team ranked ahead of them. But they were caught off-guard by
teams from provinces considered to be weak curling powers, and
were disappointed to finish tied for third.

Kerry was only 18 that June when the team headed to Brandon for
their first men's spiel. A summer spiel was a novelty, and they were in
high spirits, planning to camp and party. They met Paul Gowsell in
the campground, and the first round of competition—in touch football and in partying—was on. The two teams met again in the final
of the spiel.

Burtnyk and the boys lost both encounters, but they realized they
belonged in the league, and they saw how much fun they could have.
They also saw the potential of push brooms and made an immediate
switch.

The next year Kerry was too old for juniors but he did have a
chance to redeem 1978's disappointment. Instead of heading into
men's, he waited out a year so he could compete with his team in the
Canada Winter Games in February 1979 in Brandon. It was a very
wise decision; they won a gold medal, and the confidence that was to
carry them through the next couple of years started to soar.

Winning the Canada Winter Games in their home province made
them local heroes. That status was reinforced in the 1980 men's
playdowns when they qualified for the semi-finals of the province,
undefeated. They were 21-year-olds on a team of destiny.

Enter Earle Morris. He was a major in the Canadian forces and
would later represent Ontario and Quebec, but in Manitoba he
wasn't given much chance of winning, especially since Burtnyk's
team had already beaten him in the first round of the competition.

From the start of playdowns they'd won 17 straight games, but
now they faltered against Morris and were out on their ear. Nearly a
dozen years later that loss still rankles with Burtnyk. He resents a

system that he believes makes it very unlikely the best team will win. A double-knockout system for 32 teams is just too wide-open, he believes.

But despite the disappointing end, it had been a fabulous year for the team. At one point they'd had a 47-game winning streak going. "I don't think we were known as an arrogant team," says Olson, looking back. "But we were very, very confident and we thought nobody could beat us. I think we intimidated a lot of teams."

If they were filling out income tax forms in those days, the most accurate answer for occupation would have been "curler." Kerry had enrolled in the Red River Community College and started into a college career of taking and dropping a couple of courses a year. Mark's father owned a stucco-and-plastering business and he worked for him in the summers. In the winter he was on unemployment insurance.

They knew that if they were to take the next step as curlers they had to play on the bonspiel circuit, and regularly play teams like Gowsell, Lukowich and a new light on the scene, Al Hackner, who had lost the final of the 1980 Brier.

In curling it was a time of powerful young men's teams, and Bubba and the boys wanted, above everything, to be part of it. But to get out on that bonspiel circuit they needed money. Mark's dad came to the rescue. They managed to work out a deal that he would put up $6,000 sponsorship money, and if they won they would pay him back plus 20 percent of their winnings. If they lost he would chalk his $6,000 up to experience.

Kerry's parents helped them get their first invitations to the big B.C. cashspiels. In the fall of 1980 they were the least-heralded of the entries into the Vernon carspiel. And anyone watching their airport antics in Edmonton would have put their chances of doing anything at the bonspiel somewhere east of impossible. They spent the whole five-hour stopover in the bar, and when the flight was called, sprinted through the airport pushing one of their inebriated number on a luggage cart. Somehow they got tangled in the roped barrier and pulled dozens of standards down with loud clangs that echoed hideously through the airport.

With this inauspicious beginning it was no surprise they were trashed in their first two games. Burtnyk remembers people patronizing them in a kindly way, talking about how it was important experience for them. But it was a triple knockout format, and they had been counted out a trifle too soon.

They'd won eight straight by the time they faced Bernie Sparkes in the final. "He'd won the cars two or three times before," remembers Olson. "He probably looked at us as a bunch of juniors from Manitoba who stood no chance against him. But we ended up stealing one in ninth to go two up coming home, and basically ran him out of rocks."

In the tenth end Olson looked over and saw the four cars parked on the sheet beside them. "I remember thinking about all the all-night bonspiels we'd played for $100, and here were four cars. All we had to do was play that end well. I'd never owned a car in my life. We made every shot in the end.

"I remember Kerry's shot coming down, and all of a sudden those keys were dangling in front of our faces. We're all sitting in the cars and guys are offering to buy them from us for cash. I think there were three hangovers after that bonspiel as well."

Olson never drank. He functioned through those early wild years as someone to lean on for those coming home from many an all-night party.

Kerry sold his car to the bartender that night for $4,500. Mark traded his in on a Toyota Celica. For Spencer and Kammerlock it wasn't quite as idyllic a moment. After selling their cars they had to hop a plane back to Winnipeg for a few days' work before the Kamloops spiel the next weekend.

Mark and Kerry stayed. They played a few rounds of golf and drove up to Kamloops, where they found themselves in the curling limelight for the first time. Everybody wanted to meet the hot young team from Manitoba. And while Gowsell continued to outrage and delight people in equal measure, nobody could find fault with the Manitobans.

Although Mark was the fiercest on the ice, he was the most self-assured when socializing afterwards, talking to everyone—funny, articulate and open. Kerry was the personification of cool. On the ice he was all business, never for a second losing control. Upstairs behind the glass, he was easy-going, friendly and something of a lady-killer in his own quiet way. He remembers the pleasure they felt when curlers whom they'd known only by their national reputations started showing them respect and talking to them as if they were friends.

They didn't have a care in the world. They were fearless and as happy as they'd ever been in their lives.

The Kamloops spiel was almost an exact replay of Vernon. Within the first few games they had dropped to C with only one life. Then their streak started and they won everything, including the final against the legendary 1978 Brier champion, Ed Lukowich. They walked away from that with an extra $10,000 in their pockets.

In two weekends they'd won nearly $30,000. It was a feat they would never equal again. But they wouldn't have believed that in the fall of 1980. Then they were just starting out. Who knew what wonders were ahead? "What had happened already was beyond our wildest dreams before we left home." Kerry explains.

They had no concept of limitations. They were too young to be scared, had implicit confidence in each other, and knew that their growing reputation as partyers added to the psychological edge they were establishing.

As Kerry points out, stories of the alcoholic antics of teams are always exaggerated. He didn't mind a bit. As their reputation for stamina grew, they seemed even more invincible to the teams that faced them in the morning. Besides, having an outlet for fun and frolic is essential when you're in your early twenties and are operating in a tense, charged atmosphere where a few millimetres of miscalculation can throw a victory away.

The social side of curling is essential, insists Burtnyk. "If I had to fly to Thunder Bay, go to my hotel room, jog, eat wheat germ, drink milk and wait for my next game, I wouldn't do it. You can't make a living at it; it has to be fun."

It was in this relaxed frame of mind that the team qualified for the 32-team provincial championship in 1981.

"We were lucky," says Olson now. It was the same format as the year before. They got off to a good start and made it to the semifinals undefeated. There they ran into trouble against their old teammate Greg Blanchard, but this time they pulled it off. They'd learned enough in a year of fierce competition to know that nobody was going to take the win away again without a dogged fight. The final against Murray Nye was much easier.

So now they had accomplished their hearts' desire, the chance to represent Manitoba in the Brier. There's a certain mystique about the Manitoba Brier team even after an 11-year period (between 1981 and 1991) when the championship was won five times by

Ontario and Northern Ontario, four times by Alberta and only twice by Manitoba. But the buffalo province still holds the record for most Brier wins, and in the hearts of Manitobans curling still belongs to them.

What is true today was even truer in 1981 when Manitoba had won the Brier 20 times, while Alberta, their closest rival, had only 13 wins.

And so, off the Burtnyk team went to Halifax, pumped with pride and ready to take on all comers. But as confident as they were on the surface, they were still only kids. A sense of awe kept surfacing, though tinged with irreverence. Mark remembers at the first practice trying to picture the arena full of 6,000 fans and finding the effort beyond him. He remembers shivering in apprehension and watching the goosebumps rise on his arms.

Kerry found that it helped to be hung over. He remembers that practice primarily for how awful he felt. He threw four rocks. None came remotely near the broom, so he gave up, telling the driver who was holding the broom for him not to worry, he'd be all right.

The next day, when competition started, the Burtnyk team was neither awed nor awful. They strode out to play with their heads high and their shoulders square. Burtnyk called for a freeze for their very first shot of the Brier. They were serving notice they had arrived.

They finished 8-3 in the round robin—one win behind Hackner. In the semi-final they beat Saskatchewan in an extra end and set up the miracle game that gave them the 1981 Brier.

It was a Cinderella story. In every province but Manitoba they were considered the underdogs. The year before, Hackner had lost in the final to Rick Folk, and in this Brier he'd already beaten Burtnyk once in an extra end in round-robin play. But nobody, except Burtnyk's team, and possibly Hackner's, remembered that the Manitobans had been successful every one of the nine times the two teams had met throughout the year.

Olson remembers lying awake at 5 A.M. on the morning of the final, trying to come to grips with the sheer size of the event. "I remember staring at the ceiling and thinking if there's ever a day in my life that I want to come out and play really well, this is it. I knew I had it. 'Just close your hand and you've the Brier,' I kept telling myself."

Olson laughs now about the CBC's attempt to take a head shot of him before the game. He was supposed to say his name and his province. Three times they tried it and every time he said his age too. Finally they gave up and left his age as part of his introduction.

But the funny thing was that he didn't realize until afterwards, when someone told him that he had been making a mistake in saying his age. "It was just total focus on the game. I don't even remember saying that."

Today he can go through that game shot by shot with the speed of an auctioneer. He points out the delicate moments, the mistakes and the near misses. But it's the tenth end that still makes his throat constrict and brings tears to his eyes.

For Al Hackner this end was a disaster. For the Burtnyk team it was the most beautiful end of curling ever played. "I've watched it 50 times and I still get emotional every time when I see how everything happened," says Olson.

They hadn't had control of the game since the early ends. Hackner was having a fabulous game, curling in the middle nineties. But now, suddenly, the tenth end had unfolded, so that by the time Kerry got into the hack for his last shot, it was theirs to win.

Mark, sitting behind the sheet, saw this as "the shot we'd talked about for years. The shot to win the Brier." He grabbed Kerry's arm and tried to calm him. "Take a few deep breaths," he cautioned. "The ice is keen, the guys [sweepers] can get it there. Watch your weight."

Kerry, with his coolness perfectly intact, walked down the ice. One of their rocks was biting by the tiniest fraction on the left behind the T-line, and Kammerlock from the other end of the rink couldn't tell. He broke one of the cardinal rules of curling by talking to Kerry as he settled into the hack. "Is it in?" he said, scarcely moving his mouth.

"Yeah, it's in," Burtnyk replied without looking at him.

Olson now regrets it, but as he held the broom for this most crucial shot, he motioned for the crowd to be silent. And although that little touch of gracelessness might have distracted some skips, Burtnyk was unflappable.

And even as he slid out, very, very slowly, the sweepers kept with him and talked. Somebody said "More" before he let go and then immediately "Whoa!"

But all this confusion and chat, which would have thrown Hackner, Lukowich or even Werenich, didn't have any discernible effect on Burtnyk. The throw was perfect, and even before it hit the house Kerry had started jumping. Olson, picking his cue from his skip, leapt onto the adjoining sheet and started running up and down madly.

Kammerlock, who with Jimmy Spencer was still sweeping the rock, thought the ecstasy a little premature. "It wasn't even in the rings yet. It could have picked a hair. Anything could have happened."

Besides, he still wasn't convinced that the other rock was really biting. Before he'd start jumping, he'd wait for the measure Hackner called for. Meanwhile, with all the uncontained excitement, a photographer almost kicked the rock before the measure.

"I don't know what would have happened then," says Kammerlock darkly. But Ron's moment of grumpiness soon passed when it became apparent, even to him, that they had taken three and won the Brier.

They were all in shock for at least an hour afterwards. But today every detail of the handshakes, the rings, the tankard, the ceremony is burned into their memories.

"Now I don't like to sit back and say I won it all, and have that attitude," says Kammerlock cautiously, "But sometimes when I'm lying awake at night, that final game will pop into my head and it keeps me awake thinking about it. I appreciate it more, looking back."

For Olson, nothing in his life except the birth of his children compares with the final moments of that game. "And I even look back today and wish for an opportunity like that again," he says.

The carpers had their usual complaints afterwards: the Burtnyk rink was too young and hadn't paid their dues. The strength of that opinion increased a few weeks later when the foursome lost to Switzerland in the final of the world championship in London, Ontario.

That loss put an ugly episode on a beautiful year. But for the nearly three weeks between the Brier and the worlds the Burtnyk rink lived in a delighted daze. There were TV cameras and 4,000 people at the Winnipeg airport to welcome them home. They were on the front page of the *Free Press* and there were instantly 50 dinners and banquets lined up for them to attend.

"All of a sudden you had the recognition of the whole curling world of Canada," says Mark with a touch of wistfulness. "It was a feeling of total ecstasy. We thought we'd win 20 times after that."

The pace was exhilarating for the apparently nerveless youngest-team-ever-to-win-the-Brier. By the time they got to London with their new made-to-measure suits, their Maple Leaf shirts, the rings and all the other Canadian paraphernalia—they felt like kings.

They still remember the opening ceremonies; how the darkened arena exploded in a deafening cheer when the Canadian team was finally introduced. They remember the kids tugging at their sleeves and asking for autographs, and how they felt when they looked down and saw themselves as they had been a few years before.

But all that emotionalism was going to take its toll. They had prepared to play the Brier but they had never even thought of world curling. In fact, like most Canadians, they were dismissive about it. They started the tournament on a high, pummelling Keith Wendorf's West German rink 11-2. In the first half-dozen draws the only close game was with the United States.

Socially this was a strange scene for them. In Europe curling is an elite sport played by the superrich at elaborate mountain resorts. The boys from suburban Winnipeg had trouble relating and felt the strain.

At breakfast one morning they sat beside Jurg Tanner and the Swiss team who were tucking into juicy steaks. Kammerlock ordered a grilled cheese sandwich but a few minutes later the waitress was back. They couldn't do grilled cheese, it wasn't on the menu, she said. Ronnie was grumpy again. Why, he wanted to know, could the Swiss have steak then? Steak wasn't on the menu either.

"I was told they brought their own food and their own chef," he says now. It didn't really matter if the story was true or not, it summed up the edginess the team felt. Here they were in their own country playing their own sport, and somehow they sensed they were out of sync. The rules and customs seemed to have subtly shifted out of their realm of understanding.

This was particularly true of rule infractions. The Swiss talked about the Canadians—particularly Olson—taking liberties with the hogline. The Canadians had a much bigger complaint about the tricky sweeping they felt was going on. In the round-robin game with the Swiss, which the Canadians won 8-3, they were so angry about what they considered "dumping" that Olson slammed a rock into the corner. But afterward, when the media pounced, both Kerry and Mark kept their mouths shut. "We didn't want to give them any more incentive to beat us if we met again," Mark says.

But Ron, in the dressing room, wasn't as discreet. He told the *Globe and Mail* what he thought of the Swiss sweeping tactics, and the tension of the week went up a notch. Still, the Canadians won their next game against Denmark and headed into the last game of the round robin unbeaten.

It had been a draining week. Burtnyk remembers how tired he felt as the week wore on. The whole thing was so overwhelming. A couple of weeks before, they had been ordinary 22-year-olds and now here they were on a pedestal, being asked for autographs, with everyone they met cheering for them.

They were close to winning it all but, as it turned out, not nearly close enough. "I could tell when we came out for that game with Sweden [the last of the round robin], we just didn't have it. I knew it," says Mark, still with a heavy sigh in his voice ten years later.

Nor did they get it back for the semi-final against Switzerland. The edginess that had been around all week was even more pronounced in that game and took its toll on both Olson and Burtnyk. They both had bad games. The breaks they'd been able to count on all year suddenly disappeared. The Swiss beat them decisively 7-4 and went on to win the final.

Olson still regrets that semi-final. It took the gloss off their Brier win. It also resurrected the LaBonte* curse, which the superstitious believed had foiled the Canadian team at the world championships from 1973 to 1980. In 1980 Rick Folk had finally won again for Canada. But now, a year later, Canada was dumped right back into the mire again. Olson, for one, felt as down as he had ever felt in his life.

"Bothersome" is the word Burtnyk uses about losing the worlds. "We were the best team there, and to let it slip away like that really bothered me," he says. Winning the world championship is still unfinished business in the back of his mind.

Looking back, he sees the loss as a pivotal point in their lives. But at the time, though it was a setback, it was not the end of the line. They'd done it once, they could do it again.

But it was the end of the line for Ron Kammerlock. His main

---

* At the 1972 Silver Broom, skip Bob LaBonte of the U.S.A. rushed down the ice to celebrate what he thought was his triumph over Canada's Orest Meleschuk. But he lost his balance and slid on his backside into the house kicking the Canadian stone as he slid. The United States lost on a measure and LaBonte swore Canada would never again win a world championship. Rick Folk broke the spell in 1980.

feeling, when the world championship was over, was relief. He didn't even go to the closing banquet.

"I'd had enough," he remembers. He just wanted out. He looked at the coming year with its trips to Europe to play in bonspiels, its frantic Canadian schedule with exhibition games and appearances at all the biggest and best bonspiels. He also saw and carefully weighed the price tag attached to being a celebrity in Winnipeg. He had already had a taste of that. There seemed to be public appearances and banquets every weekend that he wasn't away curling. For a blue-collar guy who liked a simple life, it was far, far too much and he balked.

By now he was the only one on the team who had a job. And the only one with a fiancée. Choices had to be made and he chose his relationship and his job. "And I've never regretted it," he says.

So while the others trekked to Europe, winning almost every bonspiel they entered, and crisscrossed Canada in search of curling glory, he sat out a year and waited for things to settle down.

Unfortunately for the rest of the team, things settled down with an abrupt thud. "It never clicked after that," says Olson, who believes it hurt their team enormously to lose Kammerlock.

"It was a big shock," remembers Burtnyk. "After that the special magic wasn't there anymore."

Another reason the jets failed to fire was that the special symbiotic relationship between Burtnyk and Olson fell apart over a woman. She had been Mark's girlfriend, and when she broke up with Mark, Kerry started dating her.

It was a blow their nine-year-old friendship couldn't withstand. "I was quite immature at the time and that affected me dramatically," says Mark. "Between a skip and a third there has to be communication, and Kerry and I lost that communication. I wrongly accused him. I should never have let it bother me like that."

The volatile Olson and the contained Burtnyk couldn't have a cathartic shouting match, and so after Mark fired his broadside at Kerry, wrongly accusing him of going behind his back, there was no way back. "We almost never talked again after that."

At the Brandon Brier in 1982, a mere 12 months after their great triumph, Mark and Kerry hadn't spoken for months, and the team was in ruins. Mark remembers searching all over the Brier Patch for his skip, because he was heading to Europe and he wanted to talk about next year. He never found him, and the team died.

The next year Mark skipped a team that included Ron Kammerlock. They made it to the semi-finals of the province, but after
another couple of years of near misses it became clear to Mark that
he wouldn't win as a skip. "You hear rumours," he explains.
"Friends tell you that people are saying, 'Olson doesn't have it,' and
the respect starts to diminish. That respect wins you a lot of games."

Burtnyk too suffered. It took a couple of years for him to feel
"comfortable" with another third. And when that happened it was
with Jeff Ryan, Pat's younger brother. The combination worked so
well that when Mark abandoned skipping and phoned to ask if they
could play together again in 1986, Burtnyk had no place for him.

The next year, playing for Vic Peters, the Manitoba curler who
usually wins the one-on-one shoot-out competitions, Mark sailed
past his old team and ended up "losing a squeaker 5-4" that would
have taken him back to the Brier.

The Peters rink, with Mark at third, repeated its success in 1988
and again made it to the final. But this time there was poignancy in
the game. At the other end of the rink Mark Olson faced all three of
his teammates from the 1981 Brier.

The Burtnyk rink, now reunited except for him, defeated the
Peters rink easily and finally. After seven years of struggle, Burtnyk
was on his way to the Brier.

Olson watched on TV as a strangely somnambulant Burtnyk went
through the motions, never really catching fire.

He finished tied for third and out of contention. Thinking about
his performance afterwards, he believes he had come to focus too
much on winning Manitoba. When he did it and beat Mark in the
process, he didn't seem to have enough energy left to switch goals to
winning the Brier. It felt as if the year was over.

Kammerlock is surprised at his skip's comments. For him, the
determination to win in 1988 was very strong. But Kerry, for all his
Iceman antics, knows inside there must be some fear. He wasn't
nervous enough, he confesses. Some of the games felt like club
games. The low-key atmosphere at the Chicoutimi Brier added to the
impression.

There was one game, though, that stands out, even today, as a
prized symbol of the code of curling that Kerry so admires. It came
at the very end of the week when Kerry was 7-3 and still had a
mathematical chance of making it to the playoffs. He met his old
friend Al Hackner in the final game of the round robin.

Since their dramatic encounters in the early 1980s, Al and Kerry had become good friends. Watch them walk into a room together at a bonspiel party and their similarities are striking. The two Icemen. And under the cool, solemn surface—in both cases—beats the heart of a guy who loves to party. Win or lose, the celebration is an integral part of the competition. When Hackner lost the heartbreaker to Burtnyk in 1981, their code dictated that their two teams party together all that night. For Al or any of his team to crawl away to nurse his wounds would have been impossibly weakminded.

These two aren't like Pat Ryan. They wouldn't dream of talking about "living on the edge." They don't acknowledge the edge is there. But even so, when they set up the rules for the game, they make sure the tightrope is high—and very narrow.

The two friends had talked about the 15th draw of the 1988 Brier. Going in, Hackner was 4-6 and finished. Burtnyk had his back to the wall. If everything unfolded correctly, he could force a tie-breaker by beating Hackner.

But Bubba was worried. Hackner was, as he knew very well, incapable of playing a bad game in a situation like this. In fact, what worried Burtnyk most was that he would be loose and probably more likely to have a superb game.

There had been teasing that Hackner should take it easy on them. And even when they were playing, Ronnie remembers, they were joking "C'mon, give us a chance."

But no chances were given and the game ended 6-4 with Burtnyk out of the playoffs.

But the accomplishment of getting to the Brier stood. After seven years as a big-deal contender, half of those years as the favourite, Burtnyk had begun going to the provincials with a sense of dread thinking, "How are we going to blow it this year?"

Now with that monkey off his back he was ready to get on with the decision he'd made about a career. He was 29 and he'd never had a serious job. For half-a-dozen years he worked in the winter for Asham Curling Supplies, selling and doing whatever was necessary. In the summers he didn't work, preferring instead to camp and enjoy himself around the White Shell area of Falcon Lake, Manitoba.

It was an idyllic existence, except for the fact that the world was rushing past him, and in his late twenties he began to notice. He had never worn a tie and had so little use for that symbol of the workaday world he'd never learned how to tie one.

One night Jeff Ryan dropped in for a visit and chuckled at the incongruous sight of Bubba struggling with the Windsor knot. He had a job interview in the morning. Ryan obliged his buddy and left the tie knotted and ready to be pulled over his head. Ryan remembers Kerry got the job but only lasted a day or two.

When Burtynk hit on the idea of taking the securities course and trying to become a broker, he thought it might be better than some of the grim selling jobs he'd investigated (or briefly held), but he didn't expect it to be much more than a passable means to an end.

He'd always dabbled a bit in investments, and now he realized that his name in Winnipeg was probably an asset in the business community. Even if the businessmen he met weren't curlers, they would know his name and it would give him an entrée.

In 1989 the team didn't travel much and only won $5,000. It was a little bit of a blow in the pocketbook for a team that was used to winning between $20,000 and $30,000 a year. But the break allowed Kerry to get his business going at Richardson Greenshields. As he had hoped, he got the job ahead of others with better paper qualifications because of his name in the community.

But even if he was starting to be drawn into the vortex of business, he managed to practise at the curling rink occasionally and play the odd bonspiel. In the 1989 playdowns, ironically, they almost struck paydirt for the second year in a row. They lost a close game in the semi-final.

Nobody was too surprised that math whiz Kerry Burtnyk wound up doing well at the best investment firm in Winnipeg. He'd managed his team for years, always signing a sponsor or two to help with their expenses. And despite the wildness around the edges, he had a reputation of being a solid kind of guy who knew which end was up.

The work suits him perfectly. He can take a day or two whenever he needs it for curling, and there's a win-loss ledger at the end of the week, not a salary.

Sure he felt a bit awkward for the first few months, a bit of an impostor, showing up in a shirt and tie. But he'd been through these awkward transitions before; he knew he'd learn the ropes. And very soon he knew that this predominantly male world with its own subset of rules and obligations was not a whole lot different from curling. In many ways, although more subtle in its successes and failures, he finds the business world just as competitive and just as compelling as curling—a fact that surprises and delights him.

As for curling, it remains one of the staples of his life, but only one. His winnings are down into the teens now but he remains one of the consistent forces in Manitoba. There are more changes on his team than there have been in the past, but the connection with Kammerlock continues—and will, Ron believes, as long as they curl.

But in 1990, with new players Rob Meakin at second and Dave Smith at third, he had a mediocre year. The bonspiels were "average." They made a little more money than it cost them to play, but the playdowns were very disappointing. For the first time since 1980, when Bubba entered men's competition, he didn't make the 32-team provincial tournament.

True to character, though, he's sticking with his team. He feels he has the right guys together because they get along extremely well. And he accepts that things outside of curling, his marriage plans and his career, have taken a toll on his sport.

But he doesn't waste time worrying about it. In fact, for 1991-92 he and Mark Olson have pulled off something that will leave other provinces gasping in wonder. They've organized a $250,000 Manitoba cashspiel circuit that will allow local curlers like themselves to get all the competition they want very close to home. Curling may have dropped from one to three on Kerry's priority list, but it's still a big deal in his life. The circuit will make life easier for him to juggle everything.

Burtnyk is one of the few who seem on the way to putting curling into perspective in their lives. It is no longer the only arena he has to compete in and he's won enough to be satisfied. He doesn't want to quit but he also doesn't feel there's a huge chapter of unfinished business in his life. He'd still like to win the world championship "because that's the ultimate," but he hardly ever thinks of it.

It's a sign of how different their make-ups are that Mark Olson is still weighed down by that failure so long ago in London, Ontario.

"I keep waiting for a break," says Olson now. "If we had won the world championship I can honestly say I could retire today and be happy being 33 years old. But we didn't and the drive is very, very strong—even today."

10

MIKE RILEY
The Outsider Moves On

IN WINNIPEG CURLING circles Kerry Burtnyk is as mainstream as it gets. Manitoba curling fans have watched him grow up. He's been a normal kid in every way except that his skill and competitiveness have assured him bigger successes, more fame and more fun than most. Today, perhaps a little late, he's on the verge of responsible maturity. Tall, crisp and competent, he seems to skim effortlessly along the surface of life.

Just like Burtnyk, Mike Riley has represented Manitoba at the Brier twice during the 1980s and won once. Just like Burtnyk, he's Winnipeg born and bred and has spent many years pursuing the golden fleece of the Brier. But where Burtnyk is Manitoba's curling hero, Riley is almost a forgotten man. And where Burtynk skims along without complications, Riley is complex, and driven by the need for challenge.

When the organizers of the $250,000 Moncton 100 cashspiel sent out their 16 invitations, they sent one to Burtnyk, of course, but the second Manitoba invitation went to Orest Meleschuk, a fiery showboater who last won the Brier in 1972.

Ask curlers across the country about Mike Riley and they all say the same thing: "I don't know much about him . . . I think he's got money or something." Not much more is known about him in Winnipeg. Ask the best curlers in town to rate their top players and, despite his obvious success, Riley doesn't make the top five in many lists.

The reason they write him off is that they've seen him play badly, very badly. But they've also seen him play superbly well. At cashspiels where competitive curlers gather and compare notes, Riley almost never makes an impression. He's not big on the party scene and he's often lamentably weak on the ice. This is not his scene, and for a decade or more he's avoided cashspiels except when he needs them to get tuned up for playdowns.

He doesn't care about the money and he can't crank himself up when it doesn't count. But the other curlers still shake their heads.

"I can't understand the guy," says Mark Olson, "he goes to the Bahamas or somewhere and comes back just in time for the playdowns and wins the thing. It's incredible. Nobody can do that. You have to practise."

And so when he wins, they tend to look through him and attribute his success to an inadequate playoff structure or luck or a fluke.

Ironically, considering how the elite curlers feel about him, Riley has hung around the fringes of competitive curling for a quarter-century because he enjoys what he calls the "recognition." It's not that he doesn't have anywhere else to go.

He's got a list of passions longer than Pat Ryan's, and his best friend says that even before his Brier win in 1984 he was talking about quitting. He stayed because he was winning, not, like Burtnyk and Hackner, because he was enamoured of the lifestyle, not, like Werenich and Lukowich, because he loves the game.

But at 46 this maverick champion has finally traded in his slider— at least for the time being. In 1990-91, the year he first went cold turkey from curling, he headed off to sail the Caribbean in a 38-foot schooner. With his wife and another couple he drifted through the British Virgin Islands avoiding big storms or big trouble. For a guy who had done most of his sailing on a 22-foot boat around his own beloved corner of Lake of the Woods, it was an adventure.

The trip lasted a month and when he came back there was little time to pine for the intensity of the provincial playdowns. He had to make arrangements for his spring adventure holiday—trekking in Nepal. In the end he didn't go, trading in the trip in favour of a June canoe trip down the Mackenzie from Great Slave Lake to the Arctic Ocean at Tuktoyaktuk.

Even with these diversions he expected the first winter without the jumped-up excitement of the playdowns to be "traumatic." He didn't know if he could be happy without the cachet of being an excellent curler. He looked at all the other chapters he'd recently finished in his life, and he knew that curling probably belonged to the past. But he'd talked retirement before and always ended up on the curling sheet when it counted. So he didn't know if this would be a year off or real retirement.

When you meet Mike Riley, the first impression is of a ten-speed adventurer. Here's a guy who sees life in the round, you say to yourself, somebody who wants to go around as many corners as he can in the time allotted him. You get glimpses of a guy who was born to the manor and never saw much need for any of the other trappings of business success.

He sits in front of a computer in a bland, unpretentious, pink-and-rosewood office on the 26th floor of the Trizec Building. He's 200 metres kitty-corner from and three floors below Burtnyk, and he's doing the same kind of number-crunching. But their worlds seldom collide. Riley plays a high-stakes gamble. He's an investor, and with partners he runs a venture-capital company that invests money for insurance companies like Great West Life and even the Manitoba government. Their mission: to find Manitoba companies that have potential international markets and invest in them.

He smiles cautiously. Grey beard, grey suit, wire glasses, and a slightly dishevelled look that tells you that, yes, he did ride his bike to work today. For all his silver-spoon life as a member of the powerful Riley family in Winnipeg, as a cousin of Conrad Black's and as a natural talent in curling, Mike looks like a person who understands struggle. He has none of the crisp, straight-to-the-bottom-line confidence of Burtynk. It's taken him 25 years to find the peace he now has in his life, says Dennis McCaffrey, who has been his best friend since they were engineering undergraduates at the University of Manitoba.

Mike remembers how important curling was to him as an undergraduate and through his twenties. It was how he got recognition, how he perceived himself fitting into the world. Through his twenties, curling success meant much more than his job as an engineer at Manitoba Telephone Services. "I guess I can say that now that I've resigned," he laughs.

Every year he'd add on a bit to his curling skill. Of all the sports he'd tried, curling came the most naturally. But he wasn't, he knew, despite his dark, deep dreams, Brier material—at least not yet. He hadn't come close to representing his province as a junior, but at 20, skipping three other 20-year-olds, he made it to the men's playdowns. It was a thrill that spurred him to take university curling seriously. In his final year his rink won the Canadian university championships and Riley's competitive career was launched.

Although his memories of his love affair with curling are vivid, there were other important sidelights in his life. He did, for example, manage to put enough time aside to graduate in electrical engineering, get a job and, at 28, take two winters off (from work, not curling) to do an MBA. Dennis McCaffrey recalls the shuffleboard games and long, long liquid talks in the pub that were part of both of their formative years and their developing friendship. (They still have monthly "Meaning of Life meetings" at the pub to commemorate those days.)

In the early 1970s Mike and Dennis bought 40 acres on Middle Island in the centre of Lake of the Woods. It was virgin territory and they homesteaded. Now it's the place where Mike is most at home and most comfortable. For 18 years both men have been working on their cottages, at first hauling the lumber by barge and more recently putting the fine touches to the interiors. It's a hobby and a passion and the other thing—besides curling—that has kept Mike Riley in Winnipeg.

For Riley the big kick of curling has always been the competition, performing in front of fans with a chance of winning a title or a purple heart. Cashspiels have never held much appeal. "You can make more staying home on a Sunday and licking envelopes," he says. "If Lukowich divides the number of hours he spends by the amount he wins, I bet he finds he's working for less than the minimum wage."

Of course, there are cashspiels where the pots generously line the winners' pockets, but they are few and far between, he says. He would have liked to play in the Moncton 100 but most cashspiels aren't worth the effort.

And yet, in his twenties and early thirties, long after he'd outgrown the boisterous parties, he hit as many cashspiels as he could for the competition. He didn't win much but he was building up experience or "capital" in the game, as he puts it.

In 1974, when he was 30, Rod Hunter came calling. Hunter had played third on Don Duguid's back-to-back championship rinks in 1970 and 1971. In 1973 he'd tried third with Danny Fink and made it to the Brier. By 1974 he decided it was time to strike out on his own. His choice at third was Mike Riley, a clubmate at the Winnipeg Granite and an accomplished competitor.

Mike agreed because he wanted to win. His chances with Hunter—even though he had to play third—were better than they were on his own. They got to the Brier and finished 6-5 but Riley was not happy. He tried to mould himself into the third's role but it didn't work. After a couple of miserable years he gave up. "He's not a team player," says one of his friends not unkindly. "He'd rather lose at skip than win at third."

Mike elaborates. "Skip is the most pressure-packed position in any sport. It really often comes down to one shot by the skip, in many, many games. As skip, there's more credit and more blame and it's more exciting."

Now that he was into his thirties, his independence of mind was growing. Although he kept them to himself he began to think heretical thoughts. For example, he came to believe that the great drama of sweeping the rock in curling was all show and no substance. "His theory is based on observation and a bit of engineering judgment," says McCaffrey, "but he kept it to himself. He knew it would screw up the whole game. There would be nothing for those other two guys to do and the whole excitement of the sweep would be gone."

He was also becoming more interested in health and fitness—two attributes not deeply admired in the curling world. But for Riley long, boozy nights in a smoky curling club were rapidly losing their appeal.

He was also beginning to wonder how much longer he could take working for a living—or at least working for a big company. Financially, it had always been possible for him to get by without working. But his conscience and his work ethic wouldn't allow him to quit.

But as he developed he found the corporate culture demanded too much conformity. He was too much of a loner, too independent, and he was always debating the pros and cons of working and contributing to society versus following his interests and his craving for adventure. He hadn't found his niche in the business world and McCaffrey, who worked with him at MTS, watched him struggle with work that didn't draw on his talents and never fully satisfied him.

In 1978 he started the slow withdrawal from MTS. He handed in his resignation, but he continued to work with them full-time as a consultant, doing the financial studies on engineering projects. By 1982 he and his first wife called it quits on a relationship that had never been very compatible, and he finally cut the tie with MTS.

Investing had always been a hobby of his, something he was good at and something, he insists, he works very hard at. "I don't play with investments," he says sternly.

His new direction was to become a full-time investor not only using his own money but also investing for others. He was much happier out on his own, doing something he was good at and enjoyed. It was around this time in his life that his ardour for curling began to cool. His private life now allowed for more adventure and more physical challenge. He ran, biked and swam in Tin Man triathlons. He hiked through the mountains, cycled with a friend through the islands of Cape Breton and Ireland and sailed through the Caribbean with McCaffrey.

He continued to curl, but by the fall of 1983 when he got together with Russ Wookey, John Helston and Brian Toews to form a team, he was 39 and the focus of his life had shifted. He no longer expected to win.

Six months later they were hoisting Labatt's gold tankard, and Riley told reporters: "When we started out this year we had no idea how good we'd be—I mean, we'd never played together and all of us were at the stage in our lives where we'd given up on the Brier dream. It wasn't really important anymore.

"Then we played [defending Brier champion Eddie] Werenich in a Winnipeg cashspiel and beat him. That's when we realized we had a hell of a team."

Now he talks about how they decided to play together because they liked each other. This was not a dream team, this was a bunch of friends who were available on the same night. "And since it wasn't so extremely important to do well any more, for the first time I could concentrate on the moment, not on the consequences," says Riley.

He was playing no better than he had ten years before but now he was much more in charge of himself, he believes. "There was no way I could have won the Brier at 29 because of my mental immaturity," he says. "Then if there was bad ice, I'd get angry at the ice. But by 1984 if I got on a bad sheet, I'd just concentrate on making the best of it. It's mental discipline."

He credits second John Helston and his casual, friendly style for much of the team's relaxed attitude. John was always ready to have fun, knew everyone and kept everything in perspective. He was also, at second, the best hitter Riley ever played with.

In 1975, playing third at the Brier, Mike had felt a great load of responsibility representing Manitoba. This time he felt much lighter.

He was doing this for himself and he might never be back again, especially since his life seemed to be taking off in new directions.

The maturity wasn't only in mental discipline, he knew; he was now a smarter skip, too. Curling is a slow game and skipping is a long learning process, he says. "There are a lot of real subtleties that you don't see until you've been at it for a long, long time. By 1984 I'd seen enough situations that I could play the probabilities instead of the hunches."

Clare DeBlonde, who had played in two Briers, went along as coach and fifth man. They worked together on strategy. DeBlonde scouted the other teams trying to figure out which turn the team favoured, and any other idiosyncrasies they had. Together Mike and Clare analysed their schedule and found they had five easy games first before they hit the more difficult competition. The plan was to play cautiously, wait for their chances and go in for the kill at just the right moment.

"One of the other things you learn is patience," explains Riley. "Younger skips think because this is the playdowns or the Brier you have to do something different, something exceptional. But it really is just a curling game and the chances will always come."

The first day everything went according to plan. But by the second day their composure began to unravel. In the morning they lost 7-4 to Newfoundland and, after a bye in the afternoon, went on to lose 7-6 to New Brunswick.

"They were one up coming home with last rock," remembers DeBlonde. "Mike's rock was not well thrown and New Brunswick ended up stealing two."

Mike was devastated. The Manitoba party was right after the draw and he was sure no one would want to go. But DeBlonde remembers that when he walked into the room and heard the cheering and clapping his spirits started to rise. Later, listening to his speech, DeBlonde knew Mike had made up his mind to win.

He didn't know it then, but he has since learned that when Riley turns on his laser-beam focus he is almost unbeatable. The problem is finding the switch. He can play embarrassingly badly, but when he really wants to win, there's a magic that leaves his friends breathless.

"He has an amazing ability to concentrate," says McCaffrey. "There are lots of people who can't block out the world the way he can. And he has control of his emotions to an extraordinary degree."

After that night he lost only one more game—to the home-province hero, Bernie Sparkes, and his imposing third, the big, intimidating dentist they called "Army," Jim Armstrong. Riley's rink finished tied with Alberta for first at 8-3 and secured themselves a bye to the final because they'd beaten Lukowich in the round robin.

There were the usual Brier controversies—this time over whether or not they should cover the rocks with towels to keep the heat of the TV lights off them. Everybody got hot, including DeBlonde, until Riley interrupted the bickering.

"Who cares?" he said. "Let's get the game going."

It's one of his most cherished bits of curling wisdom that there will always be external things you can't control. Whether it's warm rocks or a teammate's bad play, you have to accept it and try to play around it. "I've played with two people who I won't name who are as good as anybody I've ever seen, but they get thrown off their game by things they can't control and they forget to handle the things they can."

This attitude, he believes, helped him win the Brier. There was one problem that was much more significant than warm rocks. Each of the sheets was slightly higher in the centre than at the sides and the hump in the middle made it almost impossible to play around a centre-guard, he explains. The game had to be played around corner-guards.

Much has been made about Werenich's slip-up in the third end of the final, when he allowed Riley to steal two. "I could have missed that shot too," says Riley. "And I'd never say I picked up on the ice conditions faster than Ed Werenich. But probably on every other sheet he'd ever played on, the rock would have curled. This time it stayed straight."

By 1984, when he won the Brier, Riley believed he was drawing on the capital he'd built up in curling. He had practised and played a lot in the past but now he had outgrown cashspiels and stopped practising completely. Since 1982, when he'd finally broken with MTS, more of his passion had gone into his work life. And also he was courting the woman who would become his second wife. He met Janet in the summer of 1983. She had spent most of her adult life globetrotting, living out of a suitcase and searching for adventure. She had never so much as seen a curling rock. She watched the new man in her life play a few games of an incomprehensible ice sport and tagged along to Victoria for the Brier. All of a sudden he was Canadian champion.

"She thought that's just the way it was," laughs Mike. "She didn't understand I'd been trying for 20 years."

The team went to Duluth for the world championships and lost 9-8 in the semi-final to the Attinger rink from Switzerland. In the final Eigil Ramsfjell beat the Attingers and won his second of three world championships.

The loss did not disturb Riley the way it has so many other Canadian champions. His rink had already so far surpassed their own expectations they were riding a wave of delight. Besides, the championship organization and the fan interest were so inferior to the Brier it was hard to believe this was the ultimate championship. Afterwards, he says, he felt some regret because his team played well and they lost only because he had missed too many routine shots. "I didn't feel terrible," he says. "I have regrets but it's in the past and it's not something I dwell on."

Besides, all the curlers at the Duluth world championship had stark proof the game could be taken much too seriously. Austria has never been a curling hotbed, and at this competition the Austrian skip was hopelessly outclassed. His team didn't win a game. Part way through the competition he was gone and the teams later found out that he had been taken to a psychiatric hospital after his stress had erupted in a violent incident.

But Riley was way beyond succumbing to that punishing stress. He was having a great time as a celebrity skip and the media loved his thoughtful, intelligent answers. While others got worn out or cranky with all the attention, Riley's only negative emotion was guilt. He felt badly because his team was being ignored and he kept trying to divert some of the interviews their way.

Although his love affair with the sport was fading—even more quickly now—he had a full card of European bonspiels for 1985. At home there were guest gigs at the big Canadian cashspiels.

The team approached the year as a lark; curling was the last thing on their minds—and it showed. Riley says he was a little embarrassed: they were being hyped as a great curling power from Canada and they'd show up and never win a game. "It was one of the worst curling seasons I've ever had," he says ruefully.

His indifferent play illustrates how important focus is to Riley's game. If he had been able to muster the energy to win the European bonspiels, he probably wouldn't have been able to enjoy Europe. It's one more way he and Burtnyk are complete opposites.

He wasn't indifferent to his disappointing showing. By the time playdowns rolled around for the 1986 Brier, he felt he had something to prove. He wanted to show he deserved the Brier win, that it hadn't been just a fluke.

In 1984 they had dominated the provincial playdowns. They had gone through undefeated and only faced one tough game. In 1986 it was much tougher. Every game seemed a come-from-behind struggle and they were tired by the time they got to the Labatt Brier at Kitchener-Waterloo. But they had done it once again—defeated all the Manitoba hotshots who regularly wrote them off, and carried the provincial colours out of the province.

But the Brier wasn't the same happy experience it had been in 1984. They finished at 6-5 tied for third with three other rinks. Riley says his own play made the difference: he wasn't as strong as he'd been in 1984. And the team missed John Helston's hitting.

Clare DeBlonde is fascinated by Riley's talent. In the 86 Brier it went very badly at first, "but I remember them talking after they were mathematically eliminated," Clare says. "They didn't want to finish with a bad record." After the tenth draw they were 2-5 but they won their next four games, three of them in extra ends, to give themselves a respectable 6-5 record.

In 1985 Mike had remarried and he and his new wife had planned the most challenging adventure yet for the summers of 1986 and 1987. According to McCaffrey, Janet is perfect for Mike, a "Harrowsmith type who can live off the land—if she has to." He wasn't a bit surprised when they came up with the idea of retracing the fur traders' canoe route from Lake of the Woods to Ottawa. It took them 10 weeks over two summers (1986 and 1987) before they finally covered the 2,000 kilometres and 71 portages on the way to Ottawa.

In the winters Mike was back at the curling rink trying once again to find the focus and desire to make himself a winner. Janet took up the sport with gusto—perhaps with more enthusiasm than Mike. The investing had gone well; he could book off whenever he wanted to, and sometimes curling was the only thing that kept them in minus-forty-degree Winnipeg instead of holidaying in the tropics.

"Those were years of diminishing enjoyment," Mike admits. Ask him if he should have retired after 1986 as his third, Brian Toews, had done, and he at first agrees. But wait! He's forgotten that what he considers his greatest accomplishment in curling didn't come until

1988 when he won the largest bonspiel ever in the world. "It's in the Guinness Book of World Records," he says with a satisfied grin.

It was the 100th anniversary of the Manitoba Curling Association and more than 1,200 teams entered. "It was harder to win that than the Brier," he says, "because you had to win 'way more games."

In 1989 and 1990 Clare DeBlonde played third for him. "He really showed me something," DeBlonde says over and over, his voice full of wonder. "He doesn't work at the game like other curlers. He just has this incredible focus. I've never known Mike to go to the rink and throw rocks. You won't see him at the rink watching other teams."

But although he tosses out the things DeBlonde considers the essential tools of success in curling, Riley is always there when it counts.

"In 1989 we had a brutal cashspiel season and then Mike went to Hawaii. I was worried, but Russ Wookey kept reassuring me. 'Don't worry,' he'd say, 'when we get Mike into an arena he'll be OK,'" and he was. They went to the semi-finals of the province.

But in 1990 they didn't make it to the final tankard, an unusual and discouraging result for Riley. It helped him make up his mind to bow out for a while.

"For me the desire waned—I don't know what happened. The rest of my life expanded and curling became less important. I might curl competively again, but it won't be until I get the desire back."

11

RICK FOLK
Pudge Presses On

MIKE RILEY AT 46 is walking away from curling into something—anything—more physically challenging. He doesn't want to take wild chances (he turned down a chance to attempt a harrowing trip by canoe to South America) but he wants new horizons. Life without novelty, risk and the opportunity to stretch himself doesn't have much appeal.

Curling now seems too much effort for too little payback. He loved the recognition and the profile the sport gave him, but now he's had that, he's moving on to new challenges.

But for Rick Folk, another prairie champion, and another man in his forties, turning his back forever on curling would be inconceivable. The sport is an essential part of who he is. As for physical challenge, curling is more than enough exertion for Folk, who looks like he would much prefer an easy chair to a canoe trip down the Nahanni.

But nothing in Rick Folk's curriculum vitae hints at the stark differences in the two men. The events of his life would lead you to believe Rick Folk is even more a man of action and adventure than Mike Riley. He's won five provincial golf championships, made his living as a golf pro, a politician, a cabinet minister, a businessman, and an ad-agency executive. He's got enough chutzpah and sense of adventure to pull up his roots and transplant himself, on 45 days' notice, to another province. And while he has juggled so much change in his workaday life, he has continued to nurture a curling talent prodigious enough to win his teams $250,000 or more on the Gold Trail, a Labatt Brier and a Silver Broom, as the world championship used to be called.

His curling game is another example of a spirited approach to life. He played a draw game in a province where everyone else liked to hit, hit, hit. Even now if he has last rock, he'll gamble, court pressure and never let up on the opposition. And if an opponent is bending the rules, he'll confront him in the blink of an eye, kick the offending rock out of play and glare down the delinquent.

This is a guy who, to all appearances, loves risk, snatches opportunities and likes life on the edge.

Hello, Rick Folk?

There must be some mistake. This quiet, diffident shopkeeper cannot possibly be Rick Folk. This 41-year-old with the slight stoop and the soft voice, who has you straining to hear, could never be the skip whose team wore black and had an "Attitude" that intimidated every curler this side of the Pacific Ocean. This can't be the guy who, even without that team, at the 1989 Brier ignored the catcalls from the crowd, talked down a furious opponent and took a controversial burned rock out of play. Nor could this guy with his clear-eyed, unadorned version of the facts possibly survive in the never-say-what-you-mean waters where politicians cavort.

But yes indeed, this is the formidable Folk discussing sliders and the size of ladies' curling pants in a small store in downtown Kelowna. And if you think this mild-mannered man is just the husk that's left when the dynamo burned out, let it be remembered that in 1990-91 he skipped the "Super Team," a collection of styles, talents and egos large enough to have the curling fraternity talking from coast to coast.

And two years before that he almost won the Brier, losing in the finals to Pat Ryan 3-2.

How did the quiet third child of a successful Saskatoon furrier make it to the pinnacle of the curling world and come to represent the epitome of (to some at least) the win-at-all-costs school of competition? In the process he was booed and reviled, and in the end he came to represent—for some of his enemies—the symbol of all that's wrong with curling today.

These are not easy questions to answer in the presence of Rick Folk, a guy whose nickname "Pudge" has all the terror of a bad day on Sesame Street. Unlike his slightly ferocious second, Tommy

Wilson, his aggression doesn't stick out anywhere. He can even laugh at himself.

Still, there are a couple of obvious answers. First, to get that much notoriety in a sport dangerously thin on heroes, he had to be good. So good that he's always been virtually in a class by himself. And second, he had to have help. That is, he had to have someone on his team willing to run interference for him, someone who understood him and knew the value of intimidation in a curling game. For much of Folk's curling career, Tommy Wilson performed that function, and when he left Saskatoon in 1985 to take a big job in Toronto he was keenly missed.

But to find out how the magic soil of talent and toughness nurtured Rick Folk it's necessary to return to the old Nutana Curling Club on Main Street in Saskatoon in 1958.

Old-timers remember how that year a little kid, eight years old, would slip into the club every day after school to watch. His father, Alex Folk, was a man of substance, as they used to say, in the town of 140,000. He owned Folk's Finer Furs. Possessing one of Folk's handcrafted fur coats was an important step up the status ladder in town.

But none of that was remotely interesting to little Rick. Already he had fallen in love with one of the two sports that would dominate his life. Curling came first, and a year or two later golf established itself in his heart as the summer substitute.

In grade four he'd wait for an hour at the sidelines of the curling sheet for the chance to throw rocks for ten minutes. Sometimes he'd be lucky and there'd be an unexpected break. Heaven was two hours alone on the curling sheet to throw rocks. He was quickly getting good. Occasionally high-school teams would be short a player and they'd ask the little four-footer to spare for them.

Young as he was, nothing about curling bored him. Nor did he need a playmate at the rink. Nobody—not even his father—really understood his singular passion.

By the time he hit grade seven his father considered him good enough to play men's at the regular club level. Until he made the high-school team four years later, he played men's with his dad. Rick remembers Alex as the guy who taught him everything he knows about both curling and golf. Alex knew his spot in the curling hierarchy, though; he was very competitive in his home town but never quite good enough to make it to the next level.

Rick was another story altogether. By high school he was an obvious choice for the curling team. In grade 10, he played third for Tom Wilson, an energetic, competitive boy two years ahead of him. "He saw the error of his ways," laughs Wilson 34 years later, leaning back in a chair in his Scarborough, Ontario, office with his hands clasped firmly behind his head. "That was the only time he ever played any position but skip. Now he's one of the three greatest skips in the world." (The other two in Wilson's pantheon are Ernie Richardson and Ed Lukowich.)

Rick and Tom have remained best friends ever since their high-school days and a large part of the Rick Folk success story depends on the synergy between them.

But back in grade 11, none of that was obvious. All Rick knew was that his good friend and skip had moved on to college, and he was going to have to move up to skip if he wanted to get anywhere with this game. It didn't take long. The next year, 1968, he won the provincial schoolboys' championship and almost bagged the Canadian title, losing in the playoffs.

In the summer he took his talent and his plus-one handicap to the golf course, where he was recognized as the best the province had to offer as a junior golfer. Three big-time American universities came calling, brandishing impressive golf scholarships. He was tempted, sorely tempted. His brother Ron had taken such a scholarship seven years before and had even played on the PGA tour for three years. But you'd have to be a fool not to see that the odds on making a splash on the American golf scene are very, very long if you live in Saskatchewan—even if you're a five-time provincial champ. In curling, the Saskatchewan champion has almost a bye to greatness.

From Ron's experience Rick knew how tough a life the suitcase grind of the PGA can be—and how expensive. "If I hadn't tasted some success in curling, I might have done it," he says now. He knew, he says, that passing up the scholarship killed his hopes of playing big-time professional golf. Playing on the golf team of a big American university was the best way for a Canadian kid to polish his game to professional standards. Without that tutelage there wasn't much hope.

And yet, the other side of the coin was that missing three or four critical years of curling by being at college in the United States would do similar damage to his prospects in that sport. His skills were about equal in the two sports. And even though he liked golf a little better, he knew which one a Canadian prairie boy should choose.

His buddy, Tom Wilson, who used to caddy for him at big tournaments because he loved being so close to the action, still believes it was a "huge mistake" not to follow golf. "I'm not kidding," he says. "Going around the course with him is like following one of the professionals on TV, except you're there in person. He considers everything, the slight breeze, the small incline, because he's that good he can put it anywhere."

But Rick preferred the safer course. He enrolled in the University of Saskatchewan and signed on—as skip—with his Dad, his brother and another man to play in men's. For Rick this was an intense learning experience, even though the calibre of play wasn't lofty. He had taken a giant step up in strategy.

"Before [in junior] I could pretty much dictate strategy. In men's play it was much harder, they knew so much more about the game. It was quite an eye-opener, how much more I had to learn, and it wasn't just in strategy but in how to conduct myself and control my emotions. I never was a hothead but my tendency was to feel sorry for myself and mope around."

As he learned maturity on the curling sheet, he also picked up trophies on the golf links. Altogether he has played on five Willingdon Cup teams. Like Russ Howard, Rick believed the most desirable job after he'd finished his education was to be a golf pro. Like Russ, he signed on at his home club, the Riverside Golf and Country Club, right out of school. He was the assistant pro and believed that when the club pro retired, his future was assured.

But he'd only been in the job about 18 months when the club pro died suddenly and the board of directors passed over their young assistant pro and hired someone from Montreal. Rick, the local hero and hometown Saskatchewan boy, felt slighted and walked out.

But instead of accepting another assistant pro's job, he decided to help his father in the family business. The idea of moving away from Saskatoon held no appeal.

In 1973 he and Tom Wilson had put together a team they had great hopes for. Intimidation was a given in Saskatchewan curling and the young team was taking lessons from the masters. Rick was so sure they were on the right track that he turned down an offer to play with one of the most successful skips Saskatchewan had produced in many years. Wilson glimpsed then the depth of his friend's commitment and he smiled to himself.

The 1973 team included Ed Lukowich at third and Rick's younger brother Dave as lead. Until then Ed Lukowich had always played third for his brother, Mike, but he was getting interested in the finesse game and very few in the province could play with the touch and maturity of the 23-year-old Rick Folk.

Luke was the big name. He was the one who was doing them a favour by throwing in his lot with them. Their plan was not to worry much about winning but to get over the jitters of playing the big names by going after everyone. They were learning the mental discipline they needed to be an intimidating team and in the process some of their little idiosyncrasies were hardening into legend. Although they had yet to win big, there was a lot of talk about the team's future.

Their first major win came at an Edmonton carspiel. Wilson remembers it as a harbinger of the future and a testament to Folk's finesse. They were playing Gil Svenson in the final. He was much more seasoned and on an incredible winning streak, "something like 86-1 as I recall," laughs Wilson.

But as it came down to the last rock, Folk knew Svenson's streak was about to end. He still had to draw to the button to win. It was a big pressure shot. The four cars stood temptingly on the sheet beside him as Folk walked down to the hack to throw his last shot. Wilson, tugging at his collar and feeling the pressure, watched in amazement as a huge grin spread across his friend's face. He walked down to find out what in the name of God was so funny.

"Tom, she's all over," was all Rick said as he got into the hack and threw a perfect shot.

For Wilson that was vintage Folk, a guy who loved the pressure of throwing the last rock, a guy whose touch was as fine as anyone's in the game. "His confidence really made curling fun," says Wilson. "It took a lot of the pressure off. You knew you could miss a couple and it wouldn't matter."

But they didn't miss very many and in 1976 they found themselves in the provincial final in Kindersley, Saskatchewan. By then Lukowich was gone, convinced that the Folk team wasn't ready yet to win a Brier, and Bob Thompson had signed on as third.

Bob Thompson was an old friend who had been new to curling when he played with Folk the first time in the early 1970s. He was an impressive guy, a natural athlete and a born entrepreneur. After university he took his C.A. training in Toronto where the big money was. In curling, even though he was a virtual novice, he was good enough to step around Werenich and wind up as third on Paul Savage's Ontario championship rink in 1973 and 1974. But the team had a falling-out at the London Brier when Thompson came up with a "new concept on how to win that we didn't agree with," remembers Savage picking his words carefully.

But in Saskatoon, Folk had no such reservations. By 1976 the new team had begun to jell. Thompson and Folk worked well together and the front end of Wilson and Rodger Schmidt (Schmidt would later go on to make a name for himself skipping for West Germany in the Silver Broom) were powerful sweepers. Thompson had learned some things about winning as a high-school football hero and an All-Western, All-Star basketball player, and they thought all of this combined would make a very potent team.

But they were about to be disappointed. "We came up really cold," remembers Folk. "We weren't the best-liked team around because we were real sticklers for the rules, and if a person was cheating, we let them know."

He remembers that things in Kindersley got "really ugly." People sitting 10 feet away in the stands were calling them names. "It really shook up the whole team," Folk recalls.

In 1977 the same thing happened at the provincial finals in Weyburn. They were used to not being the favourites, but being everybody's favourite target was another matter. Again they were thrown off their game and unable to bear down in their usual relentless fashion.

By 1978 there was a certain ferocity about their desire to win the provincial title. This was the third consecutive time they'd been to the finals. They were neither surprised nor hurt by the fan reaction. They poured extra concentration into the games and forgot about the fans.

The one section they did pay attention to was the deep and distinctive, "thump, thump, thump," of fur-lined mitts banging together. This was the encouragement of a front-row cheering section of sisters, wives and girlfriends wearing mitts (courtesy of Folk's Finer Furs) and T-shirts that read "Folk's Finer Fans."

This time they did win and were Brier-bound. It was to be a championship dominated by two old teammates—the Rick and Ed show. Lukowich and Folk skipped teams representing Alberta and Saskatchewan respectively. The only other skip in the competition who was in their league was home-province hero Bernie Sparkes, who tied with Folk for second in the round robin.

One of the most enduring bits of Brier wisdom is that you can't always win the same way you get there. This could have been the epitaph for their hopes in 1978. In hindsight, the Folk team now knows they gambled too much in the early games of the Brier. Before they knew the ice, the rocks or anything about their opponents, they took unwise chances. Since they prided themselves on being able to play both the hitting and the draw game, they now believe they should have just kept it clean and waited for their chances. But in 1978 they had yet to learn the lesson of patience the roaring game can teach.

After three early losses they caught on and finished on a streak 8-3. But they had lost one too many, and in the days before Labatt's and Brier playoffs it was all over.

By 1978 the Folk team's style was well established. They wore black and they looked menacing. Big Tommy Wilson's headband was a regular and much-discussed feature of the team's image, as was his habit of planting himself, arms akimbo, on the hogline. It was as if he were defying the opposition to foul.

"My role was to keep my own team up and the other team honest," he explains with a grin. The headband was necessary to keep the sweat out of his eyes because the exuberant sweeper usually lost five pounds in perspiration every game. "They used to keep sweeping even after the rock had stopped, just to let you know they weren't tired," remembers one former opponent with a chuckle. Rick used to tease Tom that he swept until the rock reached the hack, but the slap, slap, slap of the corn brooms was one of the things that kept him in the game and let him know all was well.

Tommy also knew he didn't want his superlative skip upset by any irritations the other team could manufacture. His brusque style was designed to manoeuvre the opposition into docility. "Rick's so good you don't want him thinking about anything but the game," he explains. "John McEnroe thrives on the tension and the upset but Rick's not like that."

It was an interesting time in curling. There were even screaming newspaper headline messages like "Violence in Curling." One story in the *Vancouver Sun* described a situation in which Tommy Wilson first warned Kelly Horrigan about sliding over the hogline and then, when it happened again, kicked the rock right out of the B.C. curler's hand.

"Who the hell was going to stop me?" he demands. More than a decade later he's still furious that, as the innocent party, he should have to defend himself. In his darkened, scowling face you can glimpse something of the ferocity he must have shown in the game. No wonder he made his opponents queasy.

The incident happened in a big $50,000 spiel, and in the absence of umpires Wilson saw himself as a policeman for his team. "I certainly wasn't going to lose because somebody cheated on me," he says with finality.

Asked if he believed sliding over the hogline was a significant advantage to the other team he snaps: "I don't care if it's an advantage or not, it's against the rules. It makes me mad: the rule is there and yet I'm put in the position of feeling like a villain when we're not the ones breaking the rules."

In the late 1970s, as the prize money started to mushroom, the sport seemed to be breaking down into factions of those who could and would play intricate mind games and those who felt that such a win-at-all-costs philosophy defiled the "spirit of curling."

A curling credo called "The Spirit of Curling," written by Fergie Ferguson of Madison, Wisconsin, is reprinted in Paul Savage's book *Curling: Hack to House.* In part it says:

> The heart of curling is in its incomparable spirit.

> Without that spirit, curling is just another pastime. Played in that spirit, it is the king of all games. The spirit of curling is reflected in its most cherished traditions.

> Curlers play the game to win, but not to humble their opponents. Every curling game ends with a hearty handclasp and good will to both teammates and opponents.

> Every true curler would rather lose than win unfairly.

> A good curler never attempts to distract an opponent or otherwise prevent him from playing his best.

> No curler ever deliberately breaks a rule of the game, and should he do so inadvertently and be aware of it, he is the first to divulge the breach.

From time immemorial, curling has been a truly amateur sport. No curler ever plays the game for pecuniary profit either to himself or to anyone else.

The respect and honour accorded to any curler is derived neither from his wealth or social position but from his worth as a man, his skill and gentlemanly conduct as a curler, and his devotion to the game and its spirit.

Only by strict observance of these time-honoured traditions can curling be kept as a game that is played for love of it alone.

Although Savage and his friend Ed Werenich were not averse to winning money at the game, they still believed curling was a sport of amateurs and gentlemen. The Ferguson credo captured that feeling perfectly.

But in the west the pressures were different. Curling was slicker, bigger, more "professional." There was always money and prestige on the line, and quaint notions of the etiquette of winning seemed preposterous.

How could a team saturated in the "spirit of curling" cope with the Paul Gowsell rink, for example? The Gowsell foursome were currently barnstorming through the west, cutting a wide swath through everybody's curling winnings. They had no more respect for the spirit of curling than they had for any of the other traditions or the old fogeys who ran the sport.

Wilson admired the Gowsell style, and even though he's obsessively neat and a perfectionist on every front, he invited this collection of ragtag hippies to stay with him when they came to Saskatoon for the Bessborough Classic.

One-upmanship was, of course, part of the picture. Wilson remembers waking up one morning during the Classic and rubbing the sleep out of his eyes to verify that the tableau of wall-to-wall disarray in front of him was, indeed, his living-room floor. He got showered and ready for his morning game, answered the door when his brother came to collect him, and then, after careful consideration, he cleared his throat very loudly and said: "We play in 20 minutes, Paul. See you there."

The Gowsell rink arrived in time—unwashed and unshaven—and lost the game. But later in the day the two teams met again and this time Gowsell wreaked his revenge. It was not the first (or the last) time the Folk team faltered in the face of the fierce Gowsell onslaught.

Gowsell won two more Bessborough Classics, the cashspiels put on by the Nutana Curling Club. For Wilson, although he courted the situation, it was a little too much to have to entertain a victorious Gowsell after having just lost the spiel. He wouldn't go home afterwards. Instead, he'd find something to do out of town for the night to give the victors time to vacate.

Indisputably, Gowsell had Folk's number. But there was something so inventive and charming in Gowsell's style that even Wilson laughed at the showmanship of his tactics.

He remembers one incident well. Gowsell was about to throw his last rock. Tom had been talking to Rick and there wasn't time to get back to his usual spot on the hogline. When Gowsell noticed Wilson standing off to the side, he stopped the game, took Wilson by the elbow and steered him to the hogline. "It was his way of showing he didn't care where I stood. I wasn't intimidating him," laughs Wilson.

But Gowsell was only an intermittent irritant, and as the late 1970s wore on, Folk was steadily gaining in maturity, savvy and gamesmanship. In 1979 he again overcame the hostile climate in Saskatchewan to move onto the national stage in the Brier in Ottawa.

By now "Shitty" Schmidt had been replaced by Tommy's brother "Jungle Jim." As Folk's fiery front end, the brothers would soon be notorious throughout the curling world. Jungle Jim, half a foot shorter than his imposing brother, still cut a striking figure on the curling sheet with his black baseball hat and his stocky athletic body. Later he would go on to win Superjock competitions, but nobody in the curling world ever doubted his athleticism.

At a time when Gowsell's success was sparking a wholesale switch to push brooms, the Wilsons kept slapping the corn brooms and mulching up the ice with corn. Tom had always had his brooms made by the Midwest Broom Company. They were a little heavier and a little bigger than most. And the company designed the thicker handle for him, because he gripped the shaft so tightly that by the end of a game he would have had trouble prying his fingers off a thinner broom handle. The company did land-office business with Wilson. In competition he'd need a new broom after a game and a half. In regular play he replaced it about every five games.

As skip, Rick swept less vigorously and less often. However, Wilson denies Lukowich's charge that Folk always skips because "he can't sweep." In 1980, after the world championship, Folk had used the same broom all through the Brier and world championships. When he gave it away after the final game, the lucky little kid who got it said to his Dad with awe in his voice, "Look Dad, and it's brand-new too."

By 1980 the Folk rink was mentally prepared to win. One of the main things they had learned in the previous few years was how to turn a snarly crowd into a motivator. One morning in 1980 when they arrived at the rink for an 8 A.M. game, they saw it was packed with spectators. Things had been going badly and the crowd smelled blood and thought the team was going to lose.

A couple of years before, such a display of ill will might have thrown Rick. This time he just turned to Wilson with a smile and said, "This is going to make it even more fun—disappointing all these people."

After they once again collected the Saskatchewan championship, they moved on to the 1980 Brier in Calgary. They weren't expected to win. This was to be Gowsell's year and it couldn't have been more perfect. The Brier was in Calgary for the first time in 19 years and the heavy favourite was a fierce, ginger-haired "freak" named Paul.

Folk was ready. Bob Thompson was gone (he had moved to Lethbridge for business), but they had managed to replace him with Ron Mills, a very competent, if extraordinarily silent, third. Still, ready as he was, and heroic as he'd been, if he was reading the papers Folk must have thought he was just there as scenery. Interest was soaring in the rivalry between the two young teams, Al Hackner from Northern Ontario and Gowsell from Calgary. In the round robin Folk managed to just squeak past Hackner 6-5 and lose convincingly to Gowsell 8-4.

Providence, for once, was smiling on the Folk team, though. Hackner managed to outmanoeuvre Gowsell in the semi-finals and suddenly the complexion of the event changed. Now it was theirs to win. And win they did, coming up with a big three-ender in the ninth to finish off the Iceman 10-6.

Next stop Moncton for the world curling championship. This time everybody cheered for them. "For us it was like a hallowed experience," remembers Wilson. They weren't used to crowd adulation, and after it sank in that this was *the* championship for the whole world they hiked up their intensity another notch and were never in trouble. In fact, nobody beat them. They finished the tournament 10-0.

They were the first to break the 1973 "LaBonte Curse" and they did it with élan. Lukowich had often talked of the pain of losing the world championship. Wilson remembers him saying, " I wouldn't want you to have to go through what I've been through."

Wilson understood immediately.

Now just into their thirties, they had accomplished the major dream of their lives. Rick had worked since college in the family business, doing whatever was necessary, but he'd never thrown himself into a work project with the kind of intensity he reserved for curling. But in 1978 he had married Elizabeth Short of Kamloops, B.C. She already had a national title as part of the winning foursome in mixed in 1976.

At any rate, now that they were world champions, it was time for Rick to think a little beyond the next curling game. But given his nature, he wasn't likely to pull a Mike Riley and set his sights on an MBA degree or launch out into a completely different field. He knew retailing, he knew curling and he knew Saskatoon needed a curling shop. The fact that he had just won a world championship was an added bonus as he opened Rick Folk's Curling.

The next year they were great on the bonspiel scene. Wilson, particularly, loved the European travel and for a group of prairie boys it was a very big year. By playdown time they were burnt out and lost at the club level. It didn't help that Wilson was in Toronto on business when they lost their final club game.

But they were still having lots of fun and they were back the next year. As far as anybody can remember, there was no talk of retirement. But their final game of the year in 1983 would have been enough to shake lesser spirits. They were up three going into the ninth end. Kirk Ziola took two and then stole two in the 10th to beat them. Wilson's throat still tightens and his voice changes when he talks about it.

Then Rick got an offer that was too good to refuse. Grant Devine's Tories sought him out to run for them provincially. It was an interesting proposition for Folk, whose name was well known throughout the province. Wilson, who had supported him in everything he'd done so far, stepped back on this one. But curling buddies need not apply. The pros stepped in and the Devine organization helped him get the campaign under way.

Rick loved meeting people and even campaigning door-to-door. But on the business front things weren't going so well. No one suitable could be found to run the store, and just after he was elected in a Saskatoon riding, he found he had to close the store and kiss off two years of hard work.

Even though he was sought out as a celebrity candidate, he took his responsibilities very seriously. One year into his first term, the Devine government formally recognized that fact by making him Minister of Sport and Culture.

Life as a cabinet minister changed everything. Suddenly he was everywhere—representing the government at banquets here, offering government greetings there and almost always so busy he had little time for his real love—curling.

"Cabinet meetings were very interesting," he says. "I was appointed just after Colin Thatcher was arrested. (The son of the former premier was later convicted of murdering his ex-wife).

But politics wasn't really for him. "I knew part way through my first term I would run only once more and that would be the end of my political career," he says. "I wanted to do a good, thorough job, but I was never interested in making a name for myself."

The biggest drawback of political life was how little time there was for anything remotely resembling a normal life. Elizabeth Folk stayed in the riding in Saskatoon with their two small children and Rick commuted home from Regina on weekends. But every weekend it seemed there were political duties, and the time available for curling was continually shrinking.

However, in 1983 Minister of Sports and Culture Rick Folk skipped his men's team all the way to the final rock of the provincial final before they lost. Immediately afterwards, with his wife Elizabeth and Tom Wilson as the front end and Dorenda Schoenhals as third, he entered and ultimately won the Canadian mixed title.

Wilson remembers with dismay how callers to open-line shows didn't praise the accomplishments of their politician. Instead, they berated him for devoting so much time to his own leisure pursuits. Folk was angry but undeterred. In 1984 his team repeated its performance of losing on last rock in the men's provincial final.

Rick was never the type to plot his life in careful detail. When he thought of life beyond politics it was always with relief. He would be out from under the burden of official duties and he'd have more time for curling and golf. If he thought at all of what he'd do for a living, it was always in terms of retail business, probably sporting goods.

But the question of what to do next took on added poignancy when Wilson, who had curled with him for 17 or 18 years, announced that he was accepting a job in Toronto as vice-president of a firm that marketed magazine subscriptions through schools.

They had always had an us-versus-them approach to life and now the "us" was going to be seriously diminished. Rick would miss Tommy's fierce, sweeping, towering temper and great friendship.

Wilson had curled seriously for all of his adult life, but always in the back of his mind he had promised himself that curling would not be the whole story. He would, he told himself, do several things in his lifetime. Now that he had accomplished every goal he could reasonably hope for in curling, he knew it was time to shift his focus. The job offer was a chance to stretch himself in another direction. Besides, if he missed the thrill of competition, there were curling rinks in Toronto.

Jungle Jim retired from curling at the same time.

For Folk this was a time of upheaval. In the 1986 election he ran again as he had said he would, but the voters rejected him and all but one of the other urban Tories in the NDP sweep of the cities. Devine held the government only because he held the rural ridings.

It was a disappointing loss but Folk was sanguine about it. "I've had tough losses before," he says. "Sure you take it as a personal rejection, but what can you do?"

The immediate problem for any defeated politician is re-establishing himself in a career. Rick couldn't reopen his shop because his brother Dave, who now curled with him, had started up a similar store six months after he had closed his down.

He decided to try the advertising business and accepted a job selling for a friend's agency. But a year later he was once again looking to get back into the curling business. As a stopgap he worked with Dave in Folk's Curling Corner, but obviously there was not enough business to support them both.

Meanwhile, on the team front, frustration was mounting too. It seemed like a long time since they'd gone to the Brier, and although they'd had some bonspiel success since, winning a couple of sets of cars, Rick sorely missed his "fiery front end."

Clearly, Folk had reached a point in life at which he would have to make a decision for change. Unfortunately, the spot where he had arrived was more like a traffic circle than a crossroads.

For several years the Folk brothers had been talking of starting a one-stop curling store in the B.C. interior. It's a fragile business though, and if someone else beat them to it, there would be no point. They chose Kelowna as the fastest-growing city in the interior and started getting organized. The plan was that Dave would move to B.C. to get the store off the ground. He'd already made contact with local curlers to see about organizing a team.

But at the last minute Dave, whose entrepreneurial spirit was starting to blossom, had too many commitments in Saskatoon. Rick had to go.

Folk is not the chameleon Ryan is. Changing cities and provinces is not something he enjoys or would do lightly. Still, 45 days after the idea of moving to Kelowna was first broached, Rick, Elizabeth and their two children, Kevin and Andrea, were on their way.

Adjusting hasn't been easy. At first the curling was too good to be true. He signed on the team his brother had sounded out, with some adjustments because he's a skip and Dave is a lead. They had some trouble in the 1988-89 bonspiel season but then caught on, won the province "and damn near won the Brier."

With Bert Gretzinger playing third, they finished the round robin tied for first with Alberta and Ontario. They beat Russ Howard's Ontario rink in the semi-finals and came back to give another world champion who had transferred to the same Kelowna Curling club, Pat Ryan, a tough run for his money. Ryan, with his old Alberta rink's superlative hitting, ran them out of rocks. The final score was 3-2.

That was the Brier in which Howard seemed to lose control of his team and reporters contrasted their undisciplined style with Folk's absolute control of his team. But that control meant that when John Hyrich burned a rock for Manitoba late in the tournament, it was Folk who had to walk on the ice and remove the rock.

"When we played, Rick never had to deal with stuff like that," says Wilson. "The skip is the most important person and if somebody is going to get distracted, I'd rather it be the second than the skip."

That Brier success in 1989 was a blip on Folk's curling chart. It surprised everyone. But by 1990 the team had bumped back down to earth. They stayed together and made $20,000 or so on the bonspiel circuit, but the playdowns were as much a misery as, the year before, they had been a delight.

Folk got the flu and had to sit on a chair between shots. They looked vulnerable and uncertain. Their demeanour was a far cry from the intimidating attitude Folk's team had always displayed in Tommy Wilson's day.

They quickly lost the requisite two games and were out.

According to some versions of the story, Folk's front end abruptly quit or "retired" after this loss. But behind that story were several months of negotiations between Pat Ryan and Rick Folk to decide on the components of their Super Team.

The surprising rapprochement began in February when both men were invited to play in a Japanese bonspiel in Kelowna. At the dinner afterwards and later over many drinks at Ryan's house, they discussed playing mixed together with their wives. Later, when the season was over, they met for lunch and Pat proposed that Rick take over his Superleague team as skip.

"He said he had only skipped out of necessity because there was no one else," remembers Rick. "He wanted to get back to playing third."

Rick and his third, Bert Gretzinger, were close friends and Folk refused to break up the combination. Negotiations seesawed back and forth for several months. Pat and Rick each wanted to choose the team and Folk was adamant that as long as Gretzinger wanted to curl with him he would.

Eventually Gretzinger, who had been a skip and moved down to third to accommodate Folk, moved down again to second and Gerry Richards, another well-established skip, wound up at lead.

Although they'd never played a game together, their individual reputations were so well established they were quickly dubbed the "Super Team," a moniker that makes the usually placid Folk uneasy.

With good reason. The team could never quite get it together throughout the 1990-91 season. They qualified in each of the eight bonspiels they entered, but always by Monday morning play they were in disarray. They were never entirely out, but they were also never perfectly on.

Rick believes too much was expected too soon. It usually takes 30 to 50 games for a team to jell, he believes. But some who know the individuals on the team believe it's more than that. Folk needs more electricity on the team to keep his spirits from sagging, they say.

Wilson remembers that when he played with Folk his encouragement and boundless confidence in his friend took the form of constant physical patting. He focused all of his prodigious energy on the needs of his own team and disregarded everything else in his way. It didn't make him a popular guy on the circuit, but it perfectly offset Rick's occasional streak of self-doubt and admitted tendency to mope.

Everyone on the new team knew that Folk would function best with someone like Wilson in his corner. Even before the season started, Bert Gretzinger was worrying about how he would manage to fit the mould of the front end "motivator." "I've never been a big-time cheerleader," he said dubiously.

In his two years playing third for Folk, he had already had run-ins with Rick, who had been furious about his lack of decisiveness and fire. Once someone on the opposing front end casually admitted that his gum had fallen out of his shirt pocket onto the rock while he was sweeping. "Maybe I should have called a burned rock," he said after the end was over. Gretzinger said nothing and in fact didn't even tell his skip until after the game was over.

Folk exploded, roundly criticizing Gretzinger for being a "wimp." That same terminology came up in discussing Gretzinger's role in the famous stand-off with Johnny Usackis and Orest Meleschuk over Hyrich's burned rock at the 1989 Brier. Folk would have preferred it if Gretzinger had taken the heat for him.

Gretzinger accepts the argument with a defeated shrug. "It was a really unfortunate incident," he says. "The biggest problem was that not everybody understood the fine points of the rules and we got to look like dinks on national TV. But I know if they hadn't removed that rock, Rick would not have played another end. Nothing infuriates him more than teams not owning up to rule infractions."

In their first season, one of the Super Team's biggest problems was stepping around its own celebrity status. They were invited to Japan for two weeks of demonstrations in the middle of the season. It seemed as if the trip would be an ideal way to spend time together and practise. But they hadn't anticipated how hard it would be to get ice time. In the end the trip to Japan was more like a two-week hiatus in their season. A hiatus that came, unfortunately, at the most critical point in the year.

In the 1991 playdowns they seemed, at first at least, to have found their stride. They won 13 or 14 games in a row as they coasted to a win in the interior of B.C. But when they hit the provincials they were stymied. The only team they beat was the eventual B.C. champion, Gerry Kent, whose team turned out to be a surprise finalist in the Brier.

Everyone agrees the Super Team wasn't playing badly in 1990-91. They didn't lose by big margins; they were never totally out of a game, but when the chips were down they could never recover. Curiously, they have all shown this championship quality on other teams.

If ever there was a demonstration of the role chemistry plays on a team, the fate of the Super Team in 1991 is it. Pat Ryan and Rick Folk are two of the most intensely driven competitors in the game. Here they are playing on the same team, both apparently serious about seeing the team do well, and yet the team lacks the killer instinct. For both of them it's a deep and bitter irony.

And so Folk moves on, looking for a new way to win. At 41 he has a number of conflicting priorities—children to raise, a business to develop, a marriage to attend to, a new house on the golf course and a competitive spirit to satisfy.

His friend Tommy has given up on the game. He tried curling in Toronto but he could never be laid-back enough to fit in with the Savage-Werenich style. And although he played with a promising skip, they could never win enough to soothe his angry soul. "Losing just ate away at me," he explains.

And so curling is over for him, he says with sad finality. He has no mementos in his home and rarely watches the game on TV. Instead, he's running marathons now and getting into white-water rafting. He has a young son, a fancy office and an elaborate sports car with the obligatory cellular phone. The "Toronto Lifestyle" has claimed him.

But 4,110 kilometres away in Kelowna, the story is vastly different. Curling will never be done for Rick Folk. Both his business and his social life are organized around the game. He has modest tastes and he lives a quiet life that has no room for rafting or racing of any kind. For him there are no mountains of energy to be harnessed and no pinnacles of ambition to be scaled.

His horizon is tamer and his expectations more modest, and although there may be new locations and new teammates in the future, the smart money says to look for Rick Folk, by the turn of the century, to be the most dangerous skip on the seniors' scene.

EPILOGUE

CURLING'S FUTURE HAS taken a clearer shape since the hardcover edition of *Burned By The Rock* was published a year ago. As I write this, the International Olympic Committee's executive council has just accepted curling as a medal sport at future Olympics. Possibly in Lillehammer, Norway, in 1994, probably in Nagano, Japan, in 1998, and certainly wherever the Olympics are held in 2002, curling will be one of Canada's best hopes for gold.

And that small fact will have far-reaching effects on the sport in this country. First it will generate money from Sport Canada, which means Canada's finest curlers will be carded—given financial support to pursue their sport without undue worry about making a living. How this money is apportioned, who will get A carding, who B, and who C will undoubtedly feed the bushfires of politics already raging in Canadian curling. But Olympic curling will also mean sparkling new interest from youngsters who will now see the country's 1,200 curling rinks as training ground for Olympic glory. For those mostly venerable old rinks it will be a strange transformation. Once playgrounds for the wild, free and thirsty, they will become workplaces for the serious, disciplined and ambitious. And they will be places where dreams of greatness will not be idle. Certainly Canada has more curlers, more rinks and more expertise than any country in the world.

It's a wide open field and the stakes have just gotten much, much grander.

Internationally the game is also much better off than it was the day before this decision. There will now be international seed money available from the I.O.C. to allow new countries to learn the sport and train coaches. Canada's technical expertise in everything from ice-making to sweeping will likely be in high demand over the next few years. And the curlers celebrated here will be off to places like Turkey and Korea running clinics.

The decision has surprised many of curling's biggest boosters. At the Albertville Olympics, nobody would have guessed the I.O.C. was about to annoint curling as a medal sport. In February 1992 when Canada's rink of Kevin Martin, Kevin Park, Dan Petryk and Don Bartlett headed into the French Alps looking for Pralognan-La-Vanoise where curling was to be held as a demonstration sport in the XVIth Winter Olympics, they were met with a road that was almost an unnavigable track. It was an apt symbol for what lay ahead of them.

But Martin and his team wouldn't have cared about the road, wouldn't even have minded the absence of spectators or the segregation from other athletes. All that would have been disappointing, of course, but it was the curling that really disturbed them. "We lost (the Canadian men finished fourth and out of the medals) so I don't really have the right to say anything," Martin says grimly, months later. "I've been axed in the media for talking about it."

But the pain is too fresh for him to stick to his resolve. Nobody understands how badly the curling event was botched, he believes. "The conditions were unplayable," he says simply. "Everybody in the entire event curled bad. I had the high individual percentage at 74 percent. At the Brier the poorest team's average would be higher. That's the only reason I can accept it (the Olympic loss)."

The problems started with bad ice. They lost two of the four sheets before the event began and the other two varied from "ridiculously fast" to frosty. Moreover the rocks were "horribly pitted" and the draw badly organized.

Those problems were common for all curlers but Canada's rink faced other difficulties as well. The Olympics were played by free guard zone rules, a style of play that has so far been rejected for Canadian championships and one that Martin admits he doesn't enjoy. "It takes all the nerve, patience and strategy out of the game. You can't sit back and wait for the guy to crumble. It forces you on the offense and helps people who can't play the pressure game anymore," says the 25-year-old 1991 Brier champion.

Still, the Martin rink had a comfortable 3-0 record heading into the finals. Then, abruptly, they lost two games in a row, something they hadn't done for 70 or 80 games, and were out on their collective ear.

The first loss was bad enough but the second, coming as it did in the bronze medal game, stands out as the ultimate "nightmare" of the Olympics. As the Canadian team assembled bleakly for the

9 a.m. game against Bud Somerville of the United States the spectators who had come to cheer Canada to a medal suddenly noticed
only half the team was there. Coach Jules Owchar seemed to be
preparing to play front end, but who was going to throw third stone?
Nine a.m. passed in sombre discussion with officials. A tense pause.

On the rink Martin was trying to keep cool. Only one of the no-
shows was a surprise. Don Bartlett's wife was having trouble with her
pregnancy and they had an emergency doctor's appointment that
morning. They had decided the night before that Owchar would play
lead until Bartlett could get there.

But where was Kevin Park?

At 9:05 the signal was given and the game began. "It was unbelievable," Martin says now, still refusing to explain what happened.
He will say, however, that as he waited he knew this team would not
be playing together after 1992.

At 9:07 the errant third did appear but the lateness "took a lot of
steam out of us," Martin says. Canada lost and Kevin Martin, who
has described himself as "just waste" after his team lost the Junior
World Championships in 1986, had another huge disappointment to
swallow.

But as grim as the Olympics experience was, it would not be the
only frustration of the spring of 1992 for the Martin rink. They had
surprised themselves in early February by winning the Alberta provincial title for the second year in a row. As soon as they touched
down from France they had to start Brier preparations.

Considering their disappointments and what Martin describes as
the "inevitable" split that was coming, their Brier performance was
astonishing. They lost their first game to Russ Howard but after that
they won almost every game. By the time they met the Brier's surprise powerhouse, Manitoba's Vic Peters, in the final game of the
round-robin the two teams were tied for first with 8-2 records. The
game meant a bye to the final—and the hammer.

In the ninth end they were tied 4-4 but "Peters was finished,"
Martin claims. "He was uptight and falling apart. The worst we
could have been is one down coming home with the brick."

Then Martin's second stone, Dan Petryk, fell and burned a rock in
a flukey misstep. The team went down to a blazing defeat. "I felt bad
for them," Peters told the media afterwards. He (Petryk) was giving
it his all and it was one of those unfortunate things . . . I was glad to
be out of a jam though," he added with a twinkle.

Peters is that Manitoba brand of tough competitor calmly taking the breaks, good and bad, as they roll his way. When he was 19 and in love with hockey, it was all over in one afternoon. He unthinkingly had used his stick to stop a blistering shot. The wood shattered and several sharp shards went into his right eye. For a month he wore a patch and then settled for 10 percent vision in that eye, and the end of hockey.

But moping wasn't his style. Today he insists his vision isn't impaired at all. "My left eye got much stronger to compensate," he says and makes no mention of the inevitable difficulty with depth perception. His new sport would be curling, a game he'd played for fun for years in the little town of Steinbach, Manitoba, where his father was the school superindent.

The year he was 20, he moved to Winnipeg to dedicate himself to curling and work at the Rossmere Country Club as icemaker and golf-course superintendent. His hope was to play competitively at the club level. But in Winnipeg it was easy to get caught up in the curling subculture. By the time he was 26, Peters was a real force in the one-on-one shoot-outs in Manitoba, and his rink was good enough to challenge for the provincial championship.

Three times before they won in 1992, the Peters rink would have to accept the bridesmaid role in the provincial finals. "I always hoped for another chance, and I used to say to myself, 'Gee I got to four finals, most people never get to one. Maybe next time it will be our turn."

In 1992 it was. Although they'd played well all year they were unprepared for their blistering success in the Brier. Dan Carey was playing third for the first time and they felt they were a year or two away from hitting their stride. But suddenly, "everything was working. We were qualifying on the Manitoba circuit, making money every weekend," says Peters still sounding a little surprised. "When we lost, it always seemed to be by some guy making a circus shot against us."

The Manitoba final against Jim Ursel was a "real barnburner," the tensest game of the year. And when the smoke cleared the Peters rink had finally won themselves a shot at the Brier.

Next they took their systematic no-nerves approach through the round-robin in Regina, right up to the dramatic ninth end against Martin. Not surprisingly, Vic Peters doesn't see the burned rock as quite the same kind of climactic moment as Kevin Martin does. "It wasn't a win or lose situation," he says. But it did "kill their chances of winning. They were pretty upset."

In the Saturday semi-final Peters watched a great curling duel between Martin and Howard and secretly hoped for a Howard victory. He admits he didn't want to face Martin and his controversial green corn broom in the final. "We've played against corn a lot and it's not against the rules," he says doubtfully, "but with the new time limits it's hard to clean the ice perfectly. It (the corn mulch on the ice) lets him back into the game."

Howard, playing "unbelievably well," defeated Martin and earned the right to face Peters in the final. But as Sunday dawned, it seemed as if Russ had used up all his magic the day before. He came out flat, played a conservative wait-for-the-mistakes game and in the clutch missed the big shots. Peters won in an extra end. "The shot to win the Brier couldn't have been an easier one," he remembers.

The bridesmaid thing was finished; not only the Manitoba purple heart but also The Brier belonged to Peters and his rink. They looked forward to the honeymoon—the world championships in Garmisch-Partenkirchen, the beautiful resort town in the Bavarian Alps. None of them had ever been to Europe before. They saw this as a once-in-a-lifetime shot and they were determined to make the most of it.

But the unhappy fact is that Canada finished third behind Switzerland and Scotland. Twice in as many years the country that is supposed to be pre-eminent in the sport was humbled. But at least this time there were no fierce accusations of cheating as there had been in 1991. The Canadian loss came, at least in part, from what is being called the most spectacular shot ever seen at the world championships when Scotland's Hammy McMillen wicked off his own stone, removed Canada's second shot and rolled forward to ease Canada's rock out of play. The fans were on their feet, roaring with delight.

It was certainly a more pleasant spectacle for curling aficionados than the uproar at the world championships in 1991 in Winnipeg. Many Canadian curlers cringed as Martin used the rules to his advantage and littered the ice with corn mulch. The eventual champion, Scotland's David Smith, accused him of cheating, of throwing up "barrier weight" when he got ahead. And silently across Canada many elite curlers nodded their heads in agreement. Something, they insisted, should be done about Martin and his rogue broom. A few went as far as to say he doctored the broom by soaking it in sweet (and sticky) soda pop so the mulch would stick to the ice and be impossible to sweep up. This was his "emergency broom," which he switched to in the most extreme situations, they said.

Martin denies it emphatically and laughs at the uproar. "That's perfect," he laughs. "Everybody who knows curling knows I wasn't cheating." And he argues that sweeping skill is part of the game. If his opponents can't sweep well enough to clean a path for the rock, they should be practising their sweeping not calling for a rule change to outlaw corn brooms.

"The game was great as it was," he says. But in their rush to outlaw broom switching, curling officials found themselves with a diminished sport where straight ice and skillful rock throwing combined to produce blank end after blank end. Instead of admitting they had made a mistake, says Martin, they called for another rule change (the free guard zone rule) to get more rocks in play. "They fix up the first mistake with another mistake," he says with disgust.

But he takes a bemused view of the accusations against him because he owns a curling store and distributorship that sells brooms and other supplies to 327 retail outlets in Alberta and northern Saskatchewan. The controversy was "just great," he says. "I endorse and use the (green) Thompson broom and we sold out across Canada by January." It proved "kinda profitable," he admits.

Still his bemusement doesn't stretch to the specific remarks made by Eddie Werenich in an appearance on TSN's "It's Your Call" on March 5, just before the Brier. Darwin Daviduk, the president of the Northern Alberta Curling Association called to challenge comments that had been made about the primacy of Ontario curling. After all, an Alberta rink had won in four of the past six Briers, he argued. "I don't agree about the fourth," Eddie muttered and went on to rip Martin and his tactics. He called him a cheater and Daviduk, piqued, used the same adjective for Howard in the 1987 Brier final against Bernie Sparkes. At one point Werenich told Daviduk he hoped he'd "fall in the water or something silly."

It was not a pretty sight. Eddie wound up with a classic Werenich sweeping condemnation: "Alberta is the biggest problem we have in curling today: they gave us Warren Hansen and introduced what we call cheating at the Brier level."

He "worked me over pretty good," Martin says, still smarting months later. "He pretty well demolished me."

There have been calls for disciplinary action. An outspoken, Don Cherry-style straight-talker would be good for the game, says Martin, but Werenich, whom he describes as "60 or 70 pounds overweight," goes way too far."

Not surprisingly the C.C.A., armed with a new rule that nobody seems to know much about, rushed into the fray. Eddie received a phone call from a lawyer for the association explaining that he had 45 days to apologize or he would be suspended for a year. Again not surprisingly, Eddie at first thought the phone call was a gag, and refused to take the lawyer seriously.

But Dave Parkes, the Canadian Curling Association's general manager, confirms that disciplinary letters are being drafted. He argues that the 1990 rule is in a handbook for competitors and should be well known. The rule was designed to protect the image of the sport, he explains. Serious competitors should not demean either the sport, its hierarchy or its champions. If there are complaints, there are appropriate ways to lodge them, says Parkes, but sounding off on national TV is not one of them.

As this epilogue goes to print Eddie has not yet received the letter but has already vowed there will be "no apology." The phone calls are starting, pledging money for the "Werenich Defense Fund." Eddie's friends talk of mounting a legal defense under the Charter of Rights. And tempers everywhere are flaring.

"Let's see first if they do have the balls to suspend me," says Eddie. "Then we'll take them to court and baff them around real good. This is beyond curling . . . beyond everything."

Martin takes the high road: "At least a year, if not life," he says for Eddie's suspension.

Not everyone agrees. "What curling doesn't need," says Ray Turnbull, a TSN curling commentator and former Brier Champion "is another black mark. This is just one more stupid, ridiculous incident in the sport. There may not be anyone in the world who loves curling more than Eddie Werenich or who has done more for the game. Why are they (the C.C.A.) sticking their noses in this? Let Martin come after him for libel or slander or something if he wants to."

The irony is that Werenich was coming off a rough year in which his team was out of the playdowns early and placed 28th on the Gold Trail. (The Wrench won only $10,500 compared to Russ Howard's $101,000.) "Just as I was slipping into obscurity," Eddie laughs, "they found a way to make me famous again."

Meanwhile Eddie's third stone, John Kawaja, is busy working with Ed Lukowich on the World Curling Tour, a proposition that may make the Wrench's suspension from C.C.A.-sanctioned events academic. In 1991 the pro tour idea was announced, but it was loosely organized and didn't really get off the ground. In 1992-93 Eddy Lukowich, who will function as the full-time executive director and Kawaja, who describes himself as "the marketing guy," have streamlined the concept and signed Seagram's to sponsor a final for the world tour to be called the V.O. Cup. The $120,000 cashspiel will be held in Calgary in mid-February complete with six hours of live TSN telecast.

"No doubt it will be a showcase of better talent than the Brier," says Kawaja, "but it won't have the tradition of the Brier."

And will the pro tour ever eclipse the Brier? "Who knows?" says Kawaja, carefully neutral. "If, in five years, we're playing for a million bucks, it might."

For now, approximately 40 cashspiels with a total prize money of about two million dollars are collecting under the pro-tour umbrella. Merit points will be awarded based on the size of the purse in each event and standings will be released to the media weekly. At the end of the season, the top 32 teams will compete for the the $60,000 first prize.

"Our reason for starting the tour is to give some publicity to curlers who play every weekend," says Kawaja, "and also give another opportunity for guys who don't qualify for the Brier to play after Christmas."

Kawaja too is angry about the threatened suspension of his skip. "I don't know the legalities of it, but how can he be banned for speaking his mind?"

And if the C.C.A. bans Werenich for the 1992-93 season what would his rink do? "Eddie hasn't shown his hand yet . . . even to me," says Kawaja. "But personally, I don't know whether I'd play or not (with another skip in the playdowns). I've lost a lot of patience and understanding of that organization . . . I can't believe they'd be that stupid."

And so, once again in the summer of 1992, the curling warlords are tilting at each other. And now it's clearer than ever that the whole future of the amateur game is on the line—Olympics or no

Olympics. The champions and near-champions celebrated in this book are still sublunaries in the sports world, still operating in the fiefdom of the C.C.A. But it's even more clear that they, or their younger counterparts, will soon have all the burdens and pleasures of professionalism. And as the financial incentives mount—as they must—many of these 10 skips who have labored for the pure love of their game will have a new, more complex and unpredictable playing field for their struggles. And futures quite different from anything they ever dreamed.

July 1992

APPENDIX

Gold Trail Dollar Lists

1991-92

1.	Russ Howard	Penetang	$100,450
2.	Al Hackner	Thunder Bay	77,400
3.	Mark Dacey	Saskatoon	69,750
4.	Kevin Martin	Edmonton	37,750
5.	Vic Peters	Winnipeg	36,800
6.	Kerry Burtnyk	Winnipeg	34,400
7.	Brian Derbowka	Yorkton	33,500
8.	Rick Folk	Kelowna	32,000
9.	Rick Lang	Thunder Bay	32,000
10.	Jim Armstrong	Vancouver	28,950
11.	Ron Gauthier	Winnipeg	26,900
12.	Mike Vavrek	Grande Prairie	25,400
13.	John Bubbs	Winnipeg	24,000
14.	Brad Hannah	Edmonton	23,000
15.	Arnold Anderson	Shellbrook	22,200
16.	John Base	Oakville	21,750
17.	Bob Turcotte	Ajax	20,400
18.	Eugene Hritzuk	Saskatoon	18,250
19.	Jeff Stoughton	Winnipeg	18,100
20.	Ted Butler	Buckingham	17,300
21.	Barrie Sigurdson	Gimli	16,600
22.	Frank Morissette	Calgary	12,500
23.	Lorne Campbell	Grimshaw	12,400
24.	Robert Campbell, Jr.	Charlottetown	12,100
25.	Rob Ewen	Jansen	12,050
26.	Ed Lukowich	Calgary	12,000
27.	Paul Savage	Toronto	10,500

28.	Ed Werenich	Toronto	10,500
29.	Mike Harris	Toronto	10,250
30.	Harold Breckenridge	Calgary	10,000
	Doran Johnson	Lethbridge	10,000
	Doug Meger	White Rock	10,000
	Barry Smith	Kelowna	10,000
	Jeff Thomas	St. John's	10,000

Source: *Canadian Curling News*, 1992

1990-91

1.	Ed Werenich	Toronto	$61,350
2.	Brad Heidt	Kerrobert	50,250
3.	Frank Bailey	Calgary	35,000
4.	Russ Howard	Penetang	30,300
5.	John Base	Oakville	26,450
6.	Ed Lukowich	Calgary	25,000
7.	Lyle Muyres	St. Gregor	23,600
8.	Ted Butler	Buckingham	22,750
9.	Paul Savage	Toronto	22,600
10.	Dave Merklinger	Ottawa	22,200
11.	Brent Pierce	Coquitlam	19,000
	Vic Rogers	Regina	19,000
13.	Brian Penston	Winnipeg	18,100
14.	Arnold Anderson	Shellbrook	18,000
	Allan Lind	Admiral	18,000
16.	Bill Merklinger	Ottawa	17,000
17.	Rick Lang	Thunder Bay	15,000
	Les Rogers	Regina	15,000
19.	Mike Vavrek	Grande Prairie	14,500
20.	Mark Dacey	Saskatoon	14,000
21.	Eugene Hritzuk	Saskatoon	12,300
22.	Doran Johnson	Lethbridge	11,550
23.	Bob Sigurdson	Winnipeg	11,000
24.	Brent Giles	Vancouver	10,800
25.	Randy Woytowich	Regina	10,500
26.	Kerry Burtnyk	Winnipeg	10,250
27.	Gary Mitchell	Moncton	10,200

28.	Lorne Campbell	Grimshaw	10,000
	Bob Fedosa	Brampton	10,000
	Cal Fisher	Haney	10,000

Source: *Canadian Curling News*, 1991

1989-90

1.	Ed Lukowich	Calgary	$147,000
2.	Russ Howard	Penetang	74,440
3.	Al Hackner	Thunder Bay	55,080
4.	Paul Savage	Toronto	50,250
5.	Mark Dacey	Saskatoon	45,280
6.	Eugene Hritzuk	Loreburn	41,000
7.	Ed Werenich	Toronto	33,530
8.	Lyle Muyres	St. Gregor	31,000
9.	Eigil Ramsfjell	Oslo, Norway	27,500
10.	Dave Van Dine	Ottawa	27,000
11.	Rick Folk	Kelowna	21,000
12.	Larry Pineau	Thunder Bay	18,000
13.	Terry Meek	Calgary	17,780
14.	Orest Meleschuk	Lac du Bonnet	16,000
15.	Earl Blom	Vancouver	15,100
16.	Arnold Anderson	Shellbrook	14,760
17.	Kerry Burtnyk	Winnipeg	14,500
18.	Brad Heidt	Kerrobert	12,500
19.	Jim Packet	Estevan	12,000
20.	Pat Ryan	Kelowna	12,000
21.	Bob Turcotte	Whitby	10,500
22.	Mike Vavrek	Sexsmith	10,000
23.	Mark Noseworthy	St. John's	9,500
24.	Kirk Ziola	London	9,500
25.	Jim Armstrong	Vancouver	9,250
26.	Kevin Adams	Montreal	9,000
27.	Neil Okamura	Winnipeg	9,000
28.	Ian Robertson	Toronto	9,000
29.	Tim Stroh	Medicine Hat	9,000
30.	Jim Sullivan	Fredericton	9,000

Source: *Canadian Curling News*, 1990

1988-89

1.	Arnold Anderson	Shellbrook	$56,500
2.	Brent Giles	Vancouver	37,500
3.	Ed Lukowich	Calgary	20,000
4.	Mark Dacey	Saskatoon	19,400
5.	Dan Cleutinx	Vancouver	19,000
	Ed Werenich	Toronto	19,000
7.	Al Hackner	Thunder Bay	18,250
8.	Ray Talbot	Red Deer	18,000
9.	Jim Armstrong	Ft. Frances	15,000
10.	Eugene Hritzuk	Loreburn	14,600
11.	Rick Bachand	Ottawa	14,000
12.	Dave Merklinger	Ottawa	13,400
	Paul Savage	Toronto	13,400
14.	Larry Pineau	Thunder Bay	13,000
15.	Mark Noseworthy	St. John's	12,500
16.	Jim Sharples	Toronto	12,400
17.	Bill Carey	Winnipeg	12,200
18.	Eric Wiltzen	Kamloops	11,000
19.	Russ Howard	Penetang	10,900
20.	Wes Aman	Medicine Hat	10,000
	Frank Bailey	Calgary	10,000
	Gord Berthold	Grande Prairie	10,000
	Pat Ryan	Edmonton	10,000
24.	Raymond Roy	Ft. Frances	9,000
25.	Kevin Park	Edmonton	8,100
26.	Ian Brown	Dartmouth	8,000
	Lorne Henderson	St. John's	8,000
	Kevin Kalthoff	Humboldt	8,000
	Scott MacPherson	Toronto	8,000
	Ken Watson	Vancouver	8,000

Source: *Canadian Curling News*, 1989

1987-88

1.	Ed Lukowich	Calgary	$101,250
2.	Paul Savage	Toronto	58,000

3.	Rick Folk	Saskatoon	36,000
4.	Arnold Anderson	Shellbrook	32,000
5.	Kerry Burtnyk	Winnipeg	26,200
6.	Frank Bailey	Calgary	15,000
7.	Jeff Stoughton	Winnipeg	15,000
8.	Wes Aman	Medicine Hat	13,500
9.	Russ Howard	Penetang	13,125
10.	Eugene Hritzuk	Loreburn	13,000
11.	Dale Duguid	Winnipeg	12,000
12.	Vic Peters	Winnipeg	12,000
13.	Raymond Roy	Ft. Frances	12,000
14.	Bob Turcotte	Brampton	12,000
15.	Rick Bachand	Ottawa	11,700
16.	Craig Lepine	Vancouver	10,500
17.	Ron Thompson	Vancouver	10,500
18.	John Base	Toronto	10,000
19.	Earl Garratt	Milestone	10,000
20.	Mike Chernoff	Vancouver	9,000
21.	John Bubbs	Winnipeg	8,800
22.	Al Hackner	Thunder Bay	8,175
23.	Mark Dacey	Saskatoon	8,000
24.	Brent Giles	Vancouver	8,000
25.	Allan Lind	Admiral	8,000
26.	Gary Mitchell	Saint John	8,000
27.	Jamie Schneider	Kronau	8,000
28.	Ragnar Kamp	Truro	7,800
29.	John Kawaja	Toronto	7,300
30.	Bob Ellert	Assiniboia	7,200

Source: *Canadian Curling News*, 1988

1986-87

1.	Ed Werenich	Toronto	$54,675
2.	Pat Ryan	Edmonton	41,700
3.	Bert Gretzinger	Kelowna	35,824
4.	Randy Woytowich	Regina	33,400
5.	Harold Breckenridge	Calgary	32,000
6.	Kerry Burtnyk	Winnipeg	28,600
7.	Al Hackner	Thunder Bay	24,900

8.	Earl Garratt	Calgary	21,000
9.	Arnold Anderson	Shellbrook	16,700
10.	Craig Lepine	Vancouver	14,000
11.	Bernie Sparkes	Vancouver	13,000
12.	Jeff Stoughton	Winnipeg	12,300
13.	Arnold Asham	Winnipeg	12,000
14.	Mark Longworth	Winnipeg	12,000
15.	Jim Ursel	Winnipeg	12,000
16.	Eric Wiltzen	Kamloops	12,000
17.	Steve Skillings	Victoria	10,000
18.	John Basc	Oakville	9,400
19.	Don Aitken	Montreal	9,000
20.	Allan Lind	Admiral	9,000
21.	Les Rogers	Regina	9,000
22.	John Bubbs	Winnipeg	8,500
23.	Lyle Muyres	St. Gregor	8,500
24.	Raymond Roy	Fort Frances	8,300
25.	Ron Brooker		8,000
26.	Ross Tetley	Thunder Bay	7,800
27.	Rick Bachand	Ottawa	7,000
28.	Brad Clarke		7,000
29.	Brad Heidt	Kerrobert	7,000
30.	Arnie Tiefenbach	Regina	7,000

Source: *Canadian Curling News*, 1987

INDEX